LOOKING

THE BOTTOM LINE

THE STRUGGLE FOR THE LIVING WAGE!

Richard R. Troxell

Plain View Press
P.O. 42255
Austin, TX 78704

plainviewpress.net
sb@plainviewpress.net
512-441-2452

ISBN: 978-1-935514-99-2
Library of Congress Number: 2010934411

Cover photo by Allan Pogue.
Cover design by Susan Bright.

*Please note. 100% of all book sales go to further our efforts to end homelessness . . . so buy two copies and give one to a friend.

501(C)3

⚥ www.HouseTheHomeless.org www.UniversalLivingWage.org ⌂

When it comes to domestic policy, I have no more important job as president than seeing to it that every very American who wants to work, and who is able to work, can find a job that pays a Living Wage.

President Obama

My response is that I think it [raising the minimum wage ...so that every worker in America who works 40 hours in a week escapes poverty], *doesn't lower employment.* [emphasis added]

Ben Bernanke-Federal Reserve Chairman

There is nothing but short sightedness to prevent us from guaranteeing a livable income for every American family.

Dr Martin Luther King

Continuing to increase the Minimum Wage by an amount less than that necessary to reach a Living Wage only assures minimum wage workers eternal poverty.

Richard R. Troxell

National Chairman Universal Living Wage Campaign

Acknowelgements

I humbly offer my deepest heartfelt thanks:

to my wife, Sylvia Troxell, without who's invaluable help and love, this book would not exist. She encouraged and typed me through all 11 drafts of this document;

to my daughter, Colleen for her support and who at the age of seven, of her own devises, purchased Christmas tree ornaments, painted and sold them to raise money to house the homeless.

A very warm thank you —

to Michael Stoops, national organizer, who people from one end of this nation to the other, call their personal friend and guide who stopped his drive to end homelessness long enough to read and make suggestioins for the book;

to Sue Watlov Phillips who also stopped her amazing life of selfless service to others to proof the book and offer me words of encouragement;

to Carol Maderer who flew in and out of my life to review and proof read my prologue and first two chapters;

to Kurt Ericson who helped me edit my end notes. Ughhh!

to Cecilia Blanford, House the Homeless co-founder, friend, and number-one spiritual cheerleader;

to Katherine E. Kimbriel, author, friend, and www.UniversalLivingWage. org Web Master;

to Joanne Koepke who located and produced over 45,000 organizations as potential converts to the campaign;

to Tomie Holmes a "RP," Regular Person, next door neighbor, friend, and financial contributor to the publishing of this book. You are deeply missed.

to Justin Corey Webb my friend and research assistant;

to long time friend Virginia Schramm who was going to retire but found that like 50 % of our "Baby Boomers," she had not earned enough money to do so, put off retirement and gladly edited a final version of the book;

to my ever cheerful and ever optimistic publicist Melissa Weiner;

to Alan Pogue for use of his photographs, and for helping me format many of the photographs in this book;

to my Brother in Peace, Alan Graham and Mobile Loaves and Fishes for unflagging support;

to all my friends like Tom Spencer and Bill Lamar who took time to read the book, offer comments, and contribute to its completion;

and to all my thousands of friends experiencing homelessness, who through the years have seen me as their friend and someone worth telling their stories to, so that I could tell a few of them here.

> In Unity, There is Strength
> Richard R. Troxell

*Please note. 100% of all book sales go to further our efforts to end homelessness...so buy two copies and give one to a friend.

Contents

Three: The No Camping Ordinance 95

Four: Bergstrom Air Base 133

Five: Project Fresh Start

Six: The Universal Living Wage

Seven: Where Do We Go From Here ?   239

Forward

A lot of social science and policy analysis is based on hard data of one sort or another. This can, of course, be highly useful and offer profound insights if done carefully. Some of these studies strive to be objective, while others take an implicit or explicit position on the matter under consideration. When it comes to poverty and social welfare policy generally, though, few policy analysts have actually lived amongst the data: been unemployed, been on welfare, been homeless. To be sure, some journalists and novelists have spent time among the dispossessed, but it has usually been only for short stints. Thus, we often debate these issues without a qualitative feel for what life is really like for many Americans, and how social welfare policies of various sorts are perceived and working out on the ground.

Richard Troxell is a remarkable exception. Most of his adult life has been spent living and working among people who have few of this world's goods. He "knows" what most of us can only sense. But he has combined this with a keenly analytical mind, one that knows both how to probe and how things get done. Moreover, he adds a third element: An unbending optimism that change will come.

Few people will read this book without being touched by the many stories laid out in the first part. The danger is, though, that the reader will begin to feel that the whole book is a narrative of people finding hope among the wreckage of often broken lives. While that is indeed inspirational, it can seem that we have heard this before (although seldom has it been told so well). But it would be a mistake to put the book down before reaching the solution section, for he moves to a significant set of conclusions: A living wage is the best remedy for the condition of the millions of Americans who live on the margins of society; the wage should be calculated based on varying housing costs (roughly by county); and setting a wage in this way is both practical and will produce important economic benefits.

Troxell moves from narrator to policy advocate. Few people have devoted more time to carefully analyzing a social policy than he has with the housing-cost-based living wage. He knows the literature and brings it to bear on the array of questions such a policy would entail. While some might quibble with his interpretation of the data here and there or with some of the inferences he draws (I myself do in fact), no one will be able to dismiss the argument for lack of thoroughness. All things considered, it would appear that Troxell has offered a viable solution for a serious national problem.

In short, citizens of all political persuasions will gain something from pursuing this book.

Jerold Waltman

R.W. Morrison Professor of Political Science

Baylor University

Author of *The Politics of the Minimum Wage* (2000); *The Case for the Living Wage* (2004); and *Minimum Wage Policy in Great Britain and the United States* (2008).

Bridge Action. The woman next to Richard R. Troxell, Eva Adams, was one hundred years old when she joined the Universal Living Wage action on this bridge in Austin, TX.

Preface

In an effort to share my economic struggles and advocacy for the poor, I have created a unique personal narrative. It is laced with vignettes of people I have met along the way who have experienced homelessness. It is punctuated with numerous newspaper articles and photos illustrating some of the initiatives and battles of my organization, House the Homeless, Inc. It ends with my pragmatic plan to change the face of poverty for our nation's working poor with the Universal Living Wage.

Photo by Alan Pogue.

Prologue

The box was approximately 20" by 15" and about 12" deep. My father had lovingly made it so many years before. It was varnished masonite with heavy maple trim and two sturdy hinges. "Built like the Rock of Gibraltar" was a favorite description by my father of his work. It contained the last physical evidence that my mother had ever lived. It was important to me. My mother died over ten years after my father. At the time, it had been very hard to look at official documents, or small boxes of jewelry, watches, pins, and other keepsakes.

Now, almost 15 years later, I slowly passed through the papers until I found a round piece of darkened maple about an inch thick and three inches across. In the center was a half-inch ring of rich red velvet and in the center of that was mounted a 1958 Benjamin Franklin half-dollar. At first, I wondered why anyone would mount a half dollar in such a fashion and thought also that one does not see them very often anymore. It came from a different time. It came from a time when America was at its strongest. It came from a time when there was still enough gold in Fort Knox, Kentucky, to back all the paper money issued. It was made of silver, real silver.

As I held it, understanding came to me, and I realized its other significance. I was drawn into the memory it held for me.

It was 1958; I was seven years old, in my second year of military school, Porter Military Academy to be exact. My stay there had been a birthday gift that resulted in routine beatings by the older cadets and corporal punishment from my math professor. I learned the Periodic Table and the atomic weights of the elements by the third grade.

It was a life of extremes. We lived in Wappoo, South Carolina, just a few miles outside of the historic city of Charleston. This was the Deep South where I spoke in "yes, sirs" and "no ma'ams." It was the Deep South where we used to go crabbing and drop off our catch before school. My mother would turn that crab into crab meat spaghetti, crab meat sandwiches, crab meat salad and crab meat peanut butter.

My mother had lived through the depression and my younger sister Gail, my older sister Lynn and I were forced to relive it, or some variation of it, throughout our youth. To an outsider, this probably appeared odd as my father was a junior naval officer and there was probably money somewhere. Nonetheless, we pinched every penny that ever came into the household. All money went into one big pot. It was all the family money. Regardless of my father's probable income, my mother felt compelled to save money by giving us baths in buckets in the backyard so she could re-use the water on the plants in the perpetually wet backyard. My mother paid us to weed the front yard constantly. It was mandatory. It might have been OK, but she paid us in marbles. That's right, plain old, ordinary, non-cashable marbles. Looking back, I can only assume that it was a means of keeping all the other money where it belonged, in the family pot.

Therefore, it was the summer of 1958 that I was determined to go to work and make my own wage for real money. Wappoo, South Carolina, routinely produced sweltering, melting 95-degree summers with humidity so thick you had to breathe hard to pull in a full breath of air. The humidity was so intense within 24 hours it grew mildew on everything left outside. It was there that I would make my stand. I would perform my first independent act of manhood. I decided I would mow lawns for real pay, real wages.

Unfortunately, the only equipment at my disposal was an old push mower with very dull blades and very dry ball bearings. Undaunted, I charged ahead. I was going to claim my manhood. After knocking on just three doors, I found someone who was going to pay me to mow their righteously overgrown yard of grass that was no less than one half acre of land! I remember setting a price.

"Yes ma'am, whatever you think is fair."

In those days, a regular sized lawn mowing could bring as much as four or five dollars. With half an acre of yard, there was no telling how much I might make. If you factored in that I was going to do it with an inferior instrument with blades duller than butter knives and so rusted that the squeal hurt one's ears with each push, I was sure to make a small fortune. I had said, "You set the price at whatever's fair." Well, hell, that meant the sky was the limit. I was going to be rich! I was so proud. I was so clever! I had an idea, and I set out to do it. I negotiated my own fair terms and I went to work.

I mowed that field of what could easily have been classified as miniature bean stalks from early morning until just at dusk. I drank water from a hose and lost almost all of it through every pore in my body. I even sweated through the top of my head. I could feel my sweat sloshing from my sopping wet socks. Blisters formed and burst. I ignored the stinging sensation that enveloped each toe separately. I did not care. I was going to be rich! OK, so maybe not rich exactly, but I was on my way. I had worked like a man, doing a man's job. My pockets would be full. I had set my course, established a fair wage, and plied my youthful body to the task. Row after row, around each tree and shrub, I passed, sweated, grunted, groaned and pushed that demon mower again and again.

Finally, I was done. I was truly done. I was spent. I was hurting but proud. I squared my shoulders, took a double deep breath and walked up to that door.

When she came, she looked over my shoulder and said, "Oh! Wait right here." This was it! The big pay off! I could hardly contain myself. I knew I was beaming. I think she had money with her but she went back to get "the purse," the mother lode. She must have taken one look at that professionally manicured buzz cut and realized the wages she was about to pay were a pittance and wholly insufficient now that she had seen my marvelous work. She had to get that purse. When she reappeared, she reached toward me and thrust a huge amount of money in my hand, said "thank you," and, quick as you please, closed the door. It seemed so fast. She really did not have much time to admire my work. She did not pause, gaze out upon it, nor did she reflect upon how hard it must have been to cut so close about the hedges and so neatly against the raised walk. I had gone over some places two and three times to mince up the big, long cuts of grass. She did not remark and compare it to all the other less perfect mowing in the history of the yard. She did not comment on my courage to fight against the heat and struggle with the dull blades. A moment later, the door just clicked a final closing. It drew me back from my emotional letdown and caused me to refocus again on my earnings in my hand.

There of course lay the coin, the "one" coin. I did not really recognize it. I had never seen a Benjamin Franklin half dollar before that very moment. It was silver, pure silver and handsome enough but it was just one coin, just one coin. All at once, I felt chiseled and then abused. I was ashamed. How could I have been so easily duped? Wait, there must be some mistake. Yes, a mistake. That was it! But I had brought this on myself, I had negotiated the contract. I had set the terms, "Whatever you think is fair," I had said. I remember clearly the words because I was so proud when I had spoken them.

I was doing manly things, working for pay and setting my own fair and reasonable terms, honor among men as it were. I could not change the terms of the contract now!

I had deferred to her as an adult, an honest person who would pay a fair wage based on the quality of my work and her worldly experience. I was deflated, stunned and exhausted. I dragged myself home. I dropped the lawn mower on my own yet to be mowed lawn (groan). I remember smashing my knee on the foot of the bed as I pulled off my soaking wet jeans. I fell toward my sheets and was out before my face hit them.

Now, whenever I look at that fifty-cent piece mounted on carved maple, I think about my mother. With all the things she had to do, she had taken one look at that fifty-cent piece, instantly knew the entire story, and had gone into her woodshop and preserved that event forever.

I dedicate this book to you, Mom.

I realize now that every step of my life has brought me to this moment of simple realization. We are what we do. The quintessence of "us" is the things that we create and do. And in this society, we reward and show appreciation for these efforts with cold hard cash.

As they say, "money makes the world go round." As a child, I was not taught how to balance a checkbook or the meaning of compound interest. Our home ran on electricity and gas, but I was not taught what a kilowatt-hour was or what a cubic foot of gas cost or even meant. I had no idea how much money my father made or what the family "net worth" was. Money, like religion and sex, was a forbidden topic. Now, years later, all three are still hot button issues, but I have learned a little more about money.

I know that money affects every aspect of our lives. It is all interrelated, and it needs to be. Fairness, a sense of morality of what is fair, needs to come into the work place as it relates to wages.

In addition, I have learned that wages, at the lowest possible level, should relate to the necessities of life: food, clothing, shelter and access to health care.

I have learned that if every nation-state throughout the world embraced this basic moral standard, we could begin to shift the paradigm of world poverty. If, for our lowest paid workers, the world's nations were to say that, in exchange for a fair day's work, we would ensure a fair day's pay that would provide the necessities of life, we could transform the world. We would end the "welfare state" and exchange it for a compassionate world that takes care of the mentally ill and the infirm; and everyone from minimum wage workers to captains of industry would prosper. And we, the people, would all work with a sense of dignity and fairness.

We would feel respected and appreciated for the quality and consistency of our work. We would work and thrive in our own communities within our own countries and not feel compelled to travel to distant countries, traverse deserts, abandon our families for decades at a time, and live like animals, eight-to-ten people in a single room, out of financial desperation. People would be encouraged to work, and they would be pleased to do so knowing that, if they worked hard, the wage they earned would ensure them the necessities of life: food, clothing, shelter, and access to health care.

This is the vision that we present here. This is the Universal Living Wage.

Eugene Golden

Eugene Golden is an intelligent, handsome black man of 61 years. Born in Bay St. Louis, Mississippi, his family immediately moved to Canton, Ohio, where his story begins. Eugene, of sharp mind and quick wit, developed a taste for knowledge and is always reading books of an expansive nature. A high school graduate, he has held several jobs including that of a production/manufacturer/ scheduler. He later worked as an assembly and subassembly supervisor for the manufacturing of bank machine parts.

Eugene served honorably in the military as a member of an elite combat defense police unit, and he later took advantage of the GI home loan program. For the modest sum of $15,900, he was moving toward home ownership when financial disaster struck. He was laid off from his job and unable to make the $300.00 monthly mortgage payment. Counter to expectations, when Eugene ran into trouble, the VA did not reach out to help him by amortizing his loan or placing his arrearages on the far end of the mortgage. To the contrary, he was told, "You know you are responsible for your debt." Fully aware of his obligations but unable to secure another job or assistance from the VA, he lost this home through a foreclosure.

Today, Eugene's health is less than good. He suffers from Major Clinical Depression, hypertension, and a heart valve problem. He has painful bone spurs on his feet that the VA doctor says he cannot operate on because Eugene is medically unstable from the neuropathy caused by Diabetes Type II. Eugene now receives a VA Disability check for being 20% disabled. His monthly check is $128.00. This does not afford him housing.

Eugene is homeless on the streets of Austin, Texas.

ONE:

AN URBAN AWAKENING

Along the Way After Vietnam

Like many of my generation, I struggled with the issue of how to respond to the Vietnam War. Being the son of a naval officer and a product of military school training, I was the only one of my friends to choose active military duty. I remember holding my breath while watching countless hours of "Combat" with Vic Morrow. Each week I'd slip down into my parents basement and watch a 10" by 10" TV screen mounted in a wood encasement that was two feet long and two feet deep. Each week, filthy from crawling through the hill sides of hell, Sergeant Vic Morrow led his men into combat and with any luck he'd lead them all back out...wiser more seasoned. They'd emerge from the confusion, screams and explosions with a new moral perspective...ready to take on whatever new challenge life might throw at them. The deciding factor for joining the service however, came when my Marine Corps recruiter insisted that I would be able to put myself through college on the GI bill. As it turned out, the government and I ran out of money after less than two years of community college. Part of my reality is that after Vietnam, I was emotionally damaged goods anyway.

After attempting community college, I went over the proverbial edge when my father died. I rejected people and began living in the woods. I started wandering aimlessly across the United States. I had seen a commercial that showed people hang gliding, so I packed a backpack, hopped in my VW bug, and headed to some magical place in a TV commercial.

I met a man named Regalo. He had worked for Goddard Space Agency and had this crazy idea to use hang gliders as re-entry vehicles for space capsules. I met him in Kitty Hawk, North Carolina (where else?). He was standing on the sand dunes. I walked up, introduced myself, told him I wanted to learn how to hang glide.

He said, "Sure."

After two glorious weeks, I had to move on. I was driven. I felt like I might explode.

I found myself in Grand Isle, Louisiana, where marijuana entered the country by the ton in the holds of ships, and where ship welders wore very tall stovepipe hats and would only speak to you if you too wore a similar hat. I vaguely remember recognizing this as some kind of economic/class prejudice. After two weeks, I moved on. I had to go.

I then landed in New Mexico where I lived — first in my VW bug, then a truck and then a cave. I caught a job restoring trails for the US Forest Service, where I was the only Anglo among many Hispanic laborers. Then

I started serving tables for less than two dollars an hour at the one and only local bar.

I became a volunteer fire fighter and was assigned to drive the water tanker to fires. That lasted until the Thunderbird Bar, where I worked, burned to the ground one night. The owner, Ira Harge, a 6' 9" one-time professional basketball player from Anguila, Mississippi, supposedly got behind on his debt to the wrong people. A candle burned down until it met a stream of gas being released from a feed line. We fought the fire until sunrise.

Two days later, I headed north to Canada where my Springer Spaniel, Buddy, had failed to bring the necessary papers to cross the border. We landed in Philadelphia in the City of Brotherly Love.

Philadelphia

I headed to Philly to meet up with my friend, Cliff Dempsey. I slipped into an abandoned house and swiped electricity from his father's gas station next door. I was the only white person for miles in every direction. Neither I nor anyone else seemed to notice because Cliff served as emissary for my entrance into the neighborhood, which I soon grew to think of as my neighborhood. I somehow felt I could blend in and not be noticed. I needed to be alone. This was the heart of North Philadelphia, a once economically vibrant community. It had become a devastated shell of its former self with abandoned buildings standing (or what was left of them) one right after another. In the 1960s, "White Flight" had swept through North Philadelphia and all but devastated the neighborhood as disadvantaged poor people (black folks) "moved up" and in. (This occurred when the Federal Government had made home ownership possible for poor folks). Massive warehouses had long remained idle, unproductive. But there was an energy in the neighborhood. What people had was old, used, or hand-me-down, but they seemed to appreciate what they had in a way I had not experienced. Gerald from up the street, for instance, owned a Chevy Impala with the vinyl roof completely peeled off like an apple from a paring knife exposing a pocked metal under skin. But you could be sure that if you saw it coming, it would be spotlessly clean and buff-polished, inside and out.

Row houses needed roofs, but flower boxes, were carefully planted and watered daily. Everyone was working to improve their lives. Young girls with relaxed hair in curlers and fingers tied with bows sporting fresh nail polish were studying to be cosmetologists. The sidewalks, cleaned repeatedly, were always wet from a recent hosing down. The narrow, row-housed streets were a true beehive of activity literally buzzing with the latest sounds from Mo Town that carried a constant base beat.

My friend Cliff was a light skinned black man in his late twenties. He was always rolling out new ideas in an effort to make life profitable. He tried raising homing pigeons; and he read non-stop all sorts of books about business schemes. At one point, he and I tried to launch Consumer Conscious Parts, CCP, a jobber's parts store on wheels. We were going to sell hard to get sealing rings and seals and other infrequently used, but highly needed, parts to auto mechanics at local gas stations. We were sure this was a great idea, which would save auto mechanics both time and money. We even bought a used truck and refurbished it. Money or the perpetual lack of money, prevented any of these ideas from ever materializing. Banks rarely ever loaned money to people in North Philadelphia. We were no exception.

When I met Cliff's father, Garland Dempsey, the owner and proprietor of Dempsey Auto, I was instantly mesmerized. He was a big, beautiful black man with the face of God. His smile and voice were so resonating and infectious that I would linger to watch him as he spoke, listen to him talk. When he spoke, you stood a little taller and your shoulders drew back just a bit more than usual. He was an absolute optimist about everything. He spoke in broad sweeping terms, made everything seem grand and possible — *we* were the central characters in a real life drama. We were the ones who could make things happen. He spoke of always doing the right thing in that scenario of endless possibilities and about respecting every human being. This was decades before Spike Lee. He spoke of how one needed to do for others and how that if we act like men, we will be respected like men.

A man is a man, is a man, he would say.

Somehow, when he spoke those simple words he conveyed volumes of knowledge about respect. He never spoke of race unless it was the human race, and that is exactly how I heard him...respect for the work of others and the worth of others.

Garland Dempsey bought gasoline and sold it for a few pennies above the price he had paid for it. Every day was an economic challenge. He was in a constant struggle with the distributors. They were always attempting to raise prices or put new demands on him. I remember that we had this 20 foot long measuring stick that we treated like the king's scepter which we lowered into the tank at least twice a day to check and see that we hadn't been ripped off, or sprung a leak in the holding tank, or made some mathematical miscalculation.

Cliff ran an auto repair business in the shop where we sold this gas. People would drive in to get gas. We provided full service — a check under the hood, oil and washer fluids checks. In this way, we could get a look at belts and ball joints and offer helpful suggestions about timely repairs. Cliff was a great salesman. He gave me a job and taught me the auto repair business. I worked twelve hours a day; we ate at his aunt's home, where I ate the best southern cooking of my life. Cliff had let me know right away that I needed routinely to make a little financial gift to his aunt, so I quickly came to realize this was consistent with everything in North Philadelphia. His aunt didn't mind cooking and loved to please others with her down-home culinary magic, but it takes money to fill the pot. Everyone struggled constantly to not quite make ends meet. These folks took me into their homes without a question or a second thought. "People on the river are happy to give."

The good folks of North Philadelphia near 20th and Glenwood are America's working poor. Good, righteous, God fearing, generous, hard working people.

In retrospect, I realize that these folks, my brothers, my sisters, my extended family, were living and working on the edge of financial disaster. They were in a constant struggle to not slip over the edge. They worked hard every day obeying the laws of the land and taught right and wrong to their children and the children of their neighbors. Every day they worked hard so they would not slide deeper into debt, to hold off despair. The struggle was endless. You could see it etched into their faces but you could *feel* their determination to climb out and their resolve was palpable.

It turned out that Garland Dempsey was the best friend of the late, great Max Weiner. Max was a small, elderly Jewish man who was as pale as a Philadelphia porcelain tub. He was about 5'4" but when he spoke, you knew you were in the presence of an intellect of great stature. I didn't know it at the time, but that one strand of electrical wire that Cliff and I secretly ran from his father's auto repair shop to power my beige 5" x 8" bake-o-lite AM-FM radio would lead me to Max Weiner, founder of the Consumer Education and Protective Association, CEPA, and the Consumer Party.

CEPA

Max had been a member of MENSA, a real estate agent and an honest to God Communist in the 1930s.

While Max had known Ralph Nader, referred to as our nation's Consumer Advocate, it was Max's dealings in the real estate world that had led him to coin the term "Consumerism" and to eventually carry the flag of the Consumer into battle in our nation's market place. Max had seen one too many little guys get a raw economic deal at the hands of others who sat in a greater position of power. This included Philadelphia lawyers who ended up rich by taking up to 50 percent of some poor guy's settlement after he had already been taken in by some deal that, "seemed too good to be true."

No sir. Max saw no reason for a hard working person to get the short end of a deal only to turn around and compound one's economic problems by then giving away more money to some legal savior. Max always spoke of "people power." He would always say that "we already had the power; we just needed to realize it and then learn how to use it." Everywhere you looked people were getting themselves taken advantage of.

Max recognized that folks had often purchased something in good faith only to find that the product didn't work. Often the response on the part of the buyer was to just slink away in shame and embarrassment when that used car broke down five blocks from the car dealer.

Most often the seller's response was, "What do you expect me to do? It worked when you drove off the lot!"

For Max, it all came to a head when his wife, Bess, told him of the plight of Ms. Anatine Tyson, a domestic worker with beautiful high cheek bones and a thick South Carolinian accent, who had worked for a mutual friend. She purchased a freezer, which came with a "life time supply of meat." After receiving only a small supply of the promised meat, the freezer broke down and stopped running completely. It turned out the same thing happened to the woman who had told Ms. Tyson about the original, "wonderful deal." A contract obligated Ms. Anatine to pay $29.95 each month for another 15 years!

When Ms. Anatine had tried to reason with the man at the appliance store, he told her it was her problem. She had bought the freezer fair and square, and she was obligated to accept the shipments of meat (which she could not do because her new freezer was no longer working). She would have to continue to make payments in spite of the fact that the shipments of meat had stopped and the freezer didn't work.

Max was outraged. He decided to champion the woman's cause. He took Ms. Anatine and her contract to the local sheriff to register a complaint. The sheriff, after a quick glance at the paper, declared that the contract seemed to be in order and Ms. Anatine would have to keep her end of the bargain. He added that, "things could get much worse for Ms. Anatine if she failed her contractual obligation." Max tried unsuccessfully to call the owner of the store on her behalf. Max knew that Mrs. Anatine had little or no chance in the courts even if she could afford a lawyer. He thought about how outraged he had felt when he had heard the story and knew therein lay a course of action.

He and Ms. Anatine wrote out her story on one side of a single sheet of paper. They mimeographed 100 copies and painted two signs that declared "UNFAIR!" in thick, bold, black letters. They headed downtown to the main office of the department store, not the local branch where Ms. Anatine had bought her troubles.

They started marching back and forth and passing out their educational leaflets to would-be consumers as they entered the premises. Within 5 minutes, the storeowner stormed out, red-faced, leaflet crushed in his right hand, and demanded to know what they were doing!

Max explained that Ms. Anatine had been ripped off. The owner demanded that they stop picketing and leave immediately. Max had been involved in dozens of labor disputes in his union days and declared that it was their right to picket. Then, Ms. Anatine, getting into the swing of things, declared that it was her "civil right" to speak her peace.

The year was 1982, so coming from an elderly back woman this struck a cord with the owner as it did with a Sheriff's Deputy, who had shown up and now stood speechless beside the owner. Thirty minutes into the demonstration, something amazing happened.

Another woman who had reluctantly taken a flyer, came running back up the street with her husband in tow, waving the flyer yelling, "They done me too! They done me too!"

It was at that moment that Max began to realize the gravity of the situation. They had just unearthed what the newspapers would later refer to as "The Great Freezer Scam of North Philadelphia." They contacted the local media and a small story appeared in the Philadelphia Enquirer. In three days, twenty-three families contacted Ms. Anatine and Max. In the emotionally tight woven fabric of the neighborhood, word of the action spread quickly. Garland Dempsey heard of the scam and came to investigate. Instantly, Garland had grasped the situation.

After reading the flyer, he began approaching people as they passed the store. In his rich resonating voice, he started to tell them about Ms. Anatine's story and how a "poor, God fearing, woman of little formal education had been taken advantage of by those unscrupulous scoundrels." Garland molded the story into a tale and he began to preach her story to the people. Dozens of folks stopped and listened, enraptured by the tale. Garland, in his best going to church, sermon-preaching, righteous, baritone voice, spoke of truth, God, and country.

He told how Ms. Anatine, in good faith, with no knowledge of legal contracts or the working mechanics of a freezer, had been duped and had her hard-earned money taken out of her very own pocket and out of the mouths of her three small children. It was a crime against humanity! The owners of the appliance stores tore up all of the contracts and all the purchasers re-negotiated their contracts or totally cancelled them and the buyers got full refunds. It was victory of the poorest of the poor in the heart of North Philadelphia!

Later Garland invited Max back to his home for cookies and punch. It was there at the old worn pine kitchen table in the house at 20th and Glenwood (where I now found shelter in an abandoned house) that Max and Garland founded CEPA, Consumers Education and Protective Association.

Max said that in our society if you were not selling, then you were buying and as a buyer, you were a consumer. He said that everyone was a consumer at one point or another. He said that unless you were rich enough to hire a lawyer and had endless amounts of time on your hands, then you had no rights. In fact, a Latin phrase put the whole responsibility on the consumer, *Caveat Emptor*, or *Let the Buyer Beware*. The way Max and Garland figured it, if folks did not stand up for themselves, no one else would. The term Consumer was coined, and an international movement was born promoting the voice of consumers and their economic rights everywhere.

CEPA followed a simple three-step procedure: 1) investigate; 2) negotiate; and 3) demonstrate (if we had to). CEPA was located at 6048 Ogontz Ave., Philadelphia, PA, where it exists to this day. For decades Max rented space there where people from all walks of life would enter through a rickety lead-based painted green door into a unique world of camaraderie. They came with their tales of economic woes, hat in hand, feeling ashamed and wronged. Max would hear their stories, ask for a contribution of $23.50

and then help them reduce their tale to a one-page leaflet. I never asked how he had established the amount but as far as I know this contribution amount never changed.

If we won a complaint, we asked for 10% of the value of the case and some volunteer time.

We would say, "Someone came to your aid and walked the line for you and now it was time for you to do the same."

Max would then get on the phone and discuss how Mr. Jones or Mrs. Johnson had bought some used car only to have it billowing smoke just days after the purchase. Or, he called an appliance repair store explaining how some washing machines had simply stopped working after only three days of use, or how a toaster had caught fire and nearly cost someone their home.

Sometimes the seller of the item would hang up; other times, they would listen, talk and then hang up. We would then send a certified letter, return receipt requested, outlining our concerns and asking to set up a face-to-face meeting. These were mostly ignored in hopes that we would go away, but we never went away. We were *right*. *We had the power of justice on our side*. When the green return receipt came back acknowledging that the letter had been delivered, we would make a final attempt to reach the seller of the goods on the phone. Failing a response, we would pull out our sheets of cardboard.

We would get our jet-black paint and paint our truth as clearly as possible.

"Apple Auto sells Lemons!"

"Dealer won't talk with Consumer!"

"Mr. Jones sold lawn mower that won't!"

"James Brothers Builders takes over 1 year to build Kitchen…job still not done."

"Mrs. West ripped off by Central Appliance!"

Signs were painted in big block black letters. We tried to catch the eye, personalize the story and put the entire story on a bumper sticker.

"Ms. Tess was sold rotten meat!"

"Mr. Brown sold vacuum that won't!"

We would take our signs and our one-page leaflets, with no embellishments, and spend our lunch hour in front of a business showing our signs and talking to potential customers (consumers). The idea was to get people mentally to place themselves in the position of the aggrieved consumer.

We wanted them to think twice about how they might be treated if they ran into a problem with the same product at the same store. Why should they expect to be treated any differently?

We would do our best to get an empathetic fellow consumer to approach the manager or owner and ask what they were doing to resolve the situation. This was so effective that it often took only three or four people and one busy lunch hour to settle most complaints. Sometimes there would be fifty or more people on an educational picket line and sometimes complaints would take weeks to settle.

As CEPA's reputation grew, we found that just by showing up we would often be met on the sidewalk with a settlement offer. We were not suing, so we only asked our fellow consumer to be "made whole." If they had bought a set of encyclopedias that was missing volumes N and P we just wanted volumes N and P replaced or a full refund given in exchange for the return of the other volumes. We never asked for lost time or lost wages due to the recovery process. We never asked for pain and suffering or other compensation. We asked only to be made whole on the original purchase. This seemed the fairest thing to do. It was important that we were able to take the moral high ground and that all who witnessed our actions perceived our calls for fairness as justified. Our strength lay in the truth. Our strength grew from us championing the little guy — David against Goliath. Our strength grew from the fact that we stood up for ourselves and for every other little guy who just wanted a fair shake —*We The People*.

As time went on, CEPA had more work and more success. Unscrupulous businesses owners fought back by claiming that we were anti-business. They asserted that we should be prevented from conducting our educational pickets as they interfered with the business' right to conduct unimpeded commerce. We maintained that we were defending consumers. CEPA was sued. We won. It was established in a court of law that we had the right to our entire process of consumer complaint resolution. After the lawsuit, a special police task force for civil disobedience protection was created and our process was *sanctioned*.

Max felt that, as consumers, we had a right and an obligation to become involved with general price increases and business transactions that affected our lives on a daily basis. When SEPTA, the South Eastern Public Transportation Agency, set out to raise our fares from fifty cents to sixty-five cents, we got in gear. We set-up petition tables in the heart of the city in the area surrounding City Hall at 16th and Chestnut Streets. While people waited for pedestrian lights, we had almost two minutes to get on an amplified bullhorn and speak about our rights and obligations as consumers. We would talk about the lack of improvement on the buses and subways and decry the fifteen-cent fare increase as unjust.

We described it as a form of taxation over which only politically connected members of the SEPTA Oversight Board had any say. We called for people for the first time to take control of unbridled capitalistic forces that were running roughshod over our lives. We had a broad view of the intersection. People came to the pedestrian stop light from all directions. We could see them gathering like Pachinko balls. Captivated, they heard our message and stared at us paying rapt attention. Our sense was that they were being almost hypnotically drawn to our words of justice. The swelling crowd inspired our speech of economic freedom. The volume of our speech would invariably increase along with our sense of righteousness. As the light would turn green, people would bust out into the roadway. They hurriedly moved in our direction. We would invite them to "take a second, stop at our table and sign the petition to say fifty cents…no more!"

As busy as folks were, they would stop, two to three deep, quickly, sign up, give us their address and phone numbers. As they left, they would smile and gladly toss nickels, dimes and quarters or even a dollar or two into our keep-it-going jar. In this fashion, we collected tens of thousands of signatures, which we ultimately presented to the SEPTA oversight board. Sometimes we won outright, sometimes we slowed down the process, and sometimes less of an increase was granted than had been asked. Each battle reminded us that it is all about the struggle itself. *The struggle, of course, is about dignity, and economic fairness.*

Max argued that, as consumers, big decisions about building nuclear power facilities like Three Mile Island and the international purchase of gas on the high seas should be subject to consumer input. Max suggested the back of utility bills be used for consumer input. As consumers, we could make a simple, check-the-box response to any number of questions affecting our lives. Today, thirty-five years later, this method of communication is often utilized, though differently than Max would have used it. Back then, everything seemed possible. We were on the move, consumers were seizing power and control of lives, only limited by our own imaginations. In fact, we formed the Consumer Party, a third political party was founded on the concept of consumer protection. It lasted until Max's death in the early 1990s.

Following the 1973 Energy Crisis, inflation hit double digits and we started to feel an economic shift in this country. Japan and Germany had been devastated in World War II, but now thanks to the Marshall plan, they had physically rebuilt their economies. The United States in the steel, automotive and even printing industries had enjoyed much of world market but now Germany and Japan had rebuilt and automation was their mantra. In an effort for Corporate America to recapture world market share without reducing shareholder profits (or so it was thought), fewer workers would have to work longer hours for less pay. Michael Moore documented this time and events in the movie *Roger and Me*. The movie depicts the closing of entire auto factories in Detroit, Michigan, as businesses abandoned entire worker communities and closed their doors overnight. The factories later reopened in Mexico where labor was cheap and unorganized. In Ohio and Pennsylvania, the same scenario was replayed in the steel and coal industries. Entire factories would shut down and hard fought, twenty-three-dollar-an-hour jobs disappeared over night.

At CEPA, hard working, blue collar homeowners started to walk through our green door clenching lawsuits — *Complaints in Foreclosure*, for failure to pay their mortgages on time. Pat McNamara, the sweetest looking, toughest consumer advocate I ever met, taught me how to negotiate with the mortgage companies. One of my classmates from Walter Johnson High School, Arthur Liebershon, had become a lawyer, and for $125 would file an Answer to the Complaints in Foreclosure. We would treat it as any other CEPA complaint with educational leaflets, signs and pickets.

The legal response gave us time to maneuver, and we would attempt to engage the mortgage company in a dialogue about re-negotiating the contract. If the mortgagee had been lucky enough to land another job, we would work to negotiate payment. If the new job brought in less money, we would offer to place the accumulated late amount on the far end of the note term and reduce the monthly payment. We became very creative in our economic advocacy. I became a self-appointed "Mortgage Foreclosure Preventionist."

CEPA met with the Sheriff of Philadelphia County and showed him there were more foreclosures occurring then, than during The Great Depression. To our amazement, after seeing the numbers, the Sheriff agreed with us and initiated a moratorium on mortgage foreclosures in the county! He refused to allow good hard-working folks to continue to lose their homes for reasons beyond their control. Max always seemed to bring the best out in folks.

Following a lawsuit filed by the Legal Services Corporation in Chicago, the U.S. Department of Housing and Urban Development, HUD, the newly formed governmental agency dealing with housing matters, launched a Mortgage Assignment program. The government had created an amortization program for people, for whom it had made homeownership possible, but who had fallen behind on monthly payments for circumstances beyond their control (i.e. loss of job, major illness, family death, etc.) More and more of CEPA's success stories involved negotiated deals with mortgage companies and banks.

Steve Gold from Law Center North Central, (a branch of the national civil legal services organization, Legal Services Corporation), read about our victories and asked for a meeting. He could not understand how we were able to save homes from foreclosure after Legal Aid had attempted a rescue and then surrendered to a loss. Steve wanted me to come work for Legal Aid, which Max agreed to, so long as I could continue to do exactly what I had been doing in CEPA. Amazingly Max, Steve, and I struck a deal. Consumers had a new full time, paid advocate, and my near three-year stint of homelessness came to an end.

Germantown, Philadelphia

Shortly thereafter, I moved into a three-story, stone, mill worker's house on Church Lane in Historic Germantown, one of Philadelphia's many neighborhoods. George Washington had resided just 500 yards from the house in the winter of 1779, while his troops wintered at Valley Forge and he struggled with a yellow fever epidemic. The house was a twin — literally two houses using a single common firewall for the purposes of conserving heat in what can sometimes be a brutally cold Pennsylvania winter. The twin was one of about twenty such structures in our 55-block area known as the Penn Area Neighborhood, so-called because the Lenapi Indians reportedly struck a treaty with William Penn nearby, beneath a huge oak tree.

Philadelphia is a city of shifting neighborhoods based on economics. As one cultural pocket of settlers achieves economic success, they slowly, but deliberately, move into a slightly better neighborhood. As I mentioned, when The U.S. Department of Housing and Urban Development (HUD) made mortgages and home ownership available to poor and low-income black people in the 1960s, white flight swept the city. Germantown, and many other neighborhoods, were devastated when white people chose to abandon their homes rather than live next door to a black family. White families were so desperate to leave that they often ended up paying two mortgage notes, just to escape the unknown.

My house in Germantown was affordable because I shared rent with several other young guys. The house was a run down, neglected stone and brick twin that had once been quite handsome. The landlord had bought it for $100 from HUD. It had six bedrooms with porcelain doorknobs, oak stair rails, and turned oak spindles on the staircase. The floors were yellow pine and honey oak. It had ornate iron grillwork in front of a fireplace that had a painted-over, solid oak fire mantel guarding the remnants of a converted, wood-to-gas fireplace. Perfectly interlaced oak wainscoting lined the walls rising from the stairs, followed the banister around the corner and into the second floor bathroom and ended just above a claw foot bath tub where it met two, his and her, ornately hand carved oak medicine cabinets. I lived there with Ed Miller, a full-time schoolteacher who was writing "the great American novel," as he referred to it. Another roommate, Doug, was a delightful young man full of insight, who later became a Sufi, and finally left to dance around corn somewhere.

Later in the house were two brothers, John and Chris McCann. They went to LaSalle University and rowed for the crew team. They were two beefed-up, blond Irish boys who, having come from a background of poverty, took the opportunity of education seriously. They combined athletic prowess with the need for a good education. Both managed to attain athletic scholarships. This, of course, required papers to be typed and neither had a predilection in this direction. They secured the help of a young female student. Once settled in the shared house, I too tried my hand at school when (for some reason) I thought I might be a physical therapist. As a result, I also needed papers typed. One evening, the smell of oatmeal cookies rising from the kitchen of a bachelor's house brought me flying down the stairs and face to face with my future and beloved wife, Sylvia. Almost a decade after leaving the military, I thought that perhaps it was possible to have a successful relationship. She was cute as a button with long brown hair and natural blond highlights that reached down to the small of her back. She was twelve years my junior, but clearly an older soul than most. Just five years later, (my perspective not hers), we married in a house on that very same street. Together, we had restored it to its original 1896 splendor and felt it symbolized our union and struggle to find one another.

The landlord, Leonard Brown, lived in the neighborhood. The area had once been a mill town and Leonard Brown lived in the manor house high on the hill over looking the mill houses. He had taken advantage of the white flight phenomenon by purchasing from HUD scores of houses at prices that ranged from $1 to $1500. Relatively speaking, Leonard was not really a good landlord nor was he a bad landlord. He lived in the area, so that was good. He interacted with his tenants socially and that was pleasant enough, but getting him to make repairs on his collection of deteriorating houses was next to impossible. And so from that perspective, he was a typical landlord.

There was more or less an open invitation to come up to his house and drink a beer or two anytime we liked. There was always someone there. As one can imagine, the neighborhood became a refuge for people who could easily be described as oblong pegs trying to fit into not such round holes. The people make-up was interracial and eclectic to say the least.

For example, Michael Bucsek was a professor who was no longer engaged in that profession for unknown reasons. Now he kept things going by doing odd jobs as an electrician and speaking French to the local women. Honey Budnick, then a single, middle-aged German woman, settled there after hiking the Appalachian Trail forward and back (by herself). Don lived down the row, and like everyone else in the neighborhood, was a little eccentric and bit of a recluse. I entered his home only once. I found almost every inch of usable space to be covered with pipe organ parts — organ bellows, brass pipes of all dimensions and in all states of unpolished green tinge. There was oak framing everywhere. There may have been as many as four entire organs totally dismembered and strewn throughout every inch of the house including all six bedrooms. I could not grasp where one assemblage began and the next ended. No matter. He seemed to be intimate with every part.

On the other side of our twin was the home of Mr. (Old Man) Tate and his wife. They were an elderly black couple who could not have been sweeter if they took lessons and worked at it. Every day of life, he wore red suspenders that curved their way over his rotund belly, then skyward to his massive chest and disappeared over his considerable shoulders. He was as gentle as any man that I have ever met. He held concern for every creature, human or otherwise. He worked from dawn to dusk doing home repairs, mostly inside house painting at which he was meticulously good. When I think of Old Man Tate, my mind quickly turns to warm thoughts of John Coffey in the movie, *The Green Mile*. Their slow deliberate actions and gentle manner mirrored one another. Mrs. Tate felt it her duty to feed you if you got within shouting distance of their house. It was hard to imagine that it was because of people like these that countless scores of people had fled the neighborhood in abject fear. Remarkably, these two gentle people had single-handedly brought one of the oldest, most historic neighborhoods in our nation to a state of abandonment. Hard to imagine.

At one point, while still only a renter in the neighborhood, I laid siege to an abandoned house on Lena Street, just across Belfield Avenue, and therefore just outside of the Penn Area Neighborhood where we all lived. I had hopes of restoring the property, acquiring title, and moving into it. For months, at the end of each day of working for Legal Aid for poor people and fighting on behalf of consumers with CEPA, I would return to the house on Lena Street.

I would slip behind a quarter-inch-thick piece of plywood that had been haphazardly nailed on one of the first floor windows in hope of keeping the "rippers" from entering the house and stripping it of valuable copper. At the time, there were over 40,000 such abandoned buildings in the Philadelphia area. In our neighborhood of 55 square blocks, we counted 110 abandoned houses. The Lena Street house had long since had all of its copper and plumbing stripped out. The walls and ceilings had been constructed of plaster slathered over 1" x 3/8" strips of rough cut pine, spaced about an inch apart, running the length of the wall or ceiling. The plaster was up to ½" thick and oozed another ½" thick through the strips in order to bind them. Now that the pipes had been ripped out, the remaining lath/plaster carnage was in need of being removed. For months I worked to prepare the house as a shell, so I could later begin to rehabilitate the house.

I planned to process the house through the tax abatement program and secure the title. In true Tom Sawyer fashion, I got Sylvia to join me in climbing through the narrow opening and cart off dozens and dozens of extremely weighty boxes of plaster and lath. She claims that it was the first test of our courtship to see if she could keep up. I swear that had not been my intent, but who knows such things. Eventually, the house was lost to me because of local politics and government red tape. Youthful and undaunted, but still without adequate resources, I continued my search for a home. I would not be deterred in my desire to acquire my own home and through the struggle, attain a sense of community. I would later realize my dream with Sylvia by my side.

The eighties were full of creative and progressive home ownership concepts. In fact, at one point I came across a progressive mortgage-lending group that was willing to loan money to four unrelated people. So, Doug from my group house, who later danced around corn, Pat McNamara, from CEPA, Terry Mashovic, who we met through mutual friends, and Buddy, my Springer Spaniel, convinced a start up mortgage company that we were financially and emotionally stable enough to pay a note on a house. Pure insanity. We purchased a great two-story house built in the late 1950's in the Logan area of Philadelphia. Our arrangement lasted for a little over a year before things unraveled. Fortunately, we managed to sell the house at a profit of $20,000. Korean immigrants had begun to converge on the area in large numbers and the neighborhood had quickly escalated in value. Once again, another neighborhood in Philadelphia did the cultural economic rotation dance.

I took my profit of five thousand dollars and moved into another Leonard Brown house in the old Penn neighborhood. Sylvia and I moved in together and started talking of buying a house in the neighborhood that we would eventually restore. I used my nest egg of five thousand dollars to buy half a twin home from Mrs. Pringle for $25,000. Together, Sylvia and I returned this home to its original beauty from 1896. Surrounded by family and friends, we were married on the oak stairs we had so lovingly restored.

Having committed myself to the Penn Neighborhood, I started to focus on its general state of disrepair. It was then that Walter Hallinan, another neighbor, and I counted the abandoned homes in the neighborhood. My good friend Karen Morris, half of the first interracial couple I had ever known, while raising two beautiful daughters, had become more and more concerned about the deteriorating condition of our neighborhood. She, Walter, and I became determined to blow on the embers of a once-active community until we blew life into the Penn Area Neighborhood Association.

The Philadelphia Stabilization Plan

Our fifty-five block neighborhood had 110 abandoned homes and dozens of empty lots, like missing teeth, where homes had once stood. It occurred to me that none of us would live long enough to see complete restoration if we tried to rehab these houses one at a time. We needed a plan! We needed a *master* plan.

First, we needed to preserve the abandoned housing stock and stop its deterioration. These homes had been had been top notch, built of stone by German artisans, carpenters and stonemasons of the first degree whose ancestors had built some of the finest castles in Europe. They had a standard to meet and they built to last! We recognized that the construction was sound. We borrowed a page out of the HUD handbook and boarded up all the doors and windows. We mounted the facing boards of plywood solidly in place. Next, we needed to place roofs on each structure.

Because Philadelphia is a union town, I had to ensure union involvement or suffer the consequences. That meant I had to involve George Zielaskowski, who helped us negotiate roofs at $1,500 each, a bulk rate. He was principally a plumber but had his hand in all the building trades. He was the son of two immigrants of Polish decent. George spoke with a thick South Philly accent and said things like "yous guys" and "waddya talkin?" George was a good worker who saw an economic angle in everything. He probably worked harder at the angles than at the work itself, but George was with us.

We needed to completely gut the houses removing any walls or ceilings where lath had been exposed or where the plaster had "bubbled and fried" from moisture. Our next step was to replace all glass with Lexan. Lexan is the material that is used in trolley cars. It is great stuff. It is impervious to yellowing, unlike Plexiglas, and you can hit it with a sledgehammer and only shatter your own teeth in the effort.

Local businesses helped. Factory outlets donated bolts of fabric that did not move well out of the warehouses. Enthusiastic support was received from senior citizen centers willing to sew the fabric into curtains to cover the windows in our house shells. Other businesses donated gallons of old, but unopened paint. We coordinated with the City of Philadelphia and their anti-graffiti program so that errant youth would apply fresh coats of gleaming new paint to all window and door trims. It's important to remember that 95% of these homes were either all stone or stone and brick.

When the houses were ready, we took pictures of the outside of each house and all interior rooms. The photos were mounted in catalogs for prospective buyers to view the inside of each house. A local bank agreed to offer a mortgage with rehab and wrap-around loans so the buyers could purchase the shells and have money to rehabilitate them.

I heard that the City of Baltimore had initiated a similar program. We traveled there and returned with pictures of a dozen homes that were perfectly coiffed shells ready to be sold on the real estate market. We got the idea to make flower boxes — painted, planted and hung the flower boxes from the window casings. We turned the pictures into a slide show and began to search for buyers. The houses were put on a rotating calendar so we could monitor and keep their lawns mowed. My housemate, Terry Mushovic, was involved with the Philadelphia Green program, and we started a community garden. Small community gardens with flowers and benches were created in spaces where abandoned buildings had become so dilapidated that they had been razed to the ground.

We began talking to HUD, the City of Philadelphia, and a City Council member about using Community Development Block Grant dollars (CDBG) to launch our Philadelphia Stabilization Plan full scale.

However, without warning and seemingly almost overnight, like the speed of the plague, drug dealers overran our neighborhood. Of course, things were tough; times were tough. The neighborhood was as economically depressed as it could be. Clearly, people were hustling both drugs and other people. Everyone was trying to get by. Jobs were scarce and good paying jobs were almost non-existent. Marijuana and cocaine was bought and sold, but it seemed to be mostly for personal use. Some heroin was also around. We pretty much knew, though, who was "using" and basically avoided contact with them on that odd occasion when our paths would cross. *Then, crack cocaine came into our world and everything changed.*

We started to see half-inch-long, clear plastic tubes with different colored rubber caps showing up on the streets. Green caps, yellow caps, blue caps, and even red ones; all the same size, just different colored caps. Once we began to see them we came to realize that they were everywhere. They literally filled the cracks of the sidewalks.

Gunshots rang out in the night. We would report a shooting, but the police took up to half an hour to arrive. It took a while to isolate and locate the shooting incidents. We discovered that drug users had begun to pull back the HUD-installed plywood and enter the abandoned houses. They were, now, using them as miniature fortresses from which to buy, sell, and ingest their crack cocaine. We learned that people who used crack lost all inhibitions and took on what sometimes appeared to be super human strength. The shootings increased at night. Single women with children, who had once found refuge in our neighborhood from abusive relationships, now slept on the floor beside their beds so as not to be killed accidentally in a drug shooting.

The drug dealers began to have drug wars. They were laying claim to our houses to practice their debauchery and having turf wars over the perfect caches we created. The reality of it was, they saw crack as their California gold rush. The sellers and impoverished locals alike, saw a meal ticket out of poverty.

Their perception was that everyone on the planet had color TVs, Nike sneakers, boom boxes, and new cars. The images on television convinced them that everyone else had unbridled credit and had absolutely anything they wanted. Their world, on the other hand, was limited to a truncated, mediocre high school education, if that, guaranteeing only minimum wage jobs and a life of drudgery. The sale of crack cocaine meant money. Instant, big money afforded recognition and validation as a person. Layers of gold chains about their necks served as evidence of the spoils of crack. With these ribbons of gold, they were successful businessmen.

As a result of this cultural economic dance, our neighborhood took a downturn, and we were faced with accepting that there would be no rehabilitation of the Penn Area Neighborhood. Roofers would not be coming to put $1,500 roofs on our structures.

No one would volunteer to mow the lawns. No youth would come to paint the window trims, no seniors would come and install their curtains. No one would come to replace the boards and glass with Lexan. Yes, we were sure that there would be no rehabilitation of the Penn Area Neighborhood. There would be no rehabilitation unless we could fully, completely, and permanently *stabilize* the neighborhood.

We met with the police, but all they could offer us was commiseration. They were short staffed; budgets had been cut, and crime was up. They were stretched to the max as it was. They assured us that they would do their best to respond as quickly as possible to all calls. They could do little else. It was an economic thing.

Mobile Mini Police Station

Clearly, we were on our own. I decided that what we needed was another creative plan. We would have to think outside of the box. I kept mulling over everything the police had said. They were short staffed. They had limited funds. They were over extended and could not be everywhere at once.

Life had taught me that the solutions to really hard problems lie in the problems themselves. I kept thinking about every cops and robbers movie I had ever seen. I thought about all of the stereotypical depictions. What did the police need? What did we need? I reviewed our problem repeatedly.

Finally, it came to me. If Muhammad cannot go to the mountain, take the mountain to Muhammad. What we needed was a police station in our neighborhood. Yes! This would offer the immediate response that we needed. But this tends to work only in theory. Police sub-stations have little or no chance of being implemented during tough economic times, which is just when they are needed most. Even with volunteer labor, and a plethora of abandoned buildings such as found in Philadelphia, a sub-station would have taken $60,000 to $100,000 dollars to rehab and outfit on the meekest scale possible. In addition, the scope of influence of such an outpost is obviously limited. One sub-station would be ineffective. It more or less sets up an invisible, circular force field of protection around the sub-station of anywhere from a quarter mile to a half mile. However, that is about it. We could not justify the cost for such a small pocket of influence. We needed greater impact at a much more affordable cost. That is when it hit me.

What we needed was an emergency response vehicle! We needed to establish a police presence, a beachhead that was both mobile and formidable at the same time, something that would virtually shout authority and stability and at the same time could move from hot spot to hot spot. We needed a Mobile Mini Police Station. It occurred to me that the most visibly impressive vehicle would be the classic Airstream travel trailer. Its gleaming sleek silver skin of industrial strength with riveted seams commanded respect. Its aerodynamic design exuded power, like a silver bullet. The idea was that when a shooting was reported, we would move into a neighborhood with great fanfare and an overwhelming police presence. It would be radio equipped with full police sub-station capabilities. Police officers would use it as a dispatch station from which we would first introduce the idea of Community Policing, where officers in black and white units and foot patrols would receive their assignments and spread out into the neighborhood. At night, officers would use it for respites and for central check in. We would outfit it with coffee makers and storage for snacks. At night, it would be a hub of activity. A police dog would be kenneled outside to prevent fire bombings. In the daytime, city representatives would join in to use it as a base of operations for community outreach. We would use it as an outpost to let local residents organize themselves into Neighborhood Watch Teams and into community organizations.

The first thing we did was scrape and paint all the fire hydrants in the entire neighborhood. This produced an outward sign that the good, God fearing, anti-crime neighbors were united and on the move. Signs went up declaring that this was a Neighborhood Watch Area. We introduced the neighbors to the City Urban Gardening program. We built our flower boxes, painted them in bright colors, and planted flowers. We leafleted every house declaring our intentions to reclaim our homeland and expose all drug activity and drive it from our neighborhood. The Mobile Mini Police Station would remain in each area for about three months. During that time, we would move it around the neighborhood, but it would be in each neighborhood for a limited amount of time so every minute counted.

We celebrated every reclamation initiative with a show of fanfare. The elected officials were invited when we finished projects like painting our fire hydrants. We had music and dancing and held block parties at the drop of a hat. We needed to become visible again. We prepared to forge an alliance with our local police officers. We made sure that they knew every person in each household. They went door-to-door with our blessing and introduced themselves. We would cook and bake for them and deliver our goodies to the Mobile Mini Police Station. The idea was like magic. It captured the imagination of the Penn Area Neighborhood Association.

We began meeting with the police chief and the captains who oversaw our sector. They were out-gunned and out-manned. They were exhausted, burnt out, and everyone knew it. In a way, we were like the cavalry. At first, the police were wary and skeptical that we would interfere with their policing tactics. They expected us to lose interest in just a couple of weeks. We surprised them. These were our homes, and we were determined to reclaim peace and quiet. They realized this brought them more troops and united them for the first time in decades with the people they were charged with serving. Everyone went to work. Letters of cooperation were written. Congressman Fogerty was approached, and we captured his imagination.

The real breakthrough came just after Sylvia and I left Germantown forever. The late great Senator John Heinz secured the funding for the Mobile Mini Police Station and at least five now exist around the country.

"What the mind can conceive, the people can achieve," Jessie Jackson.

Austin — Mother's Health

I received a phone call from my mother's friend explaining that my mother was in the hospital having suffered a serious bout with congestive heart failure. She was sixty-seven years old. I had to go. Therefore, we went. Sylvia had a college degree, and had worked three and a half years as a special education teacher. This amounted to what most considered a transferable skill. I, on the other hand, had a high school diploma and had served three years in the Marines, after which I had mostly blown in the wind.

I learned that the Legal Services Corporation had a branch office located in Austin, Texas. I learned everything I could about Austin and contacted the Executive Director Regina Rogoff. She seemed somewhat interested because Austin had begun to have people who were experiencing homelessness and the Mayor, Lee Cook, had devised a plan to deal with it.

I shared with Regina how, on Tuesday nights in Philadelphia, I had been joining others who loaded up their backpacks with sandwiches and water and spent several hours following a little street circuit on foot where homeless, mentally ill people needed help. In the winter, they would migrate individually to steam grates that used to dot the cityscape. Philadelphia may have been unique in that, when it was being industrialized, an extensive steam vent system was built underground. It used escaping steam to heat the sidewalks and help the snow melt throughout the city. One by one, the grates in the downtown area become the proprietary location of various folks experiencing homelessness, many of whom later became my friends. We had long, rambling, mostly one-sided conversations. Other times I might meet someone whose name I never learned from the individual directly. Often, they were unmotivated to speak, and I might sit silently for twenty minutes or longer just being there.

When I left I might say, "Well, I'll just leave this sandwich and drink here should you get hungry or thirsty later."

I would always add that the food and water were safe and had been prepared in a doubly safe, protective environment under the strictest sanitary conditions. I always mentioned that I had washed my hands thoroughly with soap and water before preparation. I felt this was very important as some of these folks had phobias and because others were just skittish generally.

I knew that many of these people ate directly from garbage cans. This included the ones with cleanliness phobias, but when they foraged for the food themselves, they somehow attained a cleanliness standard only they could fathom.

Part of it was about dignity and respect. These people had lost everything and had been rejected by all. Part of the reason for their presence on the streets of America had been born of the best intentions when a lawsuit filed out of Chicago by Legal Services Corporation had led to deinstitutionalization of our nation's mental health facilities. We really did not have anything to offer as an alternative to the life that had so thoroughly enveloped them. We did not have answers, shelters, or the promise of escape. We only had ham sandwiches and the testimony of our actions showing that we cared and that they were not forgotten. We were like the little Dutch boy with his finger in the dike holding back the flood waters waiting for help...waiting for help.

The second reason Regina Rogoff was interested in me was that I had been urged to submit the Philadelphia Stabilization Plan to the United Nations International Year of Shelter for the Homeless search, for best practices initiative, for which HUD was the U.S. agent, and I won recognition. This impressed her. She said she could probably use me. I explained that I would have to put my home on the market, get things together, and head to Austin.

She said, "Fine, go ahead."

To me, that meant I could conceivably be in Austin in two and a half months. To her, this meant I might arrive in a year or longer. This is where our communication broke down, right from the beginning. Austin's real estate market was stagnant following an economic bust. On the other hand, I had just received my real estate license. I was knowledgeable and very motivated to come to Austin to be with my mother. Two months later, Sylvia and I had sold the house (at a profit) and were in Austin with no jobs between us.

TWO:

THE FACES OF HOMELESSNESS

Homelessness

When we arrived in Austin, TX, it was February 1989. There were about 340,000 people in the entire Austin metropolitan area. All things seemed possible. It was a completely new environment and a completely new life. The weather was cold at night but morning doves, not grackles (as today), were the principal birds that greeted the day. The sky was clear, blue and big. The air was fresh and clear. Except for the immediate downtown area, few buildings stood above two stories. Most homes were one-story ranch style homes. The town of Austin, Texas had already had a boom in the mid 1980s involving questionable savings and loan lending practices, which had ended in a debacle. The banks had been left holding thousands of foreclosed upon houses and empty buildings across the southwest in its wake. Homelessness had already come to Austin.

There were dozens of visibly homeless people sprinkled throughout the downtown area. I was struck by the sense that I had followed my steel, coal, and autoworkers, and now Texas oil field workers into homelessness. I worked very hard to convince Regina that I knew and understood this population and could fashion a program to help them. In reality, I had only limited knowledge of the causes of the condition or the cure except that the condition was born of economics. In Pennsylvania, when the economy went bad, people's families had taken them in. For months, extended families, cousins, grandparents offered help. At first, people were looking for work of equal pay to the jobs they had just lost, but then they were just looking for work. As time dragged on, they became more desperate. Reluctantly, very reluctantly, people went on food stamps. Then the unthinkable happened, they were forced to go on welfare (although in Texas there has never been general assistance for men). For the men, the very core of their manhood was shaken. They were unable to provide for their families. The women were scared and the children were scared.

Many factors led to the full-blown homelessness in which we now see our nation embroiled. For the last several years, the number of people experiencing homelessness on an annual basis in our country has risen to three and a half million people. At times, the numbers have swollen beyond that due to disasters like hurricanes Rita and Katrina. A major increase of homelessness began with the end of the Vietnam War due to a glut of returning soldiers. Most of these young men and women were too emotionally destabilized to work even if they could find it. Many were suffering Post Traumatic Stress Disorder, PTSD. Veterans of World War II scorned Vietnam veterans. Even though there was a Department of Veterans Affairs, it was comprised of WWII veterans and there was no outreach and no welcome mat for Korean and Vietnam veterans. World War II veterans had fought in a "real war." Homeless veterans have further added to our national disgrace with the National Coalition for Homeless calculating that between 28-33% of people experiencing homelessness are veterans.

Double-digit inflation and women's liberation changed the American family structure forever. We moved from families where only our fathers worked, to families where both parents had to work. Children came home after school to empty homes and no supervision. We called them "latch key kids;" they called it abandonment. Many of our young people have grown angry, resentful and un-bonded.

Other economic pressures increased. Divorces increased in the 1980s. In keeping with cultural tradition, the courts gave principal custody of the children to mothers. The courts then awarded mothers the houses so children would have a home. The father, then out of the house, was forced to pay for his own apartment. At the same time, he was still saddled with the mortgage note and financial support of his wife and children. The pressures increased. Often drinking began or continued. Hope began to slip away. These were the stories. I heard them over and over again.

Camee Vega

Camee Vega, age 34 was born September 12, 1969 in Hastings, Nebraska. It was the same year I graduated high school and joined the Marines. Camee's hair is the color of corn silk, her demeanor is calm and her words are few. She is the loving mother of two wonderfully respectful and intelligent daughters, Trina and Talisa. They are fourteen- year-old twins. Trina wants a career in law enforcement and Talisa thinks she may want to be a pediatrician. However, she thinks she will wait and see how her sister fares in law enforcement as she may take her lead if it proves to be enjoyable.

The three of them make a team. After suffering nine years in a physically and emotionally abusive relationship, and household, the team grabbed their schoolbooks and only the clothes on their backs and slipped away in their 1974 Chevy Malibu. In a way, they were lucky. They found their way to Austin, TX and the International Hospitality Network where broken families stay with members of various churches. For them, this went on for a month. The girls were distraught and scared. Camee was determined. She immediately got a job at Garden Terrace, then Austin's only Single Room Occupancy (SRO) facility with supportive housing. Camee is the Night Audit Person/ Desk Clerk where she mothers 85 needy residents. These folks are living independently (sort of). It is considered transitional housing but no one can afford the housing to transition into. They are housed and provided food and case management for almost no rent.

On Thursdays and Fridays, Camee works 4:30 pm to midnight, and on Saturdays, she works from 8:00 am to midnight. It is a grueling 32-hour workweek at $8.00 per hour. Additionally, Camee has secured a job at the Homeless Resource Center, ARCH. Here she also works behind the front desk or takes shifts as the bathroom attendant. However, instead of 85 people, she sees up to 500 people daily. Here she adds another 50 hours to her already very full schedule for a total of 82 hours or the equivalent of two full time jobs. She takes home $647.00 every two weeks. The family team spends $750.00 per month on a three-bedroom apartment. They get a 20% discount because she works for Foundation Communities at the Garden Terrace. The team is part of the working poor and not entitled to food stamps, health care, or public assistance. They earn no paid vacation. They save nothing. They live hand-to-mouth and month-to-month. Camee says that when she gets home, the apartment is clean and food is prepared. She attributes their overall survival to the girls. She says that without their attitude and without their constant hard work, they would be lost. Camee says they don't get all the clothes or the money to do the things the other children do, but they are OK. She hopes that no one gets sick.

About this time, President Reagan pointed to our nation's Housing Authorities, which was how we housed our poor citizens, and he referred to them as ghettos. He said people were living on top of one another like animals, and selling drugs, and hurting one another. He called it a national disgrace. As a nation, we knew he was right. We were embarrassed and ashamed. Therefore, when he led the forced march to retract 75% of the funding for these programs little was said or done. Congress went along. Unfortunately, there was no alternative plan. Scores of Housing Authority apartment complexes across the nation, fell into disrepair, then abandonment.

At the same time, similar things were being said about our nation's mental health institutions. We were abusing our people. Disgruntled, underpaid workers were physically and mentally abusing our mentally ill citizens. Legal Aid in Chicago filed a lawsuit that called for deinstitutionalization. Similar lawsuits swept the country. This coincided with the advent of psychotropic drugs such as Lithium. Mental health providers faced heavy social service dollar reductions. There was the hope that these things could be balanced by treating people on an outpatient basis. They would treat people while they were on a kind of invisible tether.

This approach failed miserably. Anti-psychotic drugs must be heavily monitored and continually adjusted and tweaked. Unfortunately, a person often adapts and sometimes fails to respond over time, so dosages have to be altered. Other drugs must be substituted. In 2010 it has been conservatively estimated that a third of our nation's homeless are suffering serious mental health problems. They now live under our bridges.

Chris Byrt Lyne

Chris Byrt Lyne was born in 1957. He was one of three brothers and three sisters. His brother Mike died in Vietnam. His sister Wendy died from an overdose of prescription drugs shortly after one of her children was run over and killed. Chris tells this in a rather stoic fashion. This may be more a side effect of a head injury he suffered in 1993 when he was jumped rather than any kind of emotional comment on his part. Before the injury, Chris was a construction laborer. After the injury, Christ became homeless. He now receives $674.00 per month in federal disability benefits He gets medical benefits, so his net income drops to $650.00. He's tried to share apartment living several times through the years. The result is always the same...disaster. He either has personality conflicts or one of the roommates fails to produce their share of the rent on payday.

Or, as Chris tells it, "Someone plays their music too loud, and we get thrown out."

Chris is a sweetheart and I care about him like a brother. I helped him get his disability benefits in the beginning and have worked hard to keep them in place. But Chris, at 5'9", 240 lbs. with a harelip scar, slurred stammering speech and poor ability to modulate verbal intonations (he can become very loud) coupled with the insistence of a person who believes he's almost always right, can be a little off-putting. People have even told me that they are more than a little afraid of him.

In fact, Chris has a charge in his police record of terroristic threats. As a result of all these things, not the least of which is his remarkably limited income of $650.00 per month in disability benefits, Chris is a perfect candidate for the HOW program. HOW stands for Habitat on Wheels. It is a housing program of Alan Graham who also runs Mobile Loaves and Fishes. This is a program in Austin where we work to make affordable housing truly affordable. Money is raised to purchase a used mobile home. The tenant, in this case Chris, will spend $300.00 per month on ground rents and costs. He will spend $25.00 per month on a trailer. This will leave the remainder of his income, $225.00, available for food, heating and cooking fuel, electricity, clothing, toiletries, transportation, and emergency medical attention. Clearly, this is less than ideal, but it is a way to make the limited dollars work and provide him with a little dignity and independence. In any event, until the program takes off and a vacancy opens up, Chris will remain homeless.

Adding to the complexity of homelessness was the loss of several million SROs (single room occupancy units) when motels and cheap apartments were torn down and replaced with condominiums or made into parking lots. Another dynamic affecting our nation's poor was the decision by the YMCA, the Young Men's Christian Association, to leave the SRO field of housing. As our agrarian society yielded to industrialization, farm hands migrated to our cities looking for better paying jobs. Migrant workers and even sharecroppers might have earned only a few thousand dollars per year where a Detroit assembly worker might have earned six times that amount.

In any mid-sized or larger city, you could once find a YMCA that offered Christian fellowship and a room for rent. On a nightly basis, you could lay down your $5.00 or $10.00 and get a decent, clean room with a place to stash your things, get up to an alarm clock, go down the hall in the morning to a shared bathroom, and then head off to work — showered, shaved, refreshed and ready to put in a full day's work. You could chase the American Dream. Once up and out, you could walk to any construction site, present yourself to the foreman, tell him you were ready for work, and he would put you to work.

Today, the YMCAs do not exist in any significant number and the construction bosses hire through labor halls where, as a worker, you walk away with about fifty cents on the dollar. A business posting a twelve dollar an hour job ends up with a worker who gets about half that or six dollars per hour and the labor hall keeps the other half of the hourly wage for having recruited and presented the worker to the job site. It is a good deal for the construction boss. It is a great deal for the labor hall, and it is an outrageous abuse of the laborer who does the work. It is daylight robbery.

Ronald Keith Johnson

Ronald Keith Johnson at the age of 45 is one of only two brothers to survive the loss of both parents. Ron made it halfway through the 9th grade — special education as Ron is profoundly dyslexic but labeled retarded.

Ron's life work has been that of a painter. In fact, he helped paint the exterior of the Austin state capitol during its massive renovation in the late 1990s.

Ron would get his jobs through the local labor hall where he was paid $7.50-$8.00 per hour and received $.50 on the dollar; the labor hall received the other 50%.

He had one of the cheaper apartments in town where he paid rent of only $375.00 per month. He was just squeaking by financially when one day he was sand blasting a building in preparation for painting, and he fell 10 feet fracturing his right ankle in three places.

I watched Ron stroke his honey colored beard and reflect, "I was making it... just barely, but I was doing OK until I busted my ankle."

In Texas, businesses are permitted to opt-out of paying for workers compensation in exchange for allowing injured workers the opportunity to sue for their injury. Of course, for such a small claim, Ron was unable to find an attorney to take his case. He was on his own. He received care at the Brackenridge Hospital Emergency where you and I, as tax payers, ultimately pick up the tab. He had no follow-up care and no physical therapy for, after all, he was a member of the working poor.

The business of course was very apologetic, but the foreman let him go saying, "Well hell, it's clear you can't do nothin' son."

Ron tried to bring two other people in to help cover the rent, but that quickly fell apart, and Ron ended up on the streets where he remains to this day. He does odd jobs, but it is never enough to put together first and last months' rent plus the deposit for a new apartment.

Molly Ivans and Homer the Goose, photo by Jana Birchum, *The Austin Chronicle*

Homer's Floating Protest

The Salvation Army built a homeless facility in what had become Austin's 6th Street entertainment district. Homeless citizens had long since given up hope for real change and a couple of homeless guys, one being a young, black man known as James Williams, decided they would hold a gosling (Homer) hostage with threats of a public execution if their demands for a homeless camp ground were not met. James Williams and some of the other folks formed themselves into the Street Peoples' Action Committee.

They built two large Styrofoam boats and began to live on Town Lake (one of the five Highland Lakes along the Colorado River that flows from North West Texas, then southeast through the heart of Austin and eventually empties out into the Gulf of Mexico). There are a series of five damns that divide the river to stem the flooding that used to ravage Austin and bordering towns. One of the lakes created by the dams was Town Lake, (now renamed Lady Bird Lake after Lady Bird Johnson wife of Lyndon Baines Johnson, 36th US President). It is a seven-mile long stretch of calm water where motorboats are prohibited and canoes are the boat of the day. The jewel of Austin is the famed natural spring fed waters of Barton Springs that reclaims crystal clear, limestone-filtered water from the Edwards Aquifer. To have dared to show the severity of their needs, on these placid, beloved waters, homeless citizens were rewarded with arrest. This resulted in a lawsuit, which they won, only to have a local ordinance adopted making it illegal for anyone to use Town Lake and its surrounding parks between 10:00pm and 5:00am. Their homelessness continued.

Note: Homer's life was spared. Lori and Sabino Renteria and friends care for him to this day.

Legal Aid For the Homeless

After weeks of harassing Rod Nelson and Regina Rogoff with Legal Aid, I was hired and given the go-ahead to create an outreach office to help the poorest of the poor. I created Legal Aid for the Homeless.

After almost three weeks of field research, I reconsidered the idea of setting up shop at the Salvation Army. From scores of one-on-one interviews with people experiencing homelessness, I came to realize that there were some serious concerns among the homeless people about the services they were receiving from the Salvation Army. Complaint after complaint stacked up. I decided that rather than list the complaints as such, I would create a survey instead. I would take the hard-core accusations and rephrase them as questions. When I reached one hundred and twenty questions, "Do you get enough to eat at the Salvation Army? Is the food any good? Have you ever witnessed any staff abuse toward the homeless people? Have you ever seen any theft by the staff or the security guards? Have you ever felt intimidated by the staff or the security guards?" I stopped and abandoned that approach. In fact, I abandoned the idea of setting up shop in the Salvation Army entirely. It became clear to me that, instead of being able to provide civil and legal services, I would be inundated with specific complaints about the Salvation Army. Unable to ignore them, I would be on a collision course with the Salvation Army, itself. I figured my stay there might last about a week before I would be invited to leave.

My search led me to Marion Morris. He had started a faith based, grass roots ministry of aid for homeless men — Helping Our Brothers Out, HOBO. He was a fire-and-brimstone preacher who believed in "a hand up, not a hand out," as he would say. He had founded HOBO with Alton Dyer, whom I only met once or twice; and who I guess was in the field (with the lilies) doing the Lord's work. Marion, his wife Sherry Mastrod and her daughter gave out work clothes and sandwiches that consisted of Cheese Whiz on white bread. This was at 5th and Guadalupe in the downtown area of Austin, but back then, in 1989, it was at the edge of the warehouse district.

Marion and I struck a deal and, for half a day, I would show up in the afternoons helping folks apply for food stamps and (if they qualified) for disability benefits. I actually helped with just about every other non-criminal matter imaginable but focused on those two core items. I leaned on my new friend and attorney Rod Nelson who recognized that I had passion for the plight of these folks...he liked to refer to it as "having fire in the belly." It was hard not to feel compassion for these economically abused, discarded souls.

As time wore on, I found myself asking what the phenomenon called homelessness really was. At first I tended to see it through the eyes of Marion Morris — a bunch of unlucky guys who got off track and just needed to be redirected. However, I grew to learn it was far more complicated than that on so many levels.

I started a newsletter — *Notes From the Blues Box.* I would write my observations and folks experiencing homelessness would write about life on the streets. This was the genesis of House the Homeless, Inc., a 501(c)(3) non-porfit organization I created to educate and advocate around issues of homelessness.

It was just 1988 when the U.S. Congress had declared homelessness a national crisis. Homeless advocates from around the country had organized to get the McKinney Act passed. This was a start, but even today it is a severely underfunded response to the situation. The questions: *What is Homelessness?* and *How do we define it?* are debated endlessly.

Jamie Maldonado

Jaime Maldonado, is a 46 old male born in Corpus Christi, TX. He is a sharp, personable, charismatic, Hispanic, and gentle man. He weighs in at 327 pounds "and then some," he adds. This is a bit much for a frame of just 5'9." Being in a state of homelessness or quasi-homelessness for years, he is unable to address this growing concern. He has an easy smile and a quick laugh to match. That causes his entire torso to rise and fall rapidly from his chin to below his navel. He sports a thick, rich, salt and pepper goatee. His gleaming, olive colored head is shaved as close as a billiard ball. Jaime has the "gift of gab" and as an easy, low talker, has coasted through life by enjoying the generosity of others who enjoy being in his company. Everybody loves Jaime! He was honorably discharged from the Army where he served from 1987-1992 in logistics as a truck driver. Every now and again he gets small, low level computer repair and programming jobs. Although he self-promotes constantly, these are rare.

He recently returned to Austin from San Antonio for the economics of health care. He was living as a "house manager" for an organization called, "Beat the Streets." His pay consisted of room and board, a free bus card for transportation, TV, internet, and free long distance calling. He "had it made."

"All my needs were met," he boasted, "...except...I got an infection in one of my lower front teeth."

He couldn't eat. This deeply concerned Jaime as his brother had died in May 2009 of diabetes complications when his body became unable to digest food. Luckily, Jaime has not yet contracted diabetes, but he does suffer from GERD, gastro-intestinal reflux disease. His condition is exacerbated by stress and heat both of which are plentiful. He is forced to prepare his own food which even as the house manager was often beyond his economic reach. And unfortunately, he can't stomach shelter food as it makes his condition worse. He also takes medication for vertigo and can no longer drive a truck.

He recently returned to Austin for the dental care for his tooth. San Antonio has something called Care-Link, but he must cover 25% of the costs. Not having traditional income, he came to Austin for the local MAP card to access the medical assistance program.

His living situation has now dramatically changed as all but one or two of the shelter beds are taken every night. This leaves over 200 nightly applicants to vie for one of approximately 80 remaining floor mats in a lottery. For the moment, Jaime is in "case management" and has landed one of 20 "reserved" mats. Jaime's stress is very high as he worries about losing his floor reservation as he is not able to work.

Life (and Death) On the Streets

Of course, throughout all of these efforts people continue to live, and, as I later came to realize, die on the streets of Austin.

It was April 1992 when I was scheduled to see my four o'clock appointment. It was almost ten minutes after four, and I was preparing to move on to my next task. I was just about to mark my 4:00 as a "no show" when I looked up from my desk to see a man standing there.

"May I help you?" I asked.

He hesitated and then said, "I'm not sure."

I surveyed him while I wondered how long it would be before he was sure. He was 5'10" and gaunt. His face was drawn as if he had not slept for several days, and he was agitated. His wrinkled clothes looked like they had been put through the washer on spin cycle then put on with a layer of dirt added. I observed him rubbing the heel of each of his palms on the outside seams of his dry, mud-splattered blue jeans.

I reached over and picked up my scheduling clipboard. I asked if he would like to make an appointment.

He stammered, "I have an appointment."

My response was, "Perhaps, but not now. I have a woman slotted for this hour."

His only response was, "Yes...Diane."

I looked at the chart. "Correct, Diane Malloy."

I asked if she was with him. In response, he just handed me a water swollen calendar that I give to my clients to help them keep medical appointments and return to my office on a timely basis. He had it open to today's date and pointed with one very undernourished finger.

"I thought maybe she was here," he offered.

I said, "Not yet. Let's check the lobby."

I called out her name into the crowd of people. We walked onto the loading dock. This was at the second of the five resource centers that I would come to occupy. It was another old warehouse but this time, it was in the heart of the warehouse district. The sidewalk outside actually blended into the loading docks and vice versa. There were several people in line for work, but they were all men.

As we drifted back in, I continued to ask folks if anyone had seen Diane. With no affirmative response, I told the young man that she was welcome to reschedule.

He seemed ready to explode, "I don't know what to do. I don't know what to do!" he shot out.

His swollen red eyes extended in front of his face as if he had a mild case of exophthalmia. I thought he might cry. I guided him back into my office and closed the door.

"What's going on?" I asked. "First, what's your name?"

"Jim...Jim Tynan. I don't know, I don't know, I can't find Diane."

All at once, out came his frustration. He burst forth with the story that he and Diane, she was his finance he told me, had sought shelter at the Salvation Army because Diane was not well. She had been coughing for weeks, ever since they had met but it seemed to be getting worse. To their dismay, they had been turned away. They were told that they could stay, but not together, as couples were not allowed. Apparently, like so many others, they were clinging to one another for support, and they would not allow themselves to be separated.

They did not have near enough money to get a motel room, so they tried to find a quiet spot in a field but had gotten themselves rousted by a police officer. They then ran into *John* who told them he knew where they could stay where no one would bother them. *John* described it as the perfect place because it was right behind the police station at 7th and Red River St. but "not to worry, no one would ever find them, purloined letter and all that." *John* had led them to the arroyo. This is a dry creek bed, with thirty foot high walls that had a cave-like area carved in one side about 12 feet below ground level. John was sure it was safe as it had not rained in almost two months, the night was clear, and the police would have no reason to come back there. They stashed their gear in a little shelf-like area in the cavernous region just above their heads.

They settled in for what Diane hoped would be a peaceful sleep. Jim was not so sure. Every time she coughed now she would bring up a little bit of blood just because she had been coughing so hard and for so long. It was even beginning to dawn on Jim that she probably had walking pneumonia. She had lost weight since they had met four weeks before. She had no appetite and was so weak from coughing that eating had become drudgery. Clearly, another disabling condition had begun to settle in...depression.

According to Jim, Diane had taken the last of her Nyquil and fallen into a fitful sleep when a crack of thunder startled them upright. An immediate flash of lightning showed them that water was raging past them just six inches below the ledge upon which they were now precariously perched. In just a few hours, things had dramatically changed. The dry creek bed had been transformed. It was now filled with 20 feet of raging water. It must have been raining up north and the storm had now caught up to the waters. Just as quickly as everything had been illuminated by the shard of lightning, they were once again enveloped in complete darkness. The thunder kept pounding and then it was followed by streaks of lightning that were coming so fast it was strobe like. In terror, they tried to scramble out of the overhang and grip the land ledge above them. They kept slipping. Jim grabbed Diane. He and John pushed her up and out. John was shouting in sheer panic for them to hurry as they struggled. Jim grabbed John next and together they managed to press him up the soggy wall and into the torrents of rain that awaited him. Lying prone, John spun around and reached back through the darkness into the area where Jim remained. He desperately fumbled in the darkness for Jim's hands. They both jammed fingers as they collided in their wild arm swinging in search for one another. John pulled and Jim scrambled to the top.

The three were elated. Drenched and literally blinded by the force of the rain, they began hugging and crying. Other than silhouettes, they still could not see each other. However, they were OK. They were fine.

Suddenly Diane screamed out, "My bag, my bag!" Jim knew it had everything in it: her medicine, their money, and her doctor's appointments.

Jim shouted to John, "Hold my legs, hold my legs."

As John grabbed hold, he slid to the lip again. He reached into the opening searching for the ledge where they had stashed Diane's bag. He felt a wave of light-headedness as the blood rushed to his head. He swung his arms wildly searching for the bag. There, he got it!

"Up, up, up," he shouted, but John could not hear him. With his right hand, Jim reached back with the bag and started hitting John with it shouting, "Up! Up! Up!" John pulled him back. They collapsed onto each other.

It was several moments before Jim called out to Diane in the darkness that he had the bag. He could not hear her or find her. Initially Jim started to panic, "Where is she, where is she?" he shouted to John.

John exhausted could barely get out the words "I don't know, she must have gone up…I don't know."

They climbed the rest of the way out and collapsed behind the police parking lot. There was no sign of Diane. Jim paced back and forth along the lighted perimeter shouting her name into the darkness of the storm. He did this for over an hour with no response. He finally crouched down in a fetal position with his back against a pillar facing into the storm staring into the darkness. Eventually, he must have fallen asleep in exhaustion.

When dawn broke, Jim found himself alone. He desperately started looking for Diane. The storm had stopped. The water had receded from the cave area where they had slept... no Diane. Jim went to the homeless resource center...no Diane. He went to Brackenridge Hospital and then to the police station where he reported what had happened. Nothing. No Diane.

It was now three days later, and Jim was in my office instead of Diane telling me this story. I picked up the phone and called the hospital. No luck. I called a buddy with EMS, nothing. I then called the police station, and after fifteen minutes and half a dozen phone calls, I located the detective to whom Jim had reported the incident.

The officer verified the report, "No, we haven't turned up anything yet," he said. Something in his voice made me skeptical that they would be having any luck either.

Diane had been my last scheduled client of the day, so I told Jim we should look where he had last seen her. I told him I had a kayak and that I did not live far. I would get it and return. I dropped Jim off on the banks of what turned out to be Waller Creek. It had only appeared to be an arroyo because it had been so long between rains.

When I got my kayak, I slipped it in at the mouth of Waller Creek at Town Lake. I saw Jim on the northeast bank. The water had dropped dramatically, but I was still able to paddle 100 yards out of Town Lake and up Waller Creek in Jim's direction.

We exchanged, "Nothing."

I was still about 100 yards short of where Jim had indicated they had attempted to spend the night, but the creek was clogged with logs and debris. I turned around slowly and paddled back to Town Lake. Along the way, there were blankets, a broken canoe, hundreds of Styrofoam cups, two police cones, a sleeping bag, a basketball, and broken branches everywhere. I saw an air mattress and used my paddle to raise it and push it aside cringing and expecting the worst. Nothing. I saw an upside down tennis shoe and touched it with my paddle. It disappeared below the surface. Then it reappeared. Then half a heart beat later a second upside down tennis shoe appeared and then the two calves of a body. My heart caught in my throat. It was Diane. At least it was somebody.

I paddled over to where Jim was searching the shore. I got as close to him as I possibly could.

I simply said, "I've found a body."

He went ashen. I saw a line of flesh colored skin tone drain down his face as if a bathtub plug had been pulled. A line of pale flesh replaced it. Jim fell to a sitting position. I told him I would paddle over to the university row boathouse where they kept the rowing sculls and meet him there. When I got there, I told a young girl who was setting up her boat that I had found a body, and that she should call the police. I sat in my boat and waited. Jim met me; we spent an uncomfortable 10 minutes in silence until the police arrived. I was placed in the back of a police car and taken to police headquarters. A detective joined me. I was pummeled with questions.

"How did you find the body? Did you know the person? Who was the person? What were you doing there?"

When I started to explain what I knew, the detective became skeptical. He wanted to know how I had been on the phone with a detective inquiring about Diane's situation and then only twenty-five minutes later had found the body. At first, I just stared at him blankly. Then I started to realize the situation. My mind started racing, and I got madder and madder when I realized that I was a suspect in Diane's death. When I responded, it was his turn to pause.

Obviously, holding my anger through gritted teeth, I answered, "Because I bothered to look!"

Apparently, Jim Tynan had made yet another judgment error. When he had reported Diane's disappearance, he had been honest and told the detective that they were homeless— big mistake. Had he left that one detail out, the police would have been looking for her. We would have heard that the boy scouts, the girl scouts, the water rescue team, and the police had been searching for a young woman who may have become a drowning victim. On the evening news, we would have been told that they were temporarily calling off the search because of darkness, but would resume first thing in the morning. Instead, they never looked. They never began a search. Don't get me wrong; I support the police. I am a graduate of the Citizen's Police Academy, my wife and I contribute to the Sheriff's Association. We support the Police Athletic League, PAL. However, there are pressures and prejudices that cause people to be seen in certain lights and treated in certain ways. As a class, The "Homeless" are at the bottom of the prejudicial barrel. They are the poorest of the poor. In India, they call them the "Untouchables." Diane was homeless. That became her fate and even in death, she was disrespected.

Homelessness Hits Home

Diane Breisch Malloy had been a mother, a daughter, a sister. She had worked for MCI (the telephone company) for ten years when she became ill. It started as a cold and became bronchitis. She could not get well. She had periods of recovery, but then would take off more time. She finally used all of her sick leave. The company, while expressing extreme sympathy, explained that they needed reliability. They were sorry. Two months later, Diane's life ended on the streets of Austin, Texas.

Diane, her death, and the circumstances surrounding it haunted me. I could not stop thinking about her. I had never met her, but when I saw her picture, I was struck by her resemblance to my sister Lynn. I thought about my sister and how with just a simple change of events Lynn could have taken Deane's place. My sister is brilliant. She has a genius IQ actually. She is also talented beyond belief. Anything she touches turns to gold — sculpting, painting, all hers for pursuit, but she has a fragility about her that makes her vulnerable just as we all are at certain times. A couple of bad decisions, an illness, financial misfortune, and anyone of us could replace Jim or Diane.

As I thought about Diane and Lynn, I started to realize that Diane was not the first homeless person that I had known who had died on the streets of Austin. For the first time since Vietnam, I allowed my thoughts to dwell on death. When the tally was complete, I had counted the names of twenty-three homeless people that I had known between 1989 and 1992 who had passed away.

When I had first returned from overseas, I had been assigned to funeral detail. I was the corporal in charge of meeting bereaved family members who had just been given the news that their son or daughter had been killed in Vietnam. When the casket arrived back in the States, it was my job to meet it, connect with the parents, and coordinate with the funeral director. The casket would be draped with the American flag. My squad would carry the casket to the gravesite. A bugler assigned to our detail would play taps. We would fold the flag into a triangle. I would then hand it to the mother or father of the fallen soldier or marine. I only did this a couple of times. I was stoic as I said the words of bereavement or spoke the words of how their loved one had served the country with honor…and that I was sorry for their loss. One night I sobbed so hard that I thought I would tear the muscles from my chest. I hated it so intensely. I felt each death so passionately. Then, almost immediately, it was over. I refused to go back.

I just said, "I am ready to be reassigned...I will not be doing this anymore." While I was not court marshaled, it didn't matter. I didn't care. I was never sent back. Something in my expression told my sergeant that going back was not an option. I was reassigned.

For three years in Austin, I had apparently repressed the realization that my clients, my friends, were dying. When you help someone who is homeless get disability benefits, you get to know them. You learn about their families, their wives and their husbands; you learn about their mothers and fathers. You learn about their bad decisions, their addictions. You learn about the incredibly hard choices they had to make that meant they would leave their children. I had to watch their faces when they told me how they never got to watch their children grow up. I learned of their dreams to go back to school, get a GED, and get that job as a welder, an over-the-road truck driver or home health aide or how they wanted to be a nurse because they wanted to help people. They all want to help someone. They all seem to want to give what they did not get. Now I did not get to ignore what had happened anymore. I had to tell the story.

I stood on a chair in the middle of the Resource Center, and I asked for everyone's attention. I named the names of each one of the twenty-three people who had died on the streets. I said, "Now that I have told you, we have to tell others." That night, we marched onto the grounds of the State Capitol. We had no permit. No one stopped us. No one approached us. We lit candles. One hundred strong, we spoke of our friends. We told their stories, hugged one another, and kissed each other and we cried. Then we marched down to Town Lake to say our last goodbyes on a dock not far from where I had found Diane. We told more stories and cried some more and then we told our final truth...that we were human beings, and yet we were homeless, and we did not want to be homeless. We were homeless on the streets of one of the richest cities in the richest country in the world. We told the truth...that we are living and dying on the streets of Austin. Then the sprinklers came on and, within minutes, we were drenched. We do not know if they were turned on intentionally. We never saw anyone emerge from the Four Seasons Hotel where the sprinklers angled down on us from the hill above, nor do we know if they just were on an automatic timer. It didn't matter. We just ended our tribute. We were done. We were all but defeated. We were certainly deflated. We were emotionally spent. We just left. Those that could, went home. Everyone else simply passed into the night.

Homeless Memorial, photo by House the Homeless member.

The Homeless Memorial

That year we worked to raise money for a memorial. We raised it among ourselves, one dollar here and one dollar there. I contacted the City of Austin Parks Department and told them that we wanted to place a memorial plaque on Town Lake. The response was a deafening silence. Finally, the silence was broken with the suggestion that we buy a new metal park bench that the city had just started to promote. I was told that they would "last for years, maybe three or four times as long as the old wooden ones." The fact of the matter is that, the benches are so uncomfortable that it may not be humanly possible to sleep on them. Some suspected that was the intended reason for the design. We were told that we could have a nice plaque placed next to the bench. I was told the benches cost a mere $5,000. I was floored. I did not care about the money. When you do not have any, the rest is irrelevant. I was just amazed at how costly the benches were.

In any event, we did not want a bench, and we certainly did not want those benches. They had dividers in the middle so you could not lie down. I had convinced the guys that what we wanted was a Treaty Oak. We wanted a living tribute to our existence. We wanted a tree that would stand three hundred years. The Parks Department was pushing a Bald Cyprus. We wanted a mighty oak. They wanted to have it placed on the far side of Town Lake in the field across from the Austin Garden Center. We wanted it to be more visible. In the end, I told them exactly where we wanted our Live Oak planted…near the people. In the end, it was. In April 1993, one year after Diane had met her tragically young fate, we planted a spindly five-foot tall Live Oak sapling on the south shores of Town Lake right next to the exercise pad, the water fountain, and the outside showerhead where the homeless people get clean in the spring and summer.

On the day we planted the tree, the City of Austin lowered Town Lake one foot so that the statue of Stevie Ray Vaughn, Austin's famed guitarist, could be placed 75 yards to our west. There must have been twenty workers there. On the other hand, there was one city worker and two of us volunteering to plant our tree. The contrast seemed about normal. A ten-foot tall statue, the lowering of Town Lake, 20 paid workers for a famous person verses the three of us to commemorate twenty-three homeless persons. The city wanted our plaque to be level to the ground. We insisted that it be tilted two inches up in the back. The plaque was donated by Plaques Plus. The money we raised paid for the marble slab on which the plaque is mounted.

The First Memorial Service

The next day at 4:30 pm we held our first Homeless Memorial at the Homeless Memorial. I got a speaker's podium and invited Mayor Bruce Todd to be the keynote speaker. Sue Milam, the then head of Health and Human Services, also agreed to speak. I suppose sixty or more people came. We were too sad to advertise it like some kind of event. It just did not seem right. Therefore, we just spread the news by word of mouth. The ones that did come had been drinking and thinking. They were mad. They were mad about what had happened to Diane. They were mad about what had happened to their friends, and they were afraid. They were afraid that what we were really doing was reading their own eulogies.

All throughout Ms. Milam's words, the homeless guys had words of their own. Some louder than others. They penetrated the air. Angry sounds reached the speaker. I hated to say anything because it was their event. They were entitled to their feelings. We did need to maintain respect however, so there was a need to quiet the crowd, which I finally did. When Ms. Milam finished, a couple of guys rushed to the podium to have their say. They were not to be undone, so I just worked to keep things orderly. Loud, angry speeches came out. Some of the words were directed at the Mayor and some at the City policies generally. After all, he was the mayor who was working to pass the No Camping Ordinance. The crowd was getting rowdier and angrier.

The Mayor leaned into me and said, "Richard, perhaps I shouldn't speak."

I turned to him and, with one eye still on the guys, I said, "Mr. Mayor, I believe in this one particular instance, we are in agreement." Then quick as a wink, he was up the chimney and gone.

Now, each November, we revisit our memorial where we have a Homeless Memorial Sunrise Service without a podium but with scheduled speakers. Everyone is encouraged to speak, but they are also encouraged to sign up in advance. The tree is grown. It must be 30 feet high. It has a glorious crown. Its leaves offer cool solace. Its roots have reached the water's edge of what is now Lady Bird Lake, and it can now drink at will. City Hall has been moved from a place across town and now sits almost directly across from the memorial on the north side of the river. Couples picnic under the tree and small boys and girls climb its mighty branches.

The plaque beneath the tree has a nick in it where a mower gashed it, but the words sanctioned by Mayor Bruce Todd that day are still quite visible and deeply meaningful:

> HOMELESSNESS:
> *It is the Essence of Depression.*
> *It is Immoral.*
> *It is Socially Corrupt.*
> *It is an Act of Violence.*

Note of Prayer

We hold the Homeless Memorial Sunrise Service in November during National Hunger and Homelessness Awareness Week. We always hold it within a week of Veteran's Day. We do this out of respect for the fact that one-third of the homeless are Veterans. We still invite an elected official to preside, so they can understand that there is a very real cost, a human cost, for not ending this plague upon our nation. We read the names of the men and women who died on the streets during the past year. Each year the number grows larger. This past year, we read the names of one hundred and fifty seven more people who died on the streets of Austin.

What We Need!

We believe that in order to end homelessness, we need *national health care*. We need this because, once we get a job, we became the working poor. We become members of the working poor because the jobs we get don't include health care. Moreover, while some people experiencing homelessness are lucky enough to have access to health clinics, this ends when a person gets an entry-level job. When we have a minimum wage job, we join the ranks of the working poor. There are no vacation days, and there is no health care. When we become sick, we either work sick or find that someone has taken your place when we return to the work place.

We also need *affordable housing* in an adequate quantity nationwide. In addition, we need *livable incomes*. For people who cannot work, we need disability benefits that pay more than $674.00 per month, so people will not have to double up with strangers just to survive.

For people who can work, we need jobs, not just any job, but *living wage* jobs. We need jobs that will provide us food, clothing, shelter (utilities included) and access to health care…at the very least. In the absence of these basic items, we are clearly going to continue to live and die on the streets of America.

Pappy

I never knew his real name. His moniker always seemed enough. I guess the reason is that when you looked at him you saw an exact cross between Wild Bill Hickock and Gabby Hayes. Any other name would make no sense. Pappy stood about 5'8", had a slight West Texas drawl, and a weathered face that reflected the West Texas landscape.

One fall day, I was outside of HOBO. I was exchanging the usual greetings with the guys, when I saw Pappy and stopped to exchange a pleasantry or two. I suppose we were talking about the weather when something began distracting me.

A spot on Pappy's trousers caught my eye, which struck me as odd. It was above Pappy's left knee. Everyone's clothes were soiled, and therefore a spot was not noteworthy. But then, I realized that the spot seemed to be growing. This spot that had started at about the size of a quarter, had grown to the size of a silver dollar. Then it grew to the size of my fist.

Surprised, I came out with, "Pappy, your leg. It's bleeding...badly."

He looked down almost as if seeing it for the first time, but then remembering. "Oh, yeah, I got whacked..."

It was then that I realized that he was actually propped up on the wall not just leaning against it. He was not able to put any weight on the leg. The bottom of his right quadriceps muscle, just above his knee, had been severed. A huge hole now replaced a good-sized chunk of his leg muscle. There were crutches next to him that I had not noticed before.

Pappy had gone to sleep in the park with a friend. His friend woke up and tucked back in the woods to relieve himself. Just as he did, a black-and-white police unit came cruising by, saw Pappy and stopped his car. One of the two police officers got out of his car and started walking in Pappy's direction. Hank, Pappy's friend, froze where he stood. He then saw the police officer look around as if to see if anyone was in the area. He pulled out his nightclub. He raised it all the way above his head and brought it down on Pappy's leg while Pappy lay sleeping. It just missed smashing his kneecap. Pappy shot up into an upright position. He never fully opened his eyes and then fell back down unconscious from what must have been excruciating pain. Hank said the officer looked in every direction and then especially hard at the woods where Hank remained frozen in stark fear. The officer slowly returned the nightstick into the ring on his belt. Hank remained hidden long after the patrol car pulled off before he dragged Pappy back into the woods.

Hank managed to get Pappy to the emergency room where Pappy was treated.

Some kind of emergency procedure took place. The next day Pappy was told that he would have to have a series of skin grafts and even then he was assured that he would never walk properly again. The year was 1989.

It was in 1990 or 1991 when we learned that Pappy had died in a house fire on the east side of town. Pappy was sleeping in an abandoned house with two other guys. Someone who was owed six dollars by one of the two other fellows set fire to the house, and Pappy died in the blaze.

Pappy was one of the sweetest, gentlest men I have ever met. I remember him showing me a picture of a fourteen-year-old girl who he said was his daughter. He was just a regular person, who was down on his luck. Pappy would have gladly paid the six dollars out of his own pocket. Money, the lack of it, and feelings of being wronged make people do unthinkable things.

Harsh Reality

I remember clearly how I felt that morning when I heard that two of our guys had been beaten with two-by-four boards. They had been sleeping in front of the first HOBO at Fifth and Guadalupe. The facility offered no sleeping opportunities, but I guess the guys somehow felt it offered some form of sanctuary. Even sleeping on the sidewalk in front of the facility seemed to offer some kind of emotional protection. They were wrong. In the middle of the night, two college-age boys driving an old Chevy raced to a stop, jumped from the car, clutching two-by-fours. They then proceeded to whale on the guys. They broke one arm of each of two men who lay sleeping. One man suffered a fractured hand and a skull fracture. The other had three broken fingers. The assailants then jumped back into the car and were gone. The event really had no beginning, only an end. It was a senseless beating. No one knew why it had occurred. We only knew that if our guys had not been sleeping on the street it probably would not have happened.

Homelessness: An Act Of Violence.

It was a warm summer day when John came to me at my outreach office. He said he and three of his buddies had been beaten. Two of them were in the lobby. We went to the lobby where John waved to Tom and Bill to enter my office. All three presented an earnest and urgent presence and insisted that they and another fellow experiencing homelessness had been beaten by the police. When I asked what they had been doing, they said, "Nothing, sleeping." almost in unison. Tom stood behind the other two and nodded in the affirmative. I was skeptical, but, even if it were true, they assured me there were no witnesses. I told them to leave and come back the next day and bring the fourth man.

When they returned, they still did not have the fourth guy nor was it likely that he was coming. I had each of them strip to the waist. I was shocked at what I saw. The reason I told them to come back a day later was to allow any bruising to materialize. There were bruises all right, long cylindrical bruises about an inch wide and eight inches long. These were on their backs, stomachs and sides. The bruises resembled the shape and dimension of a police nightstick. The men's elbows had huge raised knots.

I took each of their statements separately. I took multiple pictures, each of which I identified on the back and dated. I then directed them to go to Internal Affairs — the police of the police.

At first, the officers did not want to take their statements. They told the group that they had waited too long, but I had told them that they had thirty days to report and was insistent. Finally, the police took individual statements. After they read the men's statements, the police seemed a bit taken aback. All of the statements reflected the same story. They told the guys that they would have to take lie detector tests. The guys were threatened that if they failed them there would be "serious consequences for bringing false accusations against good cops."

A few days later, the guys returned and took the test. They were scared, and they had good reason to be scared. They passed the tests. They were told to return in a few more days. They were given two more tests. They were given *three* lie detector tests each. All three passed them all. The accused officers said our guys had been resisting arrest, but there had been no arrests. There were no charges pending, no citations of any kind had been written. This would prove to be the undoing of these rogue police officers.

Considerable time went by and then Paige White, an assistant district attorney, was brought in to prosecute the police officers. I remember how shocked she had been when she first saw the pictures, heard the evidence and listened to the story.

The police are civil servants and therefore could only be tried under Civil Service Procedures. This complicates cases, protects officers, requires a greater burden of proof, and erects barriers to prosecutors.

One day, while awaiting the trial, John and Tom were quietly sitting on a curb resting. A black and white police car passing on the other side of the street, reduced speed and came to a halt. When it started up again, it made a u-turn and stopped immediately in front of the two guys. The officer identified as the principal person in the attack against the guys was staring back at them.

He looked first at John, then at Tom, then back to John and said, "You boys don't look so good. You probably need to go somewhere for a vacation." After a long period of just staring, he slowly drove off.

As soon as they could, they came and told me what happened. They were pretty shaken. I took the story to an assistant Police Chief. He told me that the officers were "probably just concerned about my client's health. They probably didn't look too good," he commented. I felt the blood drain from my head. I felt myself get really quiet. All I could think over and over again was, "This is deep shit. This is deep shit."

Previously, I had heard this very bizarre story that I had just filed away in the back of my brain. This homeless person had been getting into a confrontation with a couple of police officers, really one in particular — the other had held back and remained silent. The cop kept telling him to leave the area and not come back. The homeless guy had little choice but to return because all the jobs, the few services, and the only free meals were in the downtown sector. Therefore, he just kept ducking out whenever he saw cops.

One day he saw the officer in a paddy wagon and the officer also saw him. The officer stopped and confronted our guy and words were exchanged. The lead police officer handcuffed our guy and put him in the back of the wagon. The story then becomes troubling...very troubling. The homeless guy was bounced around in the back of the wagon. This is not the first time I had heard of some serious bruising occurring in this fashion. The wagon finally slowed down, came to a stop and began to back up on a slight downward incline. The vehicle stopped. The engine turned off; seconds passed, then a minute went by. Another minute went by. He was closed off from the front of the van, but he heard two doors open. Suddenly the two back doors of the wagon were jerked open. Our guy looked out. He blinked his eyes and looked again…he saw nothing but water. The wagon had backed down a boat ramp and was overhanging Town Lake. As our guy looked out, still handcuffed behind his back, fairly well bruised from the thrashing around in the back, he heard a voice, "Do you think maybe you've seen enough of Austin?"

A similar story was told to me by another fellow, and at first, I thought it might be an urban legend. However, I never heard it again, and so I was never sure. But, that's the story that flashed into my mind at that moment when it was suggested that our guys might need a vacation.

I got off the phone with the Assistant Police Chief as quickly as possible. I found the guys. I told them the story. I told them that this was it, the "wall of blue," and we were up against it. They said they were still prepared to press the assault case for the moment, but we all agreed that they should leave town. They did. They went to Corpus Christi and caught some work there.

When the trial came up, they came back to Austin. They told their story of the crime. The four homeless guys had gone to sleep one night in a fenced-in garbage can area off the alley on the south side of 6th Street. The gate had a simple latch that could only be operated from the inside. At some time in the middle of the night, a police officer spied them through a hole in the fence. He climbed the fence, unlatched the gate, and let the other two officers in. They closed and latched the gate and began whaling on the homeless guys with their nightsticks. The homeless guys screamed in pain and tried to climb the fence to escape the incessant beating. Over and over again, they were grabbed off the fence and dragged back down and beaten some more. Finally, the beating stopped and the officers scurried into the night.

The charges against all but one police officer were dropped or dismissed. The guys only got a clear look at the one, lead officer. He was fined and received a three-day suspension. As punishment, he became one of the first police officers assigned to bicycle patrol. The bicycle patrol area consisted of the park where the homeless sleep.

Compassion

In June of 2004, Curtis Ray Wilson, a well-loved, mentally ill homeless man, was dragged into the lobby of the Crown Plaza Hotel (now the Capitol Plaza Hotel) and beaten to death. The attacker did this in front of multiple witnesses who stood by and just watched. Reportedly, the beating was an effort by the attacker to impress his girlfriend.

After months of investigation, but no arrest, the story did not end. Detective Lisa Morrill insisted that Mr. Wilson was a "regular person and deserved to be treated as decently as anyone else" and apprehended a suspect who was later convicted. She did so in spite of great pressure from within the police department to "just close the case."

Detective Lisa Morrill was awarded the first House the Homeless — Curtis Ray Wilson Compassion Award. This was presented at the 12th Annual Homeless Memorial Sunrise Service, November 2004.

Hating People Who Are Experiencing Homelessness

The National Coalition for the Homeless has been issuing hate crimes reports on an annual basis since 1996 and has been pressing for a U. S. Government Accountability Office, (GAO), investigation and report. In each reported event, it has been shown or expressed that the victims had been targeted because they were homeless. From around the country, we, (I sit on the Board of Directors) have chronicled beatings, stabbings and shootings. Each year since we started, we've reported that one or two sleeping homeless people have been set on fire. In 2004 in Austin, Texas, three young men went on a multi-week pellet gun shooting spree targeting homeless people from the back of a pick-up truck. In Colorado, there were a series of homeless decapitations reportedly the result of gang initiation ritual.

We find that, while the majority of people experiencing homelessness may continue to reside in the same place, they are referred to as "transients." Historically, we know just how important language can be used as a weapon. Hitler used the same type of language prior to annihilation of the Gypsies and the Jews. When you label someone as "transient," it paints a picture that he or she is just passing through. It infers that such persons have no relationship to our community and, therefore, we have no relationship to, and no responsibility for them. Language labeling like "nigger, wop, spic, kike, jap, honky, transient" are all used to deface people and make them easy targets for hate. For example, "wop" is derogatory slang for Italian immigrants. Language is often the first step in the hate/violence continuum.

You may have heard of Chante Mallard in Fort Worth, Texas, who at the end of a night of hard partying, struck a homeless man with her automobile. Gregory Biggs, became impaled upside down by her broken windshield. She believed him to be homeless due to his appearance. She was correct. In a panic, she raced home, parked the car in her garage and closed the door. Ms. Mallard then had sexual relations with her boyfriend while Mr. Biggs remained pinned upside down, bleeding and pleading for help. She periodically returned to the garage to check on him. Gregory continued to beg and plead for help. She apologized, saying she was sorry, but that there was nothing she could do. Medical experts reported that he died three days after being struck with the motor vehicle from the loss of blood. In other words, Gregory slowly bled out from what otherwise would *not* have been life threatening wounds.

Ms. Mallard contacted a couple of her friends and told them what had happened. They conspired with her, took the body, and dumped it in the park where homeless people congregate. She thought no one would notice. No one did. After all, what is one more or less homeless person? She thought no one would investigate. She was right. It was not until nine months later at another party when she told the story as party banter that she was found out. Ms. Mallard was arrested and given a $10,000 bond. This meant she would have to raise $1,000 to be bailed out. Homeless advocates cried out and the judge realized that he had just devalued a human being because he had been homeless. The bail was raised.

The police found the car seat that Ms. Mallard and her cohorts had ripped out. It was partially burnt and discarded in her backyard to cover up the fact that it was soaked in the man's blood. She was so unconcerned that she had not even bothered to get rid of the car seat. After all, it was just a homeless person. Who would investigate? But Gregory was someone's son. He had been a brick mason with mental health problems. He was down on his luck. His luck ended. Ms. Mallard was a nurse's assistant. She was sorry. "There was nothing she could do." A doctor testifying at the trial had said that if Mr. Biggs had received medical treatment he would, in all likelihood, have survived…but there was nothing she could do…she was "sorry." He could have been anyone's son or brother or uncle or father. What comes to my mind is the haunting song;

> *What if God was one of us?*
> *Just a stranger on a bus*
> *trying to make his way home?*
> *-Joan Osborne*

Protection for People Experiencing Homelessness

In 1997, I wrote the Protected Homeless Class Resolution as president of House The Homeless, Inc. the non-profit advocacy group I began in 1989. It recognizes that the United States Congress declared homelessness a national crisis in 1987. It states that international treaties signed by most of the world's major nations have declared housing a Human Right. It calls for the protection of these people just like any others that might be singled out and abused or attacked merely because of their collective condition.

Civil Rights and Human Rights: The Protected Homeless Class Resolution

Because many states and cities are passing and enforcing laws targeted at poor and homeless people, and the fact that homeless people are targets of senseless assaults and murder due to their condition of homelessness, House The Homeless feels the need for the adoption of this resolution by City, State and the United States governments.

Whereas, the United States Government has adopted and is party to the United Nations Document referenced as the Universal Declaration of Human Rights, which "confers on every member of society a right to basic economic, social, and cultural entitlements, that every (nation) state should recognize, serve, and protect, of which food, clothing, medical care, and housing are definitive components of the right to a minimum standard of living and dignity," and

Whereas, the United States Government has adopted, and is party to the United Nations Document; the Habitat Agenda, which calls for certain actions that include but are not limited to: protection against discrimination, legal security of tenure and equal access to land including women and the poor; effective protection from illegal forced evictions, taking human rights into consideration, bearing in mind that homeless people should not be penalized for their status; by adopting policies aimed at making housing habitable, affordable and accessible, including those who are unable to secure adequate housing through their own means, and

Whereas, the United Nations Document: Habitat Agenda, calls for the "Effective monitoring and evaluation of housing conditions, including the extent of homelessness and inadequate housing policies and implementing effective strategies and plans to address those problems," and

Whereas, there is a shortage of affordable housing stock nationwide, and

Whereas, the national minimum wage is an insufficient amount of money to secure safe, decent, affordable housing even at the most basic financial level, and

Whereas, more than the minimum wage is required in every state to be able to afford a one bedroom apartment at Fair Market Rent, as set by the U.S. Department of Housing and Urban Development, and

Whereas, the combined effect of these and other circumstances create a group of people that have no alternatives to living on the streets of our nation, and

Whereas, it is estimated that nationwide, there are at least 760,000 persons living without a permanent, fixed, individual residence on any given night, and

Whereas, at least 28% of our nations' homeless are United States Veterans, and

Whereas, approximately 25% of the single adult homeless population suffers from some form of mental illness, and

Whereas, the fastest growing segment of the population is women with children, and

Whereas, 36.5 million men, women and children of all ages are living in poverty (many of whom are already homeless), and

Whereas, there has been a collective, concerted effort at city and county levels to devise laws and ordinances that find homeless people guilty of having committed a crime for simple acts such as sleeping in public, and

Whereas, there are certain life sustaining acts such as eating, breathing and sleeping that must be conducted by all persons including those that are homeless who must conduct these acts in public, and

Whereas, these laws and ordinances are designed to criminalize and sweep these homeless persons from our nations' streets and imprison them, without regard for their personal safety or care for their personal belongings, for no reason other than they are lacking housing and as a result, are characterized as non-citizens, and are deprived of their human rights, and

Whereas, these impoverished persons are targeted and often made victims of malicious hate crimes and selective enforcement of these laws and ordinances, and

Whereas, camping, sleeping, sitting, lying down and other anti-homeless laws are being enforced at a time when emergency housing shelters are consistently full and no housing alternatives remain available, and

Whereas, the enforcement of such laws under such circumstances constitute cruel and unusual punishment and impinge upon these persons' access to travel,

THEREFORE: BE IT RESOLVED *That persons without a fixed, permanent, individual place of residence, and those that are earning 100% of Federal Poverty Guidelines or less, are sufficient in number characteristics, and vulnerability to compromise a distinct class of people, and as a result, shall hence forth constitute a Protected Class with all rights and protections under such a designation. Herein after, this Protected Class will be referred to as the Indigent Homeless Population.*

AND FURTHER, BE IT RESOLVED, *that as a Protected Class they will be protected:*

From laws against sleeping, sitting, or lying down in public

From acts or laws interfering with their right to travel

From wages that are so low that they are denied access to housing,

From laws or practices that disregard their rights of ownership, and protections for their personal belongings,

From being made targets of hate crimes, and

From being characterized and treated as non citizens.

Richard R. Troxell
February 9, 1998 revised July 12, 2010

Note: This resolution, written by Richard R. Troxell, President of House the Homeless, Inc., was adopted by the National Coalition for the Homelessness in April of 1998, revised in 2010 and will be introduced before the U.S. Congress for legislation and ratification. Efforts to make this a reality are scheduled to begin in 2011.

The National Coalition for the Homeless continues to call for the U.S. Government Accountability Office, (GAO), to begin to collect its own list of hate crimes perpetrated against people experiencing homelessness. NCH continues to issue its own report in the meantime. States have begun to pass hate crimes legislation protecting people experiencing homelessness.

Photo by Sam Cole.

Bum Fights

Several years back, two enterprising young men found that they could make money degrading homeless men by coercing them into hurting themselves on camera. The homeless men, immersed in their disease of alcoholism and feeling life had little left to offer them, accepted pocket change to run head first into a stack of shopping carts, pull perfectly good teeth from their heads with pliers, fight each other with bare knuckles, etc. In one video called *Bum Hunters*, an unsuspecting, sleeping, homeless man is jumped by the "Bum Hunter," a take off on the internationally known Crocodile Hunter, Steve Erwin. The hapless man is tied up and gagged with duct tape. A voice-over describes in an Australian accent, "You have to be careful mate. Some of them like this one, can be pretty wily."

The Justice Department conducted an investigation in an attempt to prosecute the perpetrators with very limited success. However, the National Coalition for the Homeless, NCH, learned that Amazon.com, Target, Best Buy, Virgin Mega Stores, Tower Records, FYE Entertainment, Barnes and Noble, and Borders, all national retailers, had been selling these hate videos both in their stores and on the internet. NCH sent a certified letter outlining our complaint and asking for all sales to stop. We set a response deadline of June 1, 2004.

Several retailers responded immediately and withdrew their videos. Others, including Best Buy, failed either to comply or to respond. I personally followed up the certified letters sent by Michael Stoops, national Civil Rights Activist and friend, by making numerous phone calls to Best Buy both locally and nationally, but to no avail.

On Tuesday, June 15th at 10:00 am, House the Homeless held a full blown press conference and educational picket at the Best Buy store at Highway 290 and MoPac in Austin, TX. This is a highly visible location. Our signs, printed in large black, block letters on poster boards, were to the point, "Best Buy Sells Hate!" "Best Buy...Isn't!" "Best Buy Sells HATE Videos!" (Max would have been proud).

We attracted considerable attention. Including that of the police who kept trying to insert themselves into our business. At one point, a spokesman came out of the store and told the police, not us, that Best Buy agreed to stop selling the videos in their stores. We were upset and angry. We scoffed at both their declaration and their manner of communication. It is not the role of the police to interfere with our negotiations. Additionally, the police thought we were being unreasonable and should leave now that our requests had been met. Clearly and calmly, I explained that Best Buy had not ceased their sales until they stopped selling their filth on the internet. Best Buy protested that they were just a local store and had no control over international internet sales. We explained that as long as the sellers carried the name of Best Buy, they were part of the entire operation. We explained that they were equally responsible for all actions, and they were our only avenue of communication with their national office and their internet sales department. We would not be leaving.

The ranks of the picket line had swelled to 40 picketers when youths from Life Works (a program for homeless youth) joined the growing number of protesters from House the Homeless, Inc., Media from *Channels 36, 24, 42, News 8 Austin*, the *Austin American Statesman* and the *Austin Advocate* (the homeless newspaper) gave witness to the demonstration. Then, just hours after the public outcry for justice had begun, the following national statement was sent out on all wire services:

"Best Buy shares the community's concern about issues related to violence against the homeless, and we understand our obligation to customers to monitor the products on our shelves. We will not be carrying the videos or DVDs in the future."

Within forty-eight hours, all but FYE Entertainment had stopped the sales of these hate videos. Sweet Victory!

Note. Just one week prior to the release of the 2004 Hate Crimes report by NCH and the educational picket, a hate video destined for retail sales was confiscated, and four young American terrorists in Cleveland, OH were arrested. They were sneaking up on unsuspecting, sleeping homeless people and stunning them with 50,000 volts of electricity in their groins and throats. In some instances, water had been added to intensify the tortures. The perpetrators were arrested and prosecuted. E-Bay continued to sell Bum Fights IV for a period of time but seems to have stopped their sales.

THREE:

THE NO CAMPING ORDINANCE

No Camping

In 1995 an ordinance was written in Austin that outlawed camping. It became known as the "No Camping Ordinance." Here follows a chronicle of harassment of the homeless which, in one form or another, has played out in every major city in America.

Austin American-Statesman, March 9, 1995:

Todd tries to ban camping in public; Advocates blast the proposal, saying it is an attempt to run homeless people out of town

Austin's homeless people – both the crude skid row drunks and the hard-luck men and women who hustle for work every day – better start looking for a new place to sleep. Public bridges, dark corners and shade trees would be off limits under a proposal that soon could come before the Austin City Council.

Mayor Bruce Todd on Wednesday called for a city ordinance making it illegal to camp in public places, causing an outcry from homeless people and their advocates. They labeled it an attempt to run Austin's homeless people out of town.

Todd, during a City Council work session, said it was time for the city to show "tough love" for the city's street population and pass an ordinance that would keep transients from building makeshift homes in city parks and under bridges.

"When people need services, you don't help them by allowing them to continue this way," Todd said. "Those kinds of encampments lead to violations of public and private property rights. I hear more complaints about the litter and safety hazards coming from those camps."

The mayor's proposal follows a national trend to run homeless people out of public places. According to a study by the National Law Center on Homelessness and Poverty, one-fourth of major American cities cracked down on homeless people in 1994 by conducting police sweeps or restricting use of public places.

Todd said city staff members would work on an ordinance and bring it to the City Council at an unspecified date.

Buzzy Smith – a sunburned man with a bedroll on his back, "Harley Davidson" tattooed above the knuckles of his right hand and an open bottle of Wild Irish Rose wine in the other hand – said he was homeless, rootless and unimpressed with the proposal to outlaw camping in the city limits.

"Where else are we gonna sleep at?" Smith said, sipping his wine above a culvert along Barton Springs Road in a spot littered with cigarette butts and crushed beer cans. "Jail?"

Perhaps.

Anti-camping ordinance followed discussion of a proposal to crack down on habitual Class C misdemeanor offenders – litterers, panhandlers, disorderly people and people who are intoxicated.

The City Council asked the city staff to return to the council with a concrete proposal and costs for a 100-bed facility to jail people who habitually violate the misdemeanor ordinances.

Austin Police Sgt. Tom Schaefer, who headed a group made up of Austin police, Travis County deputies, municipal judges and the director of the Downtown Management Organization, said that, in 1994, 38,000 of the city's 45,000 arrests were Class C misdemeanor arrests, which are punishable by a fine of up to $500.

Schaefer said the system for the lowest level of criminal offense is a revolving door in which most people serve only a few hours and never pay a fine. They aren't jailed because jails are filled with more serious offenders.

Schaefer said the crackdown was aimed at "the lawless, not the homeless."

But homeless service advocates said the plan to jail misdemeanor offenders, paired with Todd's anti-camping proposal, was a two-pronged attack on the homeless people.

"They can couch it in any fashion they want to. In reality, the people we're talking about are the homeless," said Richard Troxell of House the Homeless. "The whole thrust of this is to avoid addressing the problem properly."

In January, the city began an effort to count homeless people. Social service providers estimated that 3,000 to 8,000 homeless people live in Austin.

Todd and other council members said that there are services for homeless people in Austin but that the population that is camping out refuses to be helped.

"They can always find a place to stay. They can always find three meals a day," said Council Member Ronney Reynolds.

If the City Council passes the no-camping ordinance, it won't be the first time Austin has tried to tell homeless people where they can stay and where they can't.

In 1989, the city passed an ordinance outlawing houseboats on Town Lake after activists launched makeshift crafts to serve as a reminder of the plight of homeless people.

You will recall, a group caught the city's attention in the summer of 1988 by holding a gosling "hostage" and threatening to eat it unless the city did something about homelessness. The threat lead to a meeting with the City Council, and instead of eating Homer, the group adopted him.

In a related lawsuit, a federal judge ruled that the city ordinance outlawing the rafts violated the free-speech rights of the homeless advocates, and the city settled for $38,000.

Austin is not the only city grappling with a growing population of street people.

At one point, scores of people lived in cardboard shanties under the Interstate 453 overpass near downtown Dallas. Homeless people also camped in front of Dallas City Hall, said city spokesman Mark Flake.

The city responded by declaring the area under the freeway off limits to the public and placing a midnight curfew on the City Hall block.

Flake said the city offered temporary free rent and job counseling to as many as 100 homeless people from the I-45 shantytown. "We got a lot of people living under that bridge into jobs," Flake said.

Staff writers Dick Stanley and Mike Todd contributed to this report.[1]

It was not until January, 1996, that the ordinance was passed bcause of the resistant efforts of House the Homeless and the citizens of Austin. This is that story and the story of the subsequent efforts to repeal it.

City of Austin Memorandum:

To: Joseph Lessard, Assistant City Manager

From: Deborah Thomas, Assistant City Attorney

Date: July 10, 1995

Subject: Summary of Proposed Encampment Ordinance

In accordance with your request, the following is a summary of the proposed Encampment Ordinance:

Replace existing Section 10-1-13 of the Austin City Code.

Declares camping in undesignated areas to be unlawful.

Defines public area as an outdoor area to which the public has access and includes, but is not limited to, streets, highways, parks, parking lots, alleyways, pedestrian ways, and the common areas of schools, hospitals, apartment houses, office buildings, transport facilities, and shop.

Defines camping as the use of a public area for living accommodation purposes such as, but not limited to, the following: (1) sleeping, or making preparations to sleep, including the laying down of bedding for the purpose of sleeping; (2) storing personal belongings; (3) making any fire; (4) using any tents or shelter or other structure or vehicle for sleeping; (5) carrying on cooking activities; or (6) doing any digging or earth breaking.

Declares that activity shall constitute camping when it reasonably appears, in light of all the circumstances, that the participants are in fact using the area for living accommodation purposes regardless of the intent of the participants or the nature of any other activities in which they may also be engaging.

Establishes ownership of property or permission from owner of property to be affirmative defense to prosecution.

Does not specify penalty, but carries the penalty stated in Section 1-1-99; see Section 10-1-99 which references Section 1-1-99 as penalty for violation of any provision in Chapter 10-1 for which another penalty is not stated.

The federal Fifth Circuit Court of Appeals is scheduled to hear oral argument on the City of Dallas ordinance concerning sleeping in public on July 11, 1995. There is no scheduled date for issuance of the Court opinion. The Dallas Assistant City Attorney handling the case estimates that a decision could be issued in six months. However, he also states that the Court could take up to two years to issue a decision.

Please contact me if I can provide additional information.

Sincerely,

Deborah Thomas

Assistant City Attorney

cc: Andrew Martin

Sally Henly

John Steiner

¡Todos Somos Ciudadanos de la Tierra!

We are all Citizens of the Earth! – One of the hundreds of protest signs displayed by members of House the Homeless during the campaign to stop the No Camping Ordinance.

> *TODOS SOMOS*
> *CIUDADANOS*
> *DE LA TIERRA*
> *HOUSE THE HOMELESS, INC.*

In 1995, in response to a growing number of homeless people in the city of Austin, the City Council set out to create what was to become known as the No Camping Ordinance. The ordinance read:

"Except in designated areas, it shall be unlawful for any person to camp in a public area." The No Camping Ordinance can be found in the City Code Section 7, Subsection 10-1-13. The ordinance then defined camping as *"using a public area for living accommodation such as but not limited to:*

1. Sleeping or making preparations to sleep, including the laying down of bedding for the purpose of sleeping;

2. Storing personal belongings;

3. Making any fire;

4. Using any tents or shelter or other structure or vehicle for sleeping;

5. Carrying on cooking activities; or

6. Doing any digging or earth breaking."

House the Homeless was the first to point out that there is an existing ordinance for each and every component of the single No Camping Ordinance. We stressed that there was no need to consolidate the ordinances under one heading and that in fact it would have a harmful result. The downtown business community thought otherwise.

The ensuing debate turned the City of Austin on its ear. No one who had access to a newspaper, watched television, or listened to the radio escaped the debate. In a small way; it was not unlike the U.S. Civil War in that it turned brother against brother and friend against friend. There were protests, sit-ins, camp outs, and musical ditties. The business community framed the need for the ordinance more or less as an act of self-defense.

They were trying to preserve *their* parks and *their* quality of life. They *had nothing against the homeless, per se.*

On the other hand, the homeless, who had lost everything, saw it as one more nail in their collective coffin. They, and we as their advocates, felt that the housing costs and inadequate wages controlled by the very people promoting the ordinance were symptomatic of an unsympathetic society.

Here is a full page, Sunday Ad, that House the Homeless raised money for and placed in the City State section of the *Austin American Statesman*:

Sunday, July 16, 1995:
Jail The Homeless? Or Job Train The Homeless?
   P.O. Box 92072
   Austin, Texas
   78709-2072
Dear Friend:

The City of Austin is currently considering passing a No Camping Ordinance. This will result in the arrest of homeless people for sleeping in public. We, as taxpayers, will then be asked to pay for a new Del Valle Jail facility to "house" those people. In contrast to this "jail mill" concept, House the Homeless, for the past five years, has been leading a citywide effort to create a Continuum of Care. It is designed to move single adults from an abjectly homeless state to a fully housed, reintegrated and employed condition.

Previously, HTH has successfully encouraged the Austin City Council to set aside various facilities at the Bergstrom Air Base, including the hospital, two barracks, and the non-commissioned Officers Building in an effort to create a health care and job training program. Unfortunately, we were told that the redesign of the yet unconstructed main terminal precluded our plans at Bergstrom.

Today, in a continued effort to reach our goal, we have launched a citywide Ballot Initiative to create a similar program that is not specific to Bergstrom.

Our goal is to create a comprehensive, drug and alcohol detoxification and treatment, job training/job placement program that provides limited, but continuous transitional housing for single adults. Over one thousand homeless persons have signed a separate petition declaring that if such a program existed, they would willingly enter it.

Our ten-point program is unique in its delivery of social services for several reasons. For example, it offers a seamless continuum of care without program disruption. Additionally, it requires that participants, upon reaching a certain level of success, begin to repay the program for the benefits received. As a way of preventing the possibility of attracting homeless people from outside Austin, we've included a 1 or 2 year Austin residency requirement. We believe that this thoroughly comprehensive approach provides for dignity and fairness to all concerned.

We are asking for your help in our collection of 25,000 signatures over the next three months.

Make no mistake, this program is costly, but it has already proved itself cost effective several times over as opposed to paying for police, EMS, food stamps or the continued use of the Brackenridge emergency room as if it were a City Health Clinic. This program is certainly more cost effective than the current city proposal which is to have taxpayers pay for a "jail mill" (The No Camping Ordinance) will repeatedly arrest people for sleeping in public. They will then be returned to the streets, still without job skills or housing, only to be arrested again.

It is time to stop providing for homelessness and begin to promote programs that prevent and end homelessness. Remember, one-third of the homeless population are veterans. These people risked their lives to defend our country. Don't we owe them a decent way back off the streets? This program does just that.

Join us. Sign and circulate the petition. Help us with financial support and vote with us on November 7th to create one viable option to address homelessness in our city.

> *In Unity There is Strength,*
> *Richard R. Troxell*
> *President*
> *House The Homeless*

Violation of the No Camping Ordinance would be a Class C misdemeanor/criminal offense and carry a fine of up to $500.00. To some, the idea was ludicrous, for if the homeless had $500.00 surely they would opt to sleep somewhere other than under a bridge. For others, the homeless were merely being asked to pay their "debt to society" for their crime of sleeping in public.

House the Homeless saw the ordinance as a weapon that punished people experiencing homelessness for their condition of being poor, not as a tool to deal with the underlying conditions. The number of homeless in Austin was estimated to be several thousand, which far out-numbered the few hundred beds at the Salvation Army, the only shelter in town at that time. The ordinance allowed for the ticketing and ultimate arrest of people for failure to pay fines resulting from these tickets. These people would then be returned to the streets, still without jobs, or still without jobs paying living wages. They would still have no access to affordable housing, and the only continuity in their lives was that they were assured of being arrested again…and again.

In response, we used all avenues available to oppose the ordinance and proposed alternatives. House the Homeless raised $6,000, one and two dollars at a time, to place the full-page ad in the City/State section of the Austin American Statesman. We posed the question: Jail the Homeless or Job Train the Homeless? We offered a ten-point plan that was not specific to the Bergstrom Air Base and set out to gather 25,000 signatures to create a ballot initiative in its support. House the Homeless also involved the services of the number one local cab service, Roy's Taxi, in our efforts to gather signatures. The following newspaper article sheds light on the subject.

Daily Texan, July 12, 1995
Cabbies help get petition signatures for low-cost housing

Roger Griego spends most of his time at the Auditorium Shores work center waiting to be hired as a day laborer, but his routine was broken Tuesday when he registered to vote for the first time.

Homeless for eight months, Griego said he was a professional featherweight boxer with a 20-2 record before he succumbed to alcoholism.

Griego participated in the voter-registration drive organized by House the Homeless, Inc.

"I believe in the …cause," Griego said.

The mobilization was a reaction to Austin's proposed No Camping Ordinance. House the Homeless, Inc. aims to collect 25,000 signatures by the Nov. 7 city elections from people registered to vote in Austin. The group is petitioning the city for a low cost housing program that provides job training and health care, said Richard Troxell, the organization's president.

"This will be an alternative to the city's No Camping Ordinance, which is an illegitimate response to a legitimate concern to get the homeless off the parks and streets," Troxell said. "Their plan is only going to give [the homeless] tickets of up to $500 for sleeping in public and put them in jail with taxpayers' money, only to be returned to the streets without jobs or housing."

Austin Mayor Bruce Todd has advocated the No Camping Ordinance as a way to "return public parks and sidewalks to the taxpayers that pay for them."

Much of the drive was focused on mobilizing Austin cab drivers to collect the signatures. Nelda Wells-Spears, the Travis County tax assessor-collector, was on hand to deputize cab drivers as voter registrars.

Cab drivers are a good source of feedback on complaints about the city because of the casual and often spontaneous conversations they have with their customers, said Carlos Velasquez, president of Roy's Taxi Company, which took part in the drive.

"We all need to get involved with the homeless. We're all human beings, we all face tragedies and need to help each other out," Velasquez said. "Homeless people have come in here looking for a job smelling like a brewery, and I tell them 'Get rid of the alcohol and drugs and I'll give you a job.'"

Velasquez said 11 of his cab drivers were deputized as voter registrars Tuesday. He said he has been a registrar for 15 years.

"The main goal today was to circulate blank petitions through the cabbies and not to gather signatures," Troxell said of the first-day efforts.

Tuesday's drive was the first event organized to push an alternative program to the no-camping ordinance, and Troxell said he will continue the drive on a monthly basis.[2]

We spoke in terms of government established numbers and statistics when arguing our case. We pointed out that in Travis County where Austin is located, 90,000 people were living below poverty. I pointed to an Austin Independent School District report that estimated that over 8,000 homeless youth were living in doubled up households, motels, and transitional housing. I pointed out that the homeless had no alternative to sleeping outside as the Salvation Army itself reported that it was operating at 149% of capacity and yet in the previous year, had been forced to turn away 1,200 people, 718 of whom were children. The same report submitted to the US Department of Housing and Urban Development estimated there to be over 5,500 homeless people in the Austin area with local shelters, the Salvation

Army and the Battered Women's Shelter only able to accommodate 417 people.

It is important to note that people of color are over represented in the homeless population with 49% being Afro American, 12% are Hispanic, 4% Native American and 3% being Asian. The remaining 32% is Caucasian.[3]

The debate was hot and heavy.

Mayor Bruce Todd said, "Staying in jail will enhance their lifestyle." Shocking! Nevertheless, in fairness to the Mayor, one could only assume that he meant that they would be housed, warm and dry with a place to sleep, and have food to eat. Astute perhaps — but hardly compassionate.

Assistant City Manager Joe Lessard reportedly lost his job when at a City Council work session he declared, "Make no mistake about it, our goal is to make these people leave town." (I retain the video to this day.) Paul Norris with the Barton Springs Merchants Association saw the ban "as a way to deal with those who have chosen a life style of lawlessness and illegal behavior."

Obviously, our response was that the targets of the No Camping Ordinance are people who had lost everything, had become homeless, and who were forced to live their lives in public. The acts that are acceptable behind closed doors are not acceptable when in public. When the police say that they are only targeting "behavior;" it is the behavior of conducting life activities in public areas, which this type of ordinance, specifically targets. Activities targeted included urinating in public as opposed to using the facilities in your own home; sitting on a side walk as opposed to sitting in a chair in your living room; or cooking in public as opposed to cooking in your kitchen; or sleeping in the park rather than in your own bed.

Photo by Alan Pogue

None of us were confused by this smoke screen. These are the activities that people experiencing homelessness are participating in simply because their condition dictates it. There is an irony here that must not be overlooked. It is ironic that the people driving these ordinances, the ones who are so desperately seeking relief from what they perceive to be a siege on their way of life, are the very *same business owners who are not paying adequate wages* to the very people they are telling to "Get a Job."

Given opportunity and living wage jobs, these very people would gladly be housed and become productive and contributing members of their society. According to a U.S. government report in 2000, 42% of the homeless are working at some point during the week. Given the opportunity, who among us would want to live in public, suffer the abuses of others, and live such a desolate, lonely existence?

In early 1995, Steve Martin, one of several homeless men living in a homeless camp known as Horseshoe Pit, stated, "When I make $5.00 an hour at $40 a day, it is not enough to pay for rent. We need jobs that pay $8 or $9 or $10 an hour. They just keep pushing us deeper into the woods."[4]

The City of Austin was not alone in its efforts to create a punitive response to homelessness. According to the National Law Center on Homelessness and Poverty, "One Fourth of major American cities cracked down on homeless people in 1994 by conducting police sweeps or restricting the use of public places." In Austin, Texas, police Sergeant Tom Schaefer had said that the crackdown was aimed at "the lawless, not the homeless." This sentiment was echoed in an Austin American Statesman editorial entitled "Camping Ban Not Designed as Attack on Homeless People." [5]

In 1995, an affordability report produced by National Low Income Housing Coalition, entitled, "Out of Reach," using the US Department of Housing and Urban Development standards that one should spend no more than 30% of one's income on housing, revealed that half of Austin's renters were unable to afford one or two bedroom apartments. The report stated that the conditions had forced renters into…"inhuman housing situations."[6]

Today the National Coalition for the Homeless estimates that 3.5 million people will experience homelessness. It strains credibility to believe that 3.5 million people are voluntarily subjecting themselves to various forms of abuse, indignation, beatings, humiliation and rape. [7]

Photo of Troxell wth House the Homeless members in City Council Hearings. Photos from *Austin American Statesman*.

Hot City Council Hearings

By July of 1995, House the Homeless had been publishing *Notes from the Blues Box* for several years. This was our own newsletter about homeless issues by homeless people. In the July issue, we had published information about our Ballot Initiative for a Health Care and Jobs Training Program, a few stories about the proposed No Camping Ordinance, and a reprint of a 1993 *Austin American Statesman* story by Miguel M. Salinas. He wrote about how a man experiencing homelessness, Ricardo Davila, age 35, was fighting for his life after having been set on fire.

The article told of how Mr. Davila had received second and third degree burns on 80% of his body. He had been "brutally beaten and then set on fire." Sergeant Doug Dukes of the Austin Homicide Unit described it as…"a totally inhuman act." In fact, it was premeditated.[8] When I spoke to Ricardo years later, he had told me that he had approached one of his assailants asking for a cigarette in a convenience store parking lot at 6301 North Lamar Blvd. Angry words were exchanged. The eventual assailant left the area and returned with two other guys. They began stoning, kicking, and beating Ricardo. Witnesses verified that the attackers bought lighter fluid in the very store outside of which the attack was occurring. They then set him on fire. Ricardo did survive, but it was only after years of painful suffering, endless skin grafts, and excruciating physical therapy.

Not much has changed. In May 2010, Vickie Santana was approached on Burnet Road outside a convenience store by Carlos Mates, a man experiencing homelessness. He made the almost fatal mistake of asking Ms. Santana for a cigarette. For his trouble, he was shot at twice and Ms. Santana, for her response, was charged with aggravated assault. Her boyfriend witnessed and verified her actions.

Also in the July issue of *Notes from the Blues Box*, was the announcement that on Thursday, July 13, 1995 at 5:00 pm, City Council would hold a public hearing on the No Camping Ordinance. People were urged to come testify!

In preparation for the public hearing on the No Camping Ordinance, Sue Milam, the head of Health and Human Services, provided some additional information for the City Council just before the hearing. Because the No Camping Ordinance was being proposed, in part, from a need to respond to public intoxication, she shared the following comment. "Nearly half of Austin's homeless population have addiction problems, and over one third are likely to have mental illness as well." Ms. Milam also pointed out that with only 26 detoxification beds in the community and with a meager 413 persons served in state funded facilities in Austin in 1993, only 14% of the target population were being served.

I would be remiss if I did not point out that even with the shift in substance abuse treatment dollars in recent years to the Criminal Justice Department, in 2010, there are only two substance abuse treatment beds in the Austin community available outside the criminal justice system for single adult males. The other additional piece of information provided by Ms. Milam referenced housing. Only 42% of Travis County's rental units and 15% of owner-occupied properties were affordable to poor people in 1990. Of those that were affordable, persons who were not low income occupied 41%. She concluded by saying that "in other words, the limited stock of affordable housing does not necessarily get accessed by poor people."[9]

On the day of the first hearing, hundreds of homeless people, both supporters and opponents of the ordinance, signed up to speak before city council. Members of House the Homeless filled the gallery with signs stating:

"Forgive us for being poor!"

"Fund health care and job programs, Now!"

"Please help us!"

"We're not bad people that need to be good, we're sick people who need to be well!"

"Average residency 7.5 years!" (This sign is reference to the offensive and degrading term "transient" used to describe people experiencing homelessness.)

"Jail the Homeless or Job Train Them?"

Outside of the chambers, dozens of other House the Homeless members paraded with signs:

"House the Homeless!"

"We are Citizens"

"Stop the Economic War!"

"Civil Rights not Civil War!" (That sign scares me even today.)

We were made to wait over three hours for the hearing. We were given "time certain" for 5:00 pm, but were placed after the City's budget hearing discussion, which many thought was intentional to encourage us to wander off. However, we did not wander off. While waiting, the atmosphere took on a circus like feel with motorists honking horns and shouting words of support and encouragement, insults, or meaningless directives like "Get a job!" We continued to wave our signs, either encouraged or inspired depending upon each response. We ignored the negativity. At the bottom of each sign was our name...the imperative, "House the Homeless!" Inside and outside, the crowd grew more and more restless. We felt abused and manipulated one more time by the delay and the fact that the City was holding a budget hearing during our time.

Austin American Statesman —

Homeless hearing draws crowd

Proposal would ban camping in public places; council to vote next week

Outside City Council Chambers, several dozen homeless people and their supporters waved signs exhorting motorists to "honk for the homeless."

Inside, a proposal to crack down on homeless people by restricting camping on public sites became a status equalizer, placing suited businessmen in favor of the ban on the same aisles with purple-haired homeless teens.

JoAnn Koepke, one of the 114 people signed up to speak on the ban at Thursday's public hearing, told council members that the ban "strikes terror in my heart."

Years ago as a homeless person in Oklahoma City, Koepke said, she almost lost her feet to frostbite after she was imprisoned without medical care. "I also lost my humanity, and that's a real hard thing to recover," she said.

To rousing applause, speakers called the ban a knee-jerk response to a complicated problem, while others pleaded with the council not to criminalize poverty. Many said the ban lacked compassion and was, because jail terms could result, fiscally irresponsible.

On the other side, Paul Norris with the Barton Springs Merchants Association spoke in favor of the ban as a way to deal with those who have chosen "a life-style of lawlessness and illegal behavior."

Norris also challenged the council to search for more comprehensive solutions to homelessness, including a detoxification center and job training.

Five other business leaders lauded the ban as a way to discourage destructive behavior while returning parks, green-belts, creeks and other public areas to public use.

The council adjourned the public hearing at 10 p.m. with about three hours of speakers remaining. The hearing will resume next Thursday at 5

111

p.m. No new speakers will be added to the roster, Council Member Gus Garcia said.

After the hearing, the City Council is scheduled to vote on the first reading of the ordinance. Three readings are required for passage.

About 5,500 homeless people live on Austin's streets, according to a recent study by the Community Action Network, a public-policy board of elected officials and private-sector representatives.

The proposed ordinance would ban camping in outdoor areas to which the public has access. Campers ticketed for the Class C misdemeanor would be saddled with a criminal charge and a monetary fine ranging from $200-$500. [10]

When our issue came up, we testified one by one. Our stories were sympathetic, loud, disjointed, pitiful, and often incoherent. Our pleas were desperate. They were about the abuse we had suffered and the abuse we still suffer even now. They were about our families and how we missed them. We were childlike. We stood before our "parents" having been scolded and said that we did not mean to be bad, we just needed help. We told the world that we would work, but what is the point...we still would not be able to afford housing. In addition, we railed at them. How dare they even consider doing this to us when the wages they paid were so pitiful! Some of us cried.

Our attorney, Cecilia Wood, asserted that, "To punish the homeless for their status rather than their behavior is cruel and unusual punishment." She declared that members of House the Homeless would arm themselves with a legal instruction book, which would walk our people through every step of the legal process and create a record to use in possible litigation. When I later testified, I told them that we would not pay the fines and that our people would ask for costly jury trials.

Alan Kaplan speaking for the Downtown Management Organization (DMO, now referring to itself as the DAA) summed up the testimony of the promoters when he stated, "The problem is we have transients in this community who urinate, defecate, abuse drugs, and basically confiscate [public] places." He finished with the mantra, "This is not about homelessness; it is about behavior."

No decision was made that first night. We were scheduled to return for a second three-hour hearing. Three more hours of testimony was waiting to be given. Little did we know they would combine the second and third hearings into one final session.

At the July 29th hearing with 125 people in opposition present, previous speakers were not permitted. Only twenty voices were permitted to rise in defense of the homeless as the ordinance was passed 4-2.

One newspaper columnist wrote, "There was never any doubt that the council would support the 'anti-camping' ordinance...politics is power, a field that relegates the powerless to the fringes."[11] The next vote was set for September, 1995. It was later moved back to November, but we all knew that it was only a matter of time. A Task Force was set up to study homelessness in Austin. House the Homeless participated. Considered then to be the only major newspaper in town, the *Austin American Statesman* continued to write editorial after editorial calling for enactment of the No Camping Ban.

At the November hearing, Rodney Doerscher testified, "We've gotten so arrogant with our standard of living that we expect all people to live like us, even though our economy cannot support such a system."

The *Austin Chronicle* reported that Mayor Bruce Todd and Council Member Ronny Reynolds called it "a tough love," that "will help get homeless people off the streets and encourage them to take responsibility for their lives."[12] It would seem that the council was determined to move forward. It was not about to let facts or common sense de-rail it. On the day of the final vote, in the *Austin American Statesman* lead editorial, Mayor Bruce Todd vowed to reintroduce the ordinance after new council elections if it failed to pass. It did not fail. It passed 4-2.

Mayor Bruce Todd said, "The decision is best for the city because it preserves Austin's quality of life." Perhaps... but for whom! For some, not all. And at what cost to the others?

I was the last speaker. I held up pictures of two homeless people I knew. One was Sam West the other was Jesus of Nazareth. I asked if it made sense to pray to one on Sunday and to pass laws against the other on Monday. We were all so terribly sad.

Photo of Troxell wth House the Homeless members in City Council Hearings. Photos from *Austin American Statesman*.

Austin American Statesman
Austin Bans Public Camping
Nofziger Casts Deciding Vote In Stormy Council

An Austin City Council member who spent years on the cusp of homelessness on Thursday cast the deciding vote to ban public camping in the city.

Max Nofziger, who hitchhiked around the country before landing in Austin in 1974 as a street-corner flower salesman and musician, joined Mayor Bruce Todd and Council Members Ronney Reynolds and Gus Garcia in approving the ban, which takes effect in 10 days.

Council Member Jackie Goodman voted against the ordinance, Council Member Eric Mitchell abstained and Council Member Brigid Shea was not at the meeting.

Homeless advocates said the vote represented a hardening of a traditionally progressive and compassionate city and vowed to fight the ordinance in court.[13]

Sunday, January 7, 1996
City's Heart Hard to Find in Camp Ban

It's funny how some popular expressions mean the opposite of what they say. Like when you say, "I didn't have the heart to do it," what you usually mean is you couldn't do something heartless. You had too much heart.

Where the plight of the impoverished is concerned, Austin showed on Thursday that it didn't have the heart. Literally. As the rich get richer... It's criminal that so many folks – an estimated 6,000 in Austin – have fallen between the cracks. But to make poverty itself a crime shows just how callous Austin has become.

In leaner times, this was known as a warm place, a "live and let live" kind of city, a town where drifters and artists and "slackers" could exist on the margins and where quality of life wasn't measured by one's bank statement. It was a city that opened its arms to vagabonds like Max Nofziger. These days, the message from Council Member Nofziger and the rest of Austin is clear: If you aren't here to make or spend money, don't let the door hit you on the way out.

As of Jan. 14, 1996 the crime of living in Austin without a roof over one's head will carry a maximum $500 penalty or a jail sentence. Both measures *are ludicrous. If a homeless person had $500 bucks in his pocket, he could take a suite at the Four Seasons. As for the estimated $70 per day that it'll cost to jail the criminal camper; taxpayers would spend less to provide shelter and a couple of meals.*

Austin is hardly planning to jail thousands of these softened criminals or enrich its coffers through fine collection. Instead, the city is hoping that they'll take the hint and go be homeless somewhere else, until the next city passes a similar measure, and the next, and the whole country makes it illegal to exist without a roof over one's head. And what then for the homeless: Start swimming?

Combating poverty by making it a crime makes as much sense as criminalizing cancer. We already have laws against public harassment, trespassing and intoxication, the nuisances that the anti-camping measure is intended to counter. The difference here is that the "crime" is poverty, in and of itself.

It's too easy to demonize those who have hit a bad stretch, to dehumanize them. It's so much tougher to come to grips with the realities of corporate downsizing, sickness without hospitalization insurance, rents that skyrocket while salaries remain flat, cuts in social services and so many other factors beyond the individual's control that can spin a formerly productive member of society into the shadows.

For Austin, the travails of homelessness are easier experienced through the songs of Bruce Springsteen, whose concerts in support of "The Ghost of Tom Joad" – an album-length meditation on American poverty are sure to command top dollar. We take local pride in the literary achievement of Lars Eighner, whose widely praised "Travels with Lizbeth" documents the sort of existence that the city has now chosen to outlaw.

In essence, what Austin is saying to the homeless is, "We could care less," another one of those turnaround expressions that really means we couldn't care less. In passing the anti-camping ordinance, Austin has become a colder place to live. And not just for the homeless.[14]

Cody Michaels with Amercan Flag. Photo from *Austin American Statesman*.

Camping for Justice

Folk singer Steve Fromholz and acclaimed columnist Molly Ivins decided that when the ban went into effect, they would peacefully show their contempt for the ordinance. They would camp out on the streets of Austin. Steve said, "Anytime that you see hatred and injustice, you better do something about it...otherwise, you'll live with it the rest of your life." Molly, if I recall correctly, declared that she was "a Texas gal, and Texans love to camp. It was just silly of Council to pass a law against it."

Austin Chronicle, September 13, 1996
Best Hippie Campout
Camping Ban Protest

On the first night of Bruce Todd's ordinance banning sleeping in public places went into effect, political columnist/commentator Molly Ivins and musician Steve Fromholz – Austinites both – threw a hell of a slumber party...and raised our consciousness at the same time. Long after the television cameras shut off, and the daily's reporters headed home, Ivins and Fromholz sat in sleeping bags swigging from paper bags and singing protest songs. By the time the sun rose on Congress Avenue downtown, Ivins and Fromholz were snoozing peacefully among more than 85 others lining the sidewalks, mostly homeless men, happy to have a safe place to rest for the night.

Austin Chronicle, September 13, 1996
Best Council Activist
Richard R. Troxell

The mayor can't stand him, so he must be doing something right. He's Richard Troxell, who as president of House the Homeless and a former Vietnam veteran, speaks for Austin's homeless population. Week after week at council chambers he has waged a one-man war against Todd's anti-homeless ordinance passed last January. The camping ban is still on the books, but it'll be tirelessly challenged as long as Troxell's around.

On January 25, 1996, the No Camping Ban went into effect. The citizens of Austin immediately formed the Coalition to Repeal the Ban and joined House the Homeless to do just that. Just as promised, we began distributing self-help legal packets among our citizens. The 100-page document gave systematic instructions on how to fight the ordinance and defend against the $500 fine. Additionally, the packet included procedures for requesting a jury trial.

That night, we held a rally and candlelight vigil on the grounds of the state capitol. About one hundred of us gathered on the south lawn. We were old, young, bearded, and clean-shaven. We had long hair, gray hair, green hair, and no hair. We were well dressed and disheveled. We were a motley, eclectic group of people who were loud, mum, and spoke in clear concise words. We all had one thing in common: we cared deeply about the human condition. But to sum it up, we felt damaged. Moreover, when Cody Michaels, a homeless man with beautiful auburn tresses flowing over his shoulders and ten years of homelessness under his belt, climbed a pillar and began waving a large tattered American flag, we simply felt...betrayed.

Each one of us felt a very deep loss. We felt that something pure in essence, something about who we are as a people had just slipped away. It slipped away just like a burial at sea when the flag-draped coffin slides out from underneath the flag and then in slow motion arcs out into view and then plunges into an icy sea. A small splash of foam rises up to mark its entrance but only for a moment or two and then that too is consumed by the vastness of the ocean. Sadly, we headed to the city street corner at 8th and Congress where we would join our friends Molly and Steve who were already "camping" in protest.

Some of our signs read:

> *Repeal the No Camping Ord.*
> *House the Homeless*
> *We're not Protesting...We're Camping,*

> *Austin American Statesman*
> *Foes of Camping Band Denounce it as Cruel*
> *Man arrested on 1st day of enforcement*
> *For a few moments, they let out a single yell.*

Dozens of homeless people, who gathered their bedrolls and duffel bags at the steps of the state Capitol, were screaming. They were haggard men with beards and wool caps, and teen-agers with pierced noses and green-dyed hair.

"The pain in the streets is real, man," said Amy Edwards, one of about 100 people – some with homes but many without – who gathered to protest a new city ordinance that bans public camping. "This hurts."

On the same day that the city began to enforce the ban, which the Austin City Council adopted Jan. 4, advocates for the homeless and other opponents of the ordinance held two demonstrations that denounced the ban as cruel to people who live on the streets. While some gathered at the rally, others arrived downtown for an overnight campout at the corner of Eighth Street and Congress Avenue.

At 11 p.m., at least 50 protesters remained at the campsite with the two event organizers, columnist Molly Ivins and musician Steve Fromholz. Some protesters danced to a drum beat while others cooked green beans. Still others were settling in for the night inside a teepee, which featured a hand-written sign, "We're Not Protesting – We're Camping!"

Protesters Rail Against Camping Band

Austin Police Department spokesman Mike Burgess said officers considered the campsite a political protest and did not plan to make arrests under the camping ban at that site.

However, two protesters were arrested at about 11 p.m. after a group of 30 people marched east on Sixth Street. The two were charged with being a pedestrian in the roadway, said Lt. Mike Urubek.

Earlier in the day, before the demonstration, at least one person was arrested elsewhere for breaking the ban. Police arrested Thomas Michael Sawyer, a 39-year-old homeless man, at 9:51 a.m. after an officer found him beneath a bridge on East Riverside Drive. According to arrest records, Sawyers' campsite had "two bedrolls, a few sitting chairs, several personal items and a hole dug in the ground containing trash."

Sawyer said he won't go back. "Maybe I'll go down to the Salvation Army ...maybe I'll go see some friends," he said.

The city's ordinance prohibits camping on sidewalks, city rights of way, public parks and similar places. Violating the ordinance is a Class C misdemeanor, which carries a maximum $500 fine.

If people are ticketed for camping and do not pay the fine or do community service, they can be jailed. It costs the city about $70 a day to jail Class C violators.

Sawyer pleaded "not guilty" to the charge and is scheduled to reappear before the city's Municipal Court on Jan. 30.

For John Baldwin, a painter who spent years on the streets, Sawyer's arrest was unjust. "Without sleep, you can't have a life, and without a place to sleep, where does that leave you?" he asked.

Although opponents decried the ban, downtown businesses have pushed for the ordinance as a way to keep downtown vibrant.

Alana Mallard, who came to the rally at the Capitol, said she's worried that her 22-year-old son, who lives on the streets near the University of Texas campus, could be made a target by the ordinance. She said mental illness is one of the roots of homelessness, and the city should concentrate more attention on solving that problem rather than enforcing the ordinance.

"Besides that, I don't know what the answer is," she said, as tears fell across her face.

Back at the makeshift campsite, Brother Michael stood in protest on the corner of Eighth Street lighting a cigarette that he pulled from the pocket of his brown cloak.

"This ordinance would have put Jesus in jail," said Brother Michael, who belongs to St. Anthony Centers Morning Star Monastery.[15]

Bruce Springsteen was in town that night. He was performing at the Austin Music Hall. To so many working stiffs, and especially to those of us who have hit rock bottom, he is simply, "The Boss." His words always seem to hurt us and at the same time free us. He had sent word that he wanted to meet me. When I heard this, I felt a validation for our efforts even beyond our own belief of our right actions. But all night I struggled with small rolling skirmishes between the guys and the police. Heckling words of antagonism were used like swords all night, and they needed to be calmed. I spent the night *stamping out flaming ducks.*

I never made it to meet The Boss, but the fact that he had dedicated the T-shirt and concession sales to House the Homeless satisfied me that night. More than once I have thought of that as a missed opportunity, and more than once I've wished that I had a chance to meet him and share with him our plans, even today, to turn this thing around.

Only one person was arrested for camping that night as the police basically treated our action as a "protest" not camping. Ironically, Thomas Michael Sawyer, or Tom Sawyer as we all knew him, was the first person to receive a No Camping ticket. He was underneath a bridge with two bedrolls, a couple of chairs, and some personal items. Tom Sawyer, at age 39, had lost everything but his work ethic. He was an urban recycler. He got up every morning at *o'dark-thirty* and would travel from one end of the city to the other, gathering aluminum cans. He would crush them by stomping on them and then sell them at the American Can Company for pennies a pound. He would work all day for less than ten dollars…ten dollars in the blistering Texas sun…a crying shame. When others saw Tom, they saw a bum. I saw a man whose work ethic was solidly intact. I saw a man, who for various reasons, had fallen out of the system and was operating in an abusive black market work force. I see it as a shadow system which is forcing people to work for slave wages while depriving our socioeconomic system of its tax base.

Now, years later, when I think of Tom Sawyer and how hard he worked for so little money, I connect him in my mind with that sign from that very first campout. "Forgive the Criminal Sleepers." Tom Michael Sawyer's name was one of forty other names read at our 2001 Homeless Memorial Sunrise Service.

It was becoming clear to us all that men and women were living *and* dying on our city streets. The No Camping Ordinance would not make things any easier.

Life Under the Ordinance

As time went on, we saw the ordinance applied both unfairly and unevenly. The ordinance had made it illegal to sleep in one's vehicle. However, only homeless people in their very used vehicles got the rap on the window. They were issued tickets for camping, got their vehicles towed to the impound yard, and ultimately sold by Southside Wrecking or some other reputable towing service, for outstanding storage charges. Oddly, the police never seemed to bother musician Willie Nelson and others like him for sleeping in their $100,000 buses. Therefore, in hopes of spreading awareness, we started leafleting these rolling homes with this flyer:

House The Homeless Inc.

P.O. Box 2312

Austin, Texas 78768-2312

Contact- Richard R. Troxell

Warning !

The City Of Austin Has Passed The "No Camping" Ordinance

All: Vehicles

Campers

Music Buses

Back Packers

Picnickers

Sun Worshipers

Concert Ticket Line Sleepers And

Stranded Travelers

Are Subject To Ticketing ($500) And Possible Arrest.

The Police Now Have Probable Cause To Board Your Vehicle Without A Warrant Or Warning Under The Suspicion That Someone Is Sleeping Inside. Your Mobile Home/Home Away From Home, Is No Longer Safe. You Are Now Subject To Search And Seizure!

*Contact Max Nofziger 499-2260 And Get Him *

To Repeal The "No Camping" Ordinance.

Do It Today!

There Are Laws That Free Us And There Are Laws That Enslave Us!

This was our way of crying out and soliciting their help. It did not come. Max Nofziger was a City Council member who when running (seven times before being elected) asserted that he had been homeless. He portrayed himself as a regular guy, salt of the earth, etc. As fate would have it, Mr. Nofziger turned out to be the swing vote that passed the No Camping Ordinance. To us it seemed more like salt in the wound.

We launched a letter writing campaign where each one of the homeless wrote Max a one-page letter and personally appealed to him to repeal the ordinance.

Letters like this were sent to him:

Max Nofziger
P.O. Box 1088
Austin, TX 78767
Dear Mr. Nofziger:

Thanks for trying to help the homeless. While your head and mind may be in the right place, your idea to ban camping is just wrong thinking. This is not the way to help homeless people. I am not on the streets by choice. Jobs don't pay enough to get off the streets.

Please drop the ban. I know you can. You voted good before. We have no place to live. I still camp, but awake every morning wondering where I'll be tomorrow... free or in jail. Please help.

Yours truly,
Concerned in Austin

As far as I know, he never answered a single letter.

Tom Sawyer, dazed. Photo from *Austin American Statesman*.

Selective Enforcement

The Colorado River that flows through the center of town is dammed up and creates Lady Bird Lake and is fed in part by a natural spring known as Barton Springs. This pristine water is purified by a limestone aquifer, stretching for miles underground. It is referred to as the Edwards Aquifer. There are dozens of two-hundred-year-old pecan trees that grace its shores, which offer both cool shade and fresh air in the hot Texas sun. Small children splash in the cool waters of a constant 68 degrees while men and women lounge on the gently sloping hillside and in the warm Austin air. One by one they all succumb to the warm sun and cool breezes and their eyelids close, but despite the fact that they are sleeping in public on city land, they do not receive No Camping tickets where sleeping is expressly prohibited. We pointed this out on more than one occasion.

In early March, parents of school age children are given one day of the year when they can put in a transfer on behalf of their disgruntled child and secure an inter-district school transfer. However, there are only so many transfer slots available. As a result, parents get in line and then openly sleep on the sidewalks of Austin. But regardless of the fact that they are displayed on the 5:00, 5:30 and 6:00 am and pm news, and their pictures fill the Metro section of the newspaper, they do not receive No Camping tickets.

Travelers sleep at the bus station and the airport. They sleep both openly and conspicuously. Families that picnic and barbeque in Zilker Park are conducting *food preparation*, which is expressly prohibited under the ordinance. However, none of these folks are fined. Simply put, all of this is *selective enforcement* and therefore unconstitutional.

As a university town that swells to 55,000 students three-quarters of the year, there is an endless stream of events of high desirability that "require overnight camping" to get concert tickets, Star Wars tickets, i-pod sales, basketball and football tickets. Their camping styles are often displayed on the front pages of the City and State section of the newspaper followed by considerable discussion of how uncomfortable they must have been. The students always crowd the hero's bench and brush aside any discomfort as having been insignificant sacrifices given the rewards. None of these individuals is ever ticketed.

One of the most uneven applications and perversions of the law came against Tom Sawyer himself.

The prosecutors at Municipal Court recommended that charges against Tom be dropped. Judge David Spencer agreed citing "humanitarian reasons."

Tom had been given temporary housing, which, coupled with Tom's promise to never again camp, allowed the judge to drop the charge. It was sort of like the Judge in Miracle on 34th Street who did not want to rule against Santa Claus. How could a judge rule against Tom Sawyer for camping and ever hope to get re-elected! Of course, the Mayor was furious and wrote to the chief prosecutor, "They should implement the policies that the Council has enacted." Subsequently, the chief prosecutor responded by saying, "Others [such as Tom Sawyer] who use that argument shouldn't expect to get that same treatment."[16] I am not making this up folks.

Man with sign: Repeal the Ban! Photo from *Austin American Statesman*.

Repeal The No Camping Ban

From the moment of its passage, House the Homeless called for the repeal of the No Camping Ordinance. Voices cried out from every corner of the community. Members of the City Council were declared heartless. This was not true of Council Member Jackie Goodman. She had spent time growing up in a trailer park and was always an unwavering supporter of all of Austin's poor and downtrodden.

Hundreds of young people associated with a religious ministry had held an Urban Plunge where they camped out overnight to gain a self-imposed empathy for people experiencing homelessness. They built an enormous cardboard city, which filled several vacant city blocks. They stood in their own soup lines. They stood in line for hours only to find that when they got to the other end of the line the food or the resource they were seeking was not available. They then camped out in their cardboard city. In the middle of the night they were rousted by their counselors and told that camping was illegal….they would have to tear down their cardboard city. It had taken them half a day to construct it. They took it down, but just moved to different fields and reconstructed their encampment. Imagine that. The following week they showed up with a huge sign with hand painted words to address the Council.

We the Youth
state the following:
Jesus Christ lived
with, talked to, and ate
with the outcast and
rejected people of his
day. As his followers,
We are against the
Camping Ban passed
into law by the City
of Austin. The ban
punishes people for being
homeless and offers no
solutions, assistance,
and no compassion.

We The Youth? How cool is that?

Editorials flew back and forth. I wrote, "After only a half year of manipulation and pressure tactics, the smallest possible majority of the Austin City Council managed to overcome its fear of the truth, facts and common sense to finally pass a No Camping Ordinance. The battle cry often repeated, "I know this isn't the answer, but we have to do something"… would churn the stomach of any God fearing Marine.

Edward Sledge, who later sat on the Austin Human Rights Commission, wrote, "Is it not enough that many of our citizens do not have health care, insurance, or health security…that the minimum wage is not near enough to house and feed an individual much less a family? Homeless people may have additional concerns like where, when and if their next dollar or the next meal may materialize. Now added to the list there is a city ordinance that criminalizes the act of camping when there is nowhere else to go, except to jail."[17]

Police Lieutenant Michael Urubek, charged with fielding questions about the enforcement benefits of the new ordinance, to everyone's surprise, questioned the City Council's thought process. He wanted to know, "What were the City Council's expectations after this [ordinance] was passed? The police department is not targeting the homeless. We do not have the staff to round them up or the room to put them away. Maybe the Council should have thought this through a little more. This tool is not a tool for us to clean up anything." It was reported later that he was chastised for his remarks.[18]

In the first two months after the ordinance was passed, 56 people received No Camping citations, 54 of them served time in jail instead of paying the fine or performing community service. Obviously, the City of Austin had found a way to bring back Debtors' Prison.

Our attorney, Cecilia Wood, wanting the mayor to explain the City's need for the ordinance, subpoenaed Mayor Bruce Todd, Police Chief Elizabeth Watson and Assistant City Manager Joe Lessard in the first of what would turn out to be years of court challenges. The presiding judge quashed those subpoenas (perhaps because they were his bosses…perhaps not).

With continued pressure from House the Homeless, City Council Member Gus Garcia was quoted on 4/9/97 in the Austin American Statesman as saying, "I made a mistake, and I'm willing to admit it; the Ordinance hasn't worked." He was running for City Council at that time. Kirk Watson said, "I don't think you've solved the problem of homelessness by banning it."[19] Both Garcia and Watson later became mayors of Austin and subsequently defended the No Camping ban vigorously.

Cecilia Wood argued that the ordinance infringed on freedom to travel, equal protection under the law, and constituted cruel and unusual punishment. She also argued that it discriminated against a class of people for their *economic status*. The named plaintiffs were Christopher Standage, age 40, and Terrance Flowers, also 40; both were homeless. Ironically, the judge was Judge Mitchell Solomon. In the first pretrial conference (there would be 12!), Ms. Wood called Rory O'Malley, executive director of the Travis County Housing Authority. He testified that in Travis County there were "about 16,000 more low income families in the city than the number of available low-income housing units."

Leroy Torres, the then director of substance abuse treatment services for the Travis County Mental Health-Mental Retardation (MHMR) Center presented enlightening testimony. He testified that, given recent cuts, there were only between seven and ten publicly funded detoxification beds and that "because of federal regulations, most of those are reserved for women."

I also testified as an expert witness, citing that at the time our city had a 98% fill rate in the housing rental market. Additionally, I pointed out that most landlords were requiring first and last month's rent, security deposits, and rental history references. This amounted to approximately $1,200 plus the references. The inference from all of this specific testimony was not lost on anyone in the courtroom, especially Christopher and Terrance. People needed affordable housing and living wages with which to afford that housing.

The city's prosecuting attorney, Gayle Posey, could only attack Judge Solomon's jurisdiction and his legitimacy to preside over the case in an attempt to deflect our arguments. (*City employee attacks city employee...details at 11:00.*) She could not dispute the facts that the guys, the targets of this ordinance, had no options and no alternative to their behavior, which had now been outlawed.

When Judge Solomon quashed the subpoenas to bring the mayor, the police chief, and the assistant city manager, Ms. Wood attempted to place Ms. Posey on the stand in an effort to show that city officials had people like our clients in mind when they had created the ordinance. City employee Joe Lessard had been captured on a city video tape at a Council work session declaring it was the City's intention to make sure these people leave town. (Oddly, Mr. Lessard seemed to disappear in the middle of the trial never to be heard from again…at least not by House the Homeless. Oh yes, not unexpectedly, Ms. Posey also never testified in any of the hearings.)

It was our contention that the mayor had used the police force to target homeless people with the ordinance and therefore had direct knowledge of the cases affecting each of the accused, and he should be forced to testify. The judge apparently did not agree. No elected officials were ever made to testify and explain any of their actions or motives in creating the No Camping Ordinance. We sought all records, memos, etc. relating to the case. Judge Solomon ruled that we were entitled to the documents and ordered the City to produce them.[20] After weeks of stonewalling, the City produced a few interoffice memos. Actually, we had already acquired several others that they did not produce. We asked the judge to fine the City and order the City to produce all documents. Like many other issues in those trials that transpired over the years, the issue became lost…along with truth, justice, and the American way.

Five months after the ordinance was enacted, the first major No Camping case ended. Judge Solomon ruled that the ordinance was constitutional.[21] Chris Standage changed his plea to "no contest" and was forced to pay a $150 fine. House the Homeless raised the money and paid the fine. Ms. Wood appealed the judge's ruling on the constitutionality of the ordinance. To the media I declared, "We now stand exactly where we had hoped to be. We are building our house of defense one solid brick at a time. We trust the appellate court to prove us right and rule the ordinance unconstitutional." At this point, I was losing faith in the entire court system and was wondering if my "trust" had ever been properly placed.[22]

What I was questioning was certainly not God and perhaps not even the system with its manmade imperfections. What I was questioning (just for a moment) was our ability to overcome all the obstacles, all the barriers, all the blood, sweat and tears , all the deaths, all the hatred long enough for us to win. Then the moment passed. Clarity returned once again. We had no choice. We *have* no choice. There is an injustice. No justice; no peace.

Camping Ordinance Costs

Over 2,003 people were ticketed and/or jailed during the first year of the No Camping Ban. The city spent $120,000 in direct jail time. Thousands of police hours and court hours had been invested. At 20 minutes per citation, the deputy clerk of the court calculated that over 2,000 police hours had been spent issuing No Camping tickets and appearing in court. Many people were beginning to question the effectiveness of the camping ban.

Jail Time Costs

The total number of Camping Ordinance Citations issued by the Austin Police Department totaled 2,003. Of these, 636 citations resulted in jail time. The majority of the Filings were left pending and had no outcome.

The total amount of Jail time in days was estimated at 1,584 days.

The average jail time per citation was 2.5 days.

The total cost of the jail time was estimated at $120,000. This number was derived from information supplied by the Travis County Sheriff's Office of Public Information. A cost of $75.25 was quoted as the cost per inmate per day, but it is important to remember that the City and the Sheriff's Department split this cost.

Austin Police Officer hours

The time for an Austin Police Officer to cite and jail a violator of the Camping Ordinance was estimated to be 1.5-2 hours. This included citing, cuffing, transporting, jailing and reporting on the arrest.

The time for an Austin Police Officer to issue a citation to a violator of the Camping Ordinance was estimated at 20 minutes.

Given the Camping Ordinance Filings date for the Deputy Clerk of the Court, this translated to an estimated 2,000 Police Hours.[23]

FOUR:

BERGSTROM AIR BASE

Bergstrom Decommissioned

In 1989, I learned that Austin's Bergstrom Air Base was about to be decommissioned. I set out to get the local merchants on 6th Street to sign a petition to support the creation of a substance abuse treatment/jobs/jobs training program after the facility closed. It seemed like a perfect fit with so many homeless people having been veterans, who had so honorably served our country. I hoped, in part, to convince people that these circumstances must never be repeated.

With thirty signatures of local merchants supporting the House the Homeless substance abuse/treatment/jobs training program, I went before the Austin City Council and successfully argued for a resolution in support of the program.[24] The 6th Street businesses were solidly behind the program as it worked to their advantage. They were desperate to find a way to alleviate the brewing conflict that they perceived between homeless people and their patrons. They believed this growing problem was negatively affecting their ability to conduct business. And yet, there were only limited human services available and these businesses were not providing jobs that paid a living wage. *So, from the perspective of people experiencing homelessness, the merchants were part of the problem.*

Downtown businesses felt that people experiencing homelessness were a serious detriment to conducting business. They contended that their patrons were confronted and made to feel uneasy — probably true. The business owners wanted the flow of commerce to continue unimpeded. After all, they had their mortgages to pay and their two car payments to make and their daughter's college tuition to meet. It rarely occurred to them that the $5.15 per hour that they were paying in wages was contributing to the very problem confronting them. (Actually, most of the businesses in the entertainment district were paying $2.13 per hour, as permitted under federal law, so long as the tips that people receive from patrons brought their wages up to the federal minimum wage of $5.15 per hour). The business perception of conflict and the mere presence of homeless people puts "Joe the Cop," (the local foot patrol officer), in a most awkward position. Shop owners would become frustrated after repeatedly asking the police to "move these people along" (referring to people perceived to be homeless). The homeless have nowhere to go and this would lead to greater and greater tensions between the shop owners, the police, and the people experiencing homelessness.

Therefore, the businesses were more than happy simply to sign a petition for a plan that would send the homeless to Saint Elsewhere, (you know, anywhere but here). In fact, one business owner, a purveyor of hair salon products, pledged $10,000 if the program got up and running.

Dennis Ray Williams

Dennis Ray Williams is a forty-seven- year-old male who stands 6'4" and weighs 230 pounds. He was born in 1959 in Bay City, Texas. Dennis had been living on the streets of Austin, Texas when he decided to "turn his life around." He got a job with Austin Task; whose motto is "Employing the Unemployable." He applied to enter case management at Austin's Resource Center for the Homeless, ARCH, where he would ultimately remain for four months. For the first month of his job he slept on the front porch of the Saint Ignacious Church. He did everything he was asked. He was finally brought into the shelter and into the case management program.

Dennis was a very hard worker. He started as a janitor at $5.50 per hour. He quickly moved into the position of floor tech and then became the supervisor after just four months.

When he became supervisor, he asked for a raise. Unfortunately, he was denied. He was astounded. How could they hire him and promote him twice into a position of supervisor, and not give him a raise? How could they only pay him $5.50 per hour? He asked if they had found any problems.

The sheepish response was, "No."

Dennis again asked for a raise. He was desperate to move out of the shelter; again he was refused the raise. Dennis felt he had no choice; so he quit. He felt they were taking advantage of his situation. Dennis said they were "slave wages." Dennis, seeking only a little dignity and fairness, was homeless once again.

After a very public discussion, Austin City Council passed the following House the Homeless Resolution to create the jobs/job training/substance abuse treatment program at Bergstrom Air Base.

Be It Resolved

WHEREAS, Austin's Drug and Alcohol Detoxification Task Force (the "Task Force") has recognized the community's need to create a detoxification and treatment facility, complemented with a recovery plan based on a continuum of support and rehabilitative services; and,

WHEREAS, The Bergstrom Conversion Task Force conducted a survey to determine the highest and best re-uses of the non-aviation facilities at the Bergstrom Air Force Base, and its survey indicated that the top three (3) re-uses in the highest priority are:

—health care facilities and services;

—vocational job training; and

—the need to address veterans' issues; and,

WHEREAS, approximately one-third (1/3) of the homeless population are United States veterans; and,

WHEREAS, approximately one-third (1/3) of the homeless population suffers from some abusive form of drug and alcohol use; and,

WHEREAS, the potential availability of unused facilities at Bergstrom Air Base exists, which could facilitate the creation of a job training program complemented by a drug and alcohol detoxification and treatment component program at Bergstrom; and,

WHEREAS, Bergstrom Air Force Base comprises approximately three thousand (3,000) acres that, regardless of general re-use designations, will require minimal grounds and buildings maintenance; and,

WHEREAS, there has been a clear and strong indication of support from the general community and local businesses for the Task Force Project which is proposed to be implemented at the Bergstrom site; and,

WHEREAS, the proponents of the detoxification facility are committed to working with neighborhoods most affected by the Task Force Project; and,

WHEREAS, the City of Austin holds a reversionary interest in and to the fee simple title to the original 2,940 acres purchased in 1942 for the present Bergstrom site, which reversion may occur on or about October 1, 1993; and,

WHEREAS, state and federal entities require "site control" prior to providing funds to such projects, for a project such as that proposed by the Task Force to be located at the Bergstrom site;

NOW, THEREFORE,

BE IT RESOLVED BY THE CITY COUNCIL OF THE CITY OF AUSTIN:

That as long as the City of Austin's present plan to convert Bergstrom Air Force Base into a new municipal airport is not conflicted by a proposed project for the creation of a job training program complemented by a drug and alcohol detoxification and treatment program at Bergstrom, the City of Austin will use its best efforts to make available for project purposes certain buildings located at Bergstrom Air Force Base for the implementation of such project, as it is deemed feasible, as follows: the Base Hospital Building, No. 2700 (2nd floor only); the NCO (enlisted club) Building, No. 3510; at least two (2) enlisted men's dormitories; or other appropriate Base facilities, for a period of four (4) years, beginning on or about such date when the reversion of title occurs.

Adopted: February 18, 1993 Attest: James E. Aldridge, City Clerk

18FEB93

PGR/sja/1757

The Caveat

However, the resolution passed with one caveat; that the program not interfere with the anticipated conversion of the military base into a commercial airport. Similar language and specific buildings were identified in the resolution. This did not seem to present a problem as Bergstrom was over 3,000 acres in size. If the buildings chosen later became a needed part of the commercial project, we would select others and we did.

I designed plans to use part of the military base hospital for the substance abuse treatment program. It was a very large structure. In fact, it had 18 dental chairs just for teaching purposes. The idea was to locate a local community health clinic in the hospital as an anchor. The community had begun clamoring for a health clinic and this seemed like the perfect marriage.

The NCO club, a non-commissioned officers club with a hundred foot Olympic-sized pool, would be the base for a jobs training program. Initially, we would take over grounds maintenance operations— cutting hedges, mowing lawns and trimming along walkways. This was very low tech and we were sure we could do it fairly easily. We would be *uniformed* and take pride in our work as a unit, a team. We would take over scraping and painting all exterior walls of all buildings on a regular basis. We would move on to heating and air conditioning maintenance. We were preparing to coordinate with the local community college and the Texas Work Force Commission to establish computer training. We identified a mess hall and two barracks for temporary housing. The idea had great appeal on paper. Having come from a military background, it was obvious to me that at some point down the road, the United States would have to pare back the number of military bases as the Cold War receded. I sent the idea to presidential candidate Bill Clinton who with our document in hand, touted the idea of housing and job training our nation's homeless on soon-to-be decommissioned military bases.

For almost two years, I sat in planning meetings and worked feverishly to identify new buildings in new locations each time the airport planners announced that they needed this parking area or that building. They ate up more of the base facilities with each passing month. Efforts to accommodate our plans grew ever bleaker.

A Request For Proposals (RFP) went out and the City hired a consultant for $10,000 to design the substance abuse treatment program. We were greatly encouraged until he returned with a written report stating that the base "would not be conducive to substance abuse treatment/recovery." The report said that the sound levels were too high for good health care.

We could not believe it! Were they suggesting that the hospital that had gallantly served so many of our soldiers and airmen ever since World War II was not good enough to provide health care for Austin's homeless population!? What about all the babies that had been born in the hospital birthing center? Had they been born into a traumatizing atmosphere for years? Were they now scarred for life? Moreover, what about the homeless? Were they suggesting that the alternative of living under bridges beneath our nation's highways with their unbridled disease of substance abuse was a better life choice? Were they being offered more opportunity wandering the streets of Austin than in our jobs program? Little matter, this lame perspective was apparently all that was needed to deliver the final blow to our program. They had been deliberately moving us around the base and placing us in the direct path of the bulldozer for two years. While I was out of town, in a council work session, Council took the opportunity to kill the project.

I felt betrayed ...we all did. Members of House the Homeless had played by all the rules once again. I had personally spent hundreds and hundreds of hours working, planning, collaborating and compromising my vision to adapt to the conditions that I felt would ultimately improve the lives of my fellow human beings. In the end, it was the merchants who had been right. More than once, I had been told by various business people that the city would never allow our program to exist within a commercial airport. In the beginning, it seemed as if I was just about the only one who had seen the potential for using a closing military base. However, in the end, as it drew closer and closer, everyone saw it. I had lost sight of the adage, "profits before people."

With no other alternatives at hand, we felt we were at the end of the line and had no other option but to sue. Rather than suing the mental health professional who had written the report or the city for succumbing to the forces of commerce, who probably felt a little uncomfortable with our proposal to turn homeless people into baggage handlers in their airport potentially causing them to lose money, we went to the heart of the matter.

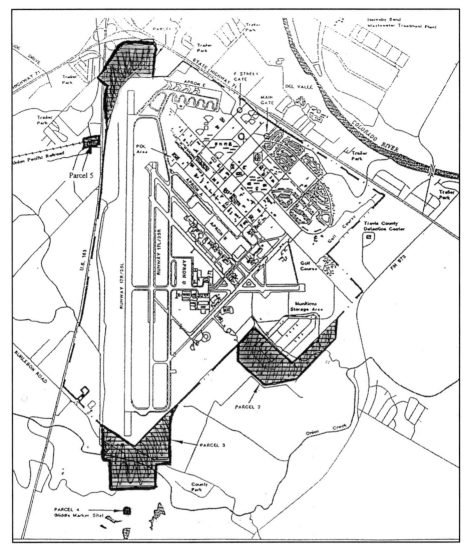

Map of Bergstrom — 3000 acres. Parcel 2-5 acres.

We the Plaintiffs

We sued the City, the United States Government, and President William Clinton. I, as President of House the Homeless, Inc. along with Chris Lyne, a homeless, person, were the named plaintiffs.

We wanted our jobs/job training/substance abuse treatment program. We did not want money. There were tax dollars involved here and the neediest of our nations' citizens were asking for help. They should benefit from years of their own labor as taxpayers. They were down and out and we, who were not, should help them.

My legal argument came from the 1988 McKinney Act which stated that after announcement in the Federal Register, *unutilized and under-utilized government property should be made available to the homeless community and their advocates.* Since 1988, the government has been operating under the assumption that "property" related only to items such as surplus military blankets that had been exposed to DDT (a toxic insecticide that had once been widely used in the United States to kill unwanted insects, but has since been banned after being identified as a carcinogen).

Being a proponent of plain language, and because I was once a licensed Real Estate Agent, I interpreted "property" to include "real property" which meant *land*. I began to look at all of the unutilized and underutilized government land that might be available to people experiencing homelessness. After considerable research, I learned that in 1941, the government decided that it needed a military base outside of San Antonio. It selected the Austin area. Austin held a bond election where it raised $200,000 for the purpose of purchasing land to create the Bergstrom Air Field.

One by one, the City of Austin bought small farms to combine to form Bergstrom Air Field. Since the land was bought with City dollars, almost all of the 3,000 acres that ultimately made up Bergstrom Air Force Base were excluded under the McKinney Act and therefore not available to the homeless. However, Bergstrom Air Field was a small self-contained city with all sorts of other property. It had roads and lights and governmental administrative buildings, mess halls, a chapel, rows and rows of barracks, the Officers' Club, the NCO Club, a day care facility, a multi-story hospital, a golf course, and a huge command center called The Donut. These structures were all bought and paid for with U.S. federal dollars! House the Homeless estimated the value at that time to be 200 million dollars. We felt it was all subject to the McKinney Act because under the law, all of these improvements were built with federal dollars and the buildings were attached to and had become part of the land under real estate law.

In addition to the buildings and the rest of the infrastructure, there were five small parcels of land bought outright with federal dollars. Two of them were specifically excluded under the Act as they lay at opposite ends of the airport runway. A third and fourth piece were very small, just a few hundred square feet in dimension, but the fifth piece, (parcel #2), was five acres in size and not in line with the existing runway.

This fifth piece, (parcel #2) was interesting…very interesting. It was five acres. By then, the FAA, Federal Aviation Administration, was being presented with three possible new runway scenarios for the conversion of the Air Force base to a commercial airport. These scenarios were based on runway length needs, other land structures, noise pollution, other private airports, and the air traffic patterns that would be required. The choice of runways was as closely guarded a secret as had been the Manhattan Project itself. I had no aviation background whatsoever, but by applying what I had gleaned during two years of sitting at the airport planners' tables, I became convinced that the airport designers would choose runway scenario #3. Runway scenario # 3 lay smack dab over the top of parcel #2!

All of this took months and months of research. I had reached out to the National Law Center on Homelessness and Poverty, NLCHP and in an eloquent letter, pled for assistance. They refused to champion our cause stating that it might endanger their hopes of great gains from the Clinton Administration. So my legal team consisted, once again, of myself and Cecilia Wood, Esq. Cecilia, our "No Camping" attorney, worked in the same Legal Aid office as I did. She was a family law attorney and a damn good one I am told. As a result, she operated in the state courts but had never once stepped into federal court to practice. It was "Us against the World,"...again.

Sue the Bastards!

Months before, Cecilia and I had been talking about the plight of the homeless and she seemed most empathetic. I am sure I was charging on about the current situation with Bergstrom and the level of intelligence needed to believe that people would be better off living under bridges and dumpster diving than receiving help in an existing military hospital. I am sure I said something like, "You're an attorney; why don't you sue them?" In retrospect, I could have said, "You have feet why don't you walk around the earth?" In any event, it turns out that in addition to House the Homeless, she had already championed an underdog in her own field. With absolutely nothing to lose, we joined forces for a second time and set out in search of windmills.

We were not totally naive; we met with Fred Fuchs, a first rate attorney at Legal Aid. He had been to federal court several times. When we told him what we were thinking, he just stared as us. He just stared for what seemed like a very, very long time. He then shook his head ever so slightly, as if to shake himself from a daydream. He looked down at notes on his desk, and a small smile slowly filled his face resting in his eyes and in his gentle west Texas accent simply said, "Well, you know, they are going to eat you alive, don't you?"

Emboldened by Fred's words of encouragement, I reached out again to the National Law Center on Homelessness and Poverty in Washington, D.C. They reminded us that Bill Clinton was the President. They also pointed out that while things had thus far not gone so well for the homeless under his administration, it was a critical time and they did not want to upset things. They would not be coming to the dance.

We never heard from Mr. Clinton on our health care/jobs program except when his lawyers answered our lawsuit. He later came out with Welfare Reform, which pushed hundreds of thousands of people off our nation's welfare rolls into minimum wage jobs. Of course, these minimum wage jobs could not sustain the workers. They simply disappeared into the ranks of the homeless, which grew simultaneously.

We first went into federal court in Austin, Texas. We went before District Judge James Nowlin. My friend Chris Lyne, you will recall, was the other named plaintiff in the case. Chris is a teddy bear, but to look at him and his rather burly 5' 9" frame, defiant stance and scraggly mustache one would not know it. Half of his upper lip was collapsed from a stroke and his speech gets masked with a slur from the same incident. I helped him get disability benefits for an injury he suffered when he fell after dangling upside down from a stairwell as a young boy. He carries a 6-inch knife on his hip and has a bit of a quick temper so, when the bailiff locked him out and refused to allow him to enter the federal courtroom for "inappropriate attire," I wasn't exactly sure where things would go. With protests from myself to Cecilia and then from Cecilia to the judge, we finally prevailed (for the first and last time) and a deal was struck. The bailiff miraculously produced a sports jacket that dwarfed Chris. He ditched his knife, and we all assembled to have the judge berate us for having dared approach him in the first place...the Great and Powerful Oz. After we were finally all assembled in his court, we were thrown out and glad of it.

It was clear that the City was probably not going to be involved in the lawsuit. While the vast majority of the land was purchased with City dollars, the City had no responsibility under the McKinney Act. Accordingly, the judge dismissed the case against the City. However, it was our contention that all the buildings and three of the small parcels of land, having been bought with federal dollars, were subject to the Act. Obviously, Judge Nowlin did not see it that way. He ruled against us.

Without hesitation, we continued our research. We didn't pause long enough to feel sorry for ourselves. We were right and we knew it. We appealed our case to the 5th Circuit Court of Appeals in New Orleans.

Cecilia kept talking about how much fun it would be to *drive* to New Orleans. I assured her that, while this indeed was exciting, I found very little of this to fit in the "fun" category. She finally divulged that she had a fear of flying and would have to drive. To commemorate the occasion, Cecilia penned the following ditty:

> "Opening Statement"
> In 1942, we bought a little base.
> And that is the reason we had to file this case.
> They would not give us buildings, and they would not give us land.
> They would not even let us have their golf course sand.
> We thought that we would get justice, but it was a big lie.
> We went before Nowlin, and it made us want to cry.
> We are headed to the Fifth, and we hope it is plenty far.
> Cause I won't fly to Washington, and he won't take the bar.
> -Sung to the melody of the "Battle of New Orleans"

We compromised and she knocked herself out with a considerable amount of Nyquil and some alcohol for good measure for the fight. The courtroom was huge. At one end, there was a semi-circle of benches. It was from these benches that the three judges sat *on high!* The benches were large enough to accommodate ten judges, which is how many would reside if a case were heard *En Banc.* I assumed this meant in full. The room was designed to make the judges seem very impressive and to make the participants feel diminutive. It worked.

Our argument came down to this: while the majority of Bergstrom land had been purchased with City bond dollars, all of the buildings and five parcels of land had been purchased with federal dollars. Under the 1988 McKinney Act, the homeless and their agents were entitled to federal property that was found to be either *unutilized or under-utilized.*

First, the federal government, through the General Services Administration, (GSA), offers the surplus property to all other governmental departments and agencies. If no other department or agency responds to the posting, the property goes to the homeless community and their agents for possible use. This occurs by posting the available property in the Federal Register. At least three of the federal properties in question, including parcel #2 had not been (as far as I could tell) posted in the Federal Register.

Our strategy was to show that the property had not been posted in the Federal Register according to law. After this, we planned to publicize the government's omission. Then, we as representatives of the "homeless community," would simply step forward, claim our parcel (directly under the soon to be constructed commercial runway) and trade it to the City of Austin for a more suitable piece of property upon which to construct our health care/jobs program. In a word, it was simple.

An Open Letter from House The Homeless, Inc. to the Citizens of Austin
January 14, 1996

Reluctantly, House the Homeless has sued the United States Air Force, the Department of Defense, and the City of Austin. In 1987, the United States Congress declared that homelessness had become a national emergency, and, in response, passed the McKinney act that made unutilized and underutilized federal properties available to the homeless population after a process.

The City of Austin asserts that it has a resultive trust for having provided $466,000.00 in 1942 so that the Army Air Corps could buy about three quarters of the land that compromises Bergstrom. This may or may not be true, but there never was a contract. There never was a signed agreement. There was, however, a series of letters and telegram discussions but the terms kept changing with each document. Fully five years after tendering the money, after failing to come to mutual agreement, the then City Council passed a one-sided "clean-up" resolution that again changed the previous terms. Nonetheless, a U.S. District Judge has recently ruled that these conflicting pieces of correspondence give the city a property interest in Bergstrom.

The court has dismissed the case against the City of Austin and denied the injunctive relief that we sought. This would have stopped the demolition and transference of Bergstrom houses because they related to our underlying case. Fortunately, the underlying case remains intact and viable. Unfortunately the City, although repeatedly cautioned by HTH, continues to run the danger of building an airport on land that Congress has set aside for the Homeless Community under the McKinney Act. We have now appealed the dismissal.

It is important to note that regardless of the City's assertion that it holds a property interest in some of the land at Bergstrom, it is undisputed that all the buildings and at least one quarter of the land was bought with federal dollars years later and in separate actions.

This land is now unutilized or underutilized and fully meets the criteria whereby it must be made available to the homeless community after a process.

House the Homeless (HTH) has repeatedly proposed programs to utilize the housing stock at Bergstrom. First, it worked for fully two years prior to the base closure to create a Drug and Alcohol Detoxification, Treatment, Job Training, Reintegration program. In fact, with the help of Council Member Jackie Goodman and Brigid Shea, the hospital, NCO club, and two barracks were designated for just that purpose. However, the city in its wisdom, hired a consultant that said due to noise consideration that the airport would not be the most conducive place to conduct rehabilitation and job training for the homeless community. Apparently, it was good enough for thousands of veterans and all the mothers that gave birth at the base hospital, but it isn't good enough for the homeless population?! Rather than deal with base construction, the homeless are somehow perceived to be better off living on the street, in our parks, eating out of garbage cans and now subject to arrest for sleeping in public!

When House the Homeless learned that the City, through the Department of Aviation, had issued contracts to demolish all the housing and infrastructure (valued by HTH at 200 million dollars); HTH lead a citywide effort to stop the demolition. The City has since devised a plan to save only about 33 houses for low and moderate income folks. Designed for highly successful renters, no homeless people will benefit from this program. The rest of the 719 units will be sold at a profit to for-profit developers. However, not one homeless person will benefit from these buildings as the U.S. Congress has intended.

Also, HTH had proposed "interim use" of the housing stock for an 18 month interim period between 1994 and 1997 when the housing had to be moved. This was a three year window. (In 2010, we have approximately only 600 transitional housing units in our entire city. We have a homeless population of approximately 4,400 people). The huge inventory of housing at Bergstrom would have gone a long way to resolve our homeless problem. However, the City staff and the Department of Aviation were terrified that, at the end of the interim use period, people might resist being returned to our streets. If the program was properly executed these people would have been reintegrated into our local society with good jobs and good homes.

Finally, there is no dispute that fully one quarter of Bergstrom and all the buildings were bought with federal dollars after the original purchase and are not subject to any reversionary concept or third party interest. This land and all of the buildings (not just the housing stock) are subject to review under the McKinney Act.

Richard R. Troxell
President

To further underscore our claim, I laminated a 24" by 30" map of Bergstrom, the runway area and the five parcels of land. In red magic marker, I outlined each of the five parcels purchased with federal dollars.

Present in the court in addition to Cecilia, myself, and the three judges were several attorneys representing the federal government. As one can imagine, the proceeding was foreign to both Cecilia and me. Only one of the judges spoke and he seemed more concerned about what efforts at resolution had been attempted than on focusing on the merits of the case. I heard Cecilia present our argument. I was poised with my graphic. I was prepared to bolster her argument the instant she indicated it was show time.

Suddenly, the judge that had been directing things, popped up like a thermometer in a turkey and said, "Ya'll work something out," as he scurried from the bench to a side door.

The other two judges-clearly taken aback-shot looks at one another. In a staggered response, they quickly, but shakily, exited close on his robe like ducklings to a mother's ducktails. I was dumbfounded. I was flabbergasted. I heard myself, in a half dream voice ask Cecilia, "What just happened?" She just gave me a look of resigned helplessness and said, "He wants us to work something out."

What did this mean? How could we have…did we lose? It was not any more clear to me then, than it is now. However, what was clear was the judge *"wasn't going to look at the twenty-seven eight by ten color glossy photos with the circles and arrows and a paragraph on the back of each one, explaining what each one was, and how each one was to be used in evidence against us. It was a typical case of American blind justice and there wasn't anything we could do about it."* (From Arlo Guthrie's *Alice's Restaurant*). The judge was not going to serve us justice. He would not be swayed by facts. He was not going to look at our laminated map, and no justice for the homeless would be dispensed that day.

Needless to say, neither the Feds nor the City found any reason to work anything out. We then filed a lawsuit with the United States Supreme Court. On review, our case made it to the 6th of the 7 review levels and was turned down. Cases that are more important were to be heard. One of those more important cases was the Jennifer Flowers vs. Bill Clinton case. The homeless after all could simply work something out.

Saving Bergstrom Housing

Meanwhile, by September 1996 House the Homeless was deeply embroiled in an effort to save 87 duplexes from demolition at the Austin-Bergstrom Air Base. While we had lost the battle to create the Health Care and Job Training operation on the base, there still existed infrastructure worth $200 million, as estimated by House the Homeless. The last of that to be scheduled for demolition were 87 duplexes. House the Homeless challenged the city to preserve this stock of housing of which the military had taken such good care. We learned that every five years, the houses got complete makeovers including new roofs.

In response, the City offered a housing lottery. In this lottery, people would pay $10.00, show proof of having a $1,500 security deposit, make a promise to move the building off the foundation by a certain date and clean the site. I did some research and found that it would cost $13,500 to move each house. A new foundation was estimated at another $13,600. Rehabilitation costs including permits and repair work such as new flooring, new siding, plumbing and electrical work were estimated by the City to cost another $3,500. Why, for just $32,100. *and* the purchase price of a piece of land, any one of Austin's 5,000 homeless could acquire a new home!

Obviously, no homeless, minimum wage workers were ever housed with this project. In fact, the Save the Duplex Project took on a different dynamic when Global Southwest Development, Inc. discovered a proverbial gold mine of slabs and construction sites in far east Austin. There, an entire suburb, the Meadows of Trinity Crossing, an undeveloped construction site which had sat fallow since the last economic bust, presented a huge opportunity. To certain developers, it appeared that this was a perfect place to move the Bergstrom duplexes.

Right from the beginning, House the Homeless had serious questions and concerns about this initiative. Who were those developers? What was their success? Had they ever moved houses? Had they ever been part of a house-moving venture?

Apparently, they had not.

The *Austin Chronicle* in a February 16, 1996 article, reported, "Neither Wood, [no relationship to our attorney Cecilia Wood] nor Johnson, the owners of Global Southwest Development, Inc., the company developing the Meadows project, had experience in the development business."

Furthermore, the *Chronicle* cited a *Fort Worth Star-Telegram* report that Wood had been "fined $123,000 by the state of New Jersey for selling health insurance policies that over stated their benefits to policy holders." Mr. Wood had been forced to surrender his insurance license to the state of New Jersey. According to the *Austin Chronicle*, a similar action had been taken against Mr. Wood by the State of Washington. The Texas Attorney General had also fined Mr. Wood's partner, Mr. Johnson, $20,000 for his part in "removing Teledated Telephone Services and substituting that of another company from which he received a commission for calls routed to it."

Unfortunately, as things progressed, our fears were realized. At first, the project was heralded as a great venture by the city and private business. Nevertheless, House the Homeless remained skeptical of the developer. We began to get detailed anonymous phone calls about some of the principals involved. This underscored our skepticism. We also learned that very sophisticated, computer balanced, house moving equipment was being used in a similar situation in Florida. We learned that the highly sophisticated equipment was necessary because old buildings, when moved, tend to respond as if they have been subjected to shaken baby syndrome. The buildings the city was "giving away" by lottery were constructed in the 1950s. The duplexes were to be cut in half and then moved. This would require the utmost care.

The Bergstrom houses were cut in half and moved. There was a big celebration. All the city officials, city council, the city manager and state officials smiled for the camera. No specialized computer moving equipment had been used. Within weeks the first problems appeared. Within six months, cracks ran up the sides of each building. Within a year, repair costs had so swamped the new homeowners that many were headed toward bankruptcy and mortgage foreclosure. Compounding homeowner problems, the general contractor Paradigm Structures, Inc. filed a $2.1 million mechanics and material lien against Global Southwest Development, Inc., the owner of the property. Global then sued Paradigm for breach of contract seeking $2.6 million for "substandard workmanship and lost profits." Then Paradigm sued Global to foreclose its lien on the 239-acre property.[25] This was a fiasco from start to finish, but, fortunately, it only affected poor people and tax payers. After all, what did they expect for $10.00?

In Search Of a Homeless Campus

Talk flew of another Homeless Task Force working on a plan to create a Homeless Campus. I became the chair of the Land Search Committee. However, while Gus Garcia, Jim Weaver, the executive director of the proposed new non-profit and I were out of town, Mayor Kirk Watson and former Mayor, Frank Cooksey held a press conference to announce the project had been shut down. They declared, "Before we get ahead of ourselves, more public education is necessary about the plight of the homeless."[26] (Have I mentioned that Kirk Watson was an active member of the Downtown Austin Alliance, DAA, throughout his tenure as Mayor?) In case you missed it, that's the Downtown Austin (*Business*) Alliance.

The reason for the Mayor's stealth move had been pragmatic. After months of in-depth searching, no downtown property had met the three-acre criteria set by the Task Force. The goal was to mirror, to some degree, a successful Orlando, Florida Homeless Pavilion. When it became clear to me as Committee Chair that there was no perfect piece of property available in the immediate downtown Austin area, I discussed it with my committee and announced that our search must now lead us slightly outside of the immediate downtown area.

Alan Kaplan, one of the committee members representing the interests of the downtown business community, and a member of DAA, without authorization of the committee, raced to contact the media in an effort to slam the door on the possibility of a permanent homeless facility being built in the immediate downtown area.[27] All the media ran with the story. The airwaves were set on fire with furious debate. The media declared... *Homeless compound to be located in Austin Neighborhoods!* It was like yelling fire in a crowded theatre. The leaders of every neighborhood of Austin could not get to the new mayor, Kirk Watson, fast enough to *express their support for the project* and underscore the need for the facility but *also* to express that "unfortunately" it would be inappropriate to have such a facility in their particular neighborhood. (You can fill in the reasons. They were all used.) The expression that covers this phenomenon is "Not in my backyard," NIMBYism. Without even discussing the situation with me, as I was in Washington D.C. advocating for Austin's homeless needs, the Mayor shut down our venture and our search for a new homeless resource center site. Efforts to build the new facility came to a screeching halt. A private ad agency was brought into the picture to put a proper/good spin on homelessness. Somehow, however, they could not figure out how to put a positive spin on families that had been ripped apart by economic forces beyond their control. Go figure.

A Public Forum

February marked the one-year anniversary of the No Camping Ordinance. Cost: 2000 Police Hours and a worsened human condition.

What was the cost to tax payers?

Council Member Gus Garcia wanted to know so he passed a resolution seeking a cost analysis from the City Manager, the Presiding Judge and the Clerk of the Municipal Court.

A partial release of the report indicated that over $120,000 had been spent to push paper in the processing of over 2000 No Camping tickets. The court costs, including down judicial time, was still unknown but it was clear that 2000 police hours had been spent issuing tickets to people for sleeping in public when there was no other alternative.[28] The Salvation Army, operating at excess capacity, could only offer seven days of shelter with a 90 day "out period" before allowing individuals to return for another seven days.

In the mean time, The Homeless Task Force struggled to find money to create a new day/night Homeless Resource Center. Central Texas Directions, an independent market research firm, conducted a poll to assess business related concerns and found that 78% of Austinites were willing to spend private/public dollars to create "a campus for the homeless" offering job training, shelter, detoxification and health care. This might have been a good use of the $120,000 plus dollars, but were Austinites willing to spend thousands of dollars and thousands of police hours to arrest poor citizens who are just too poor to have a bed while drive-by shootings and drug sales went unchecked.

Other cities had gone down this path before us. San Francisco, Atlanta, and Orlando had all abandoned this approach of arresting the poor as bad social policy and a waste of money and resources.

House the Homeless circulated a pamphlet to this effect and calling for repeal:

> *Perhaps we should consider repealing the "No Camping Ordinance" and see if we can't find another use for our limited resources and especially your police officers. Our Police Department is about 100 officers below its authorization level. The Austin American Statesman cites a recent police report stating, "As the Police Department audit indicates, increased spending has not solved our city's crime problems." Gee, with over 2000 plus hours*

being spent arresting criminal sleepers, one has to ask why that hasn't solved our crime problem and resolved this social concern.

Respectfully submitted,

Richard R. Troxell

President- House the Homeless, Inc.

For identification purposes only:

-Director- Legal Aid for the Homeless

-Chairman Austin Area Homeless Coalition

3-10-97

The House the Homeless leaflet fairly well summed up the one-year No Camping Ordinance anniversary.

HTH kept up its relentless pressure to repeal the no camping ordinance. "No Justice, No Peace" was the mantra of the day. Twenty of our members interrupted City Council Member Ronnie Reynolds' retirement speech to point out that his was one of the hands that had held the sword of Damocles above the heads of the homeless. He had pressed for the passage of the No Camping Ordinance. Like children speaking out of turn in class, we cried out for sleep, uninterrupted sleep. Stop the Abuse! It was a pitiful plea, but then ours was a pitiful situation.

A Turn in the Road

Council Member Gus Garcia, who had voted for the ordinance, led the way. He was quoted by the Austin American Statesman as saying, "It hasn't worked. There was no movement. None. Zero."

We were ecstatic. The paper reported, "The question is not if the council will repeal the camping ban, but how soon."[29]

On June 26th 1997, Gus Garcia was set to introduce a council resolution to repeal the "No Camping" ordinance!

At the council meeting, fifty of us made our case for the repeal. Our arguments were many. We cited the waste of city tax dollars, wasted police hours, the loss of human potential and the compounding of human suffering. Our signs read:

Repeal the No Camping Ordinance
Stop Bad Laws
Jail $67.50 vs. Job Training $45.00

We argued that sleeping was a physiological necessity of life. I declared that, as long as people had no other alternative, we could not possibly prevent them from sleeping in public. I described the law as being very punitive in nature and being selectively enforced. I gave an endless stream of examples. We argued, "One cannot criminalize homelessness." We stressed that it was a condition of *economic status*.

The Home Stretch

On June 28, 1997, HTH released the following:

House The Homeless, Inc.
P.O. Box 2312
Austin, Texas 78768-2312
Public Forum
June 28, 1997

We must stop abusing our homeless citizens with the No Camping Homeless Ordinance now. However, we must continue to create the means to help them achieve self-reliance. House the Homeless has been pressing for a Homeless Day/Night Resource Center since 1989. In response, in 1993, the City Council set aside various buildings at the Bergstrom for a homeless health care/job training program. The City and County hired a consultant who was paid tens of thousands of dollars to say that among the buildings, the base hospital, that had taken care of thousands of veterans "wasn't good enough" for the homeless population. Out of frustration, the Austin business community then pressed for the No Camping Ordinance.

The Austin City Council responded by passing a law that turned the homeless into "criminal sleepers." People are arrested, made to waste "time" in jail and returned to the streets only to be rearrested still with no jobs and no housing. The benefit of this jail mill? In the first year alone, close to $200,000 has been spent on processing "criminal sleepers." Additionally, the pressure and the costs to the court system have also been enormous as these victims continue to seek jury trials. Furthermore, the ban has now cost Austin well over 2000 misspent police hours.

Some people argue that if we build a comprehensive campus of services, Austin will become a magnet for the homeless everywhere. This has not happened in the other cities that have taken this approach such as Orlando, Florida. And pragmatic approaches such as establishing a waiting list starting with our own local citizens will ensure this doesn't occur. Others argue that the "No Camping" ordinance is justified because Austin's homeless population is on the streets because they want to be there. Surveys, studies and interviews have shown this to be false. It's been documented that thousands of homeless persons are denied help each year due to lack of services. Until we offer all the services necessary to help these people achieve self-reliance without any gaps in the Continuum of Care, we will not know for sure who among them will and who will not accept our offer of help. We therefore should not go on punishing all of them with the "No Camping" Ordinance.

House the Homeless Inc. has shown that the average visibly homeless person has lived in Austin for over 7.5 years, pays state sales taxes, and has contributed measurably to the Austin economy. They are mostly workers who came here during our boom, suffered during our bust, and continue to provide their labor at cutthroat wages.

The "No Camping" ordinance is punitive in nature and is being selectively enforced. Students are sleeping outside while waiting to get concert tickets without worry of being arrested. Visitors at Barton Springs and travelers in our airport and bus stations also sleep without fear of being arrested. This is obviously a crime of economic status.

Finally, the Resource Center, requiring up to 3.5 acres and now receiving citywide support, must and will be built. Other cities have all built theirs in the fringe of their downtown areas where people easily congregate. In Austin, it must be built in the most appropriate part of the City without undue pressure on site selection but with full community involvement. It needs to be built so opportunities not previously available can occur. On the other hand, the "No Camping" Ordinance has in the words of the police officer in charge of seeing its enforcement, "only driven people deeper into the woods," and should be repealed. It has been identified as unconstitutional and just a bad law. It needs to be repealed now regardless of the additional, yet separate, need to build the Resource Center.

We say "Repeal the 'No Camping' Homeless Ordinance now and continue to build the Resource Center offering shelter, job training, and health care for all our citizens."

> Richard R. Troxell
> President
> House the Homeless Inc.

Kirk Watson had replaced Bruce Todd as mayor, and he was the "golden boy." He was a lawyer who looked and talked good. He "talked Texas" with just a touch of an easy drawl served up with an engaging boyish smile. He had become a millionaire defending the rights of poor injured victims to hear him tell it. He was married with children, and he had beaten cancer! People loved him. He had fresh ideas, was a man of action, and he was going to save us all. He was the candidate of the downtown business association. That meant he came with money and political backing.

On the first day of the new City Council, the day that the No Camping Ordinance was to be repealed, Kirk Watson asked Gus Garcia for a four-month extension on the repeal question. His request was granted. What could he say; it was the "honeymoon."

In a behind the scenes meeting minutes before the opening council session the Mayor, Cecilia Wood, and I met. Cecilia and I had been summoned there in a surprise move. The Mayor laid it out. He was shutting this down. He would not be allowing a vote on the repeal of the No Camping Ordinance on that day. He wanted time. He said he needed time to bring the business community along. After all, they had all the money. If he had time, he could get them to come around, support it...even fund it. There was little to be done. There were 100 homeless people sitting in the next room waiting for the show to start. Their show. They deserved this relief. But here was the brand new Mayor asking us to give him time because it would be good for the City. It would be good for all the people. He just needed a little time, and "everyone would be happy."

The man had such charisma; you wanted to believe him. I was furious. I had no choice. I was in a box. What power did we have? We had no votes. The Council had the votes, and he had control of the Council. I knew that, privately, Gus Garcia was wavering again, vacillating between the demands of the DAA and the ineffectiveness and cruelty of the ordinance. He was now saying that we needed to build our new Homeless Resource Center *before* the repeal of the ordinance. We no longer had assurance of the votes for repeal.

In exchange for time, I insisted that the Mayor give us a drop dead date of October 16th, 1997, for an up or down vote on the No Camping Ordinance. Reluctantly, very reluctantly, he agreed.

We proceeded to have two days of public hearings. People spoke passionately on both sides. People from the neighborhoods wore green badges and spoke in defense of their beloved parks. The homeless spoke about needing living wage jobs and the need for opportunity; they wore their rags.

One of our guys, Jerry Marlow, explained how he had received seven tickets and paid none. They had all gone to warrant and he had sat in jail each time. He called it a waste. The head of the Downtown Austin Alliance, DAA, said that the ordinance had helped authorities keep the parks and greenbelts free of "transients."

While it was clear from the derogatory epithets that civilities were still in short supply, the media at least started to write about the specific lack of *affordable housing*. I pointed to studies that showed that a person must earn twice the minimum wage to afford a basic one-bedroom apartment in Austin. They then went on to print specific numbers. This was our first small victory.

Everyone had an opinion and a perspective. Ronnie Earle, the Travis County District Attorney, said, "The ordinance is not targeted at the homeless population — it penalizes behavior."[30] He followed those comments with a lengthier rehash of the position of those calling for the No Camping Ordinance, as just "one more tool needed by the police to keep order." These became often-repeated themes.

We're Not Bad People That Need To Be Good;
We're Sick People That Need To Be Well
House The Homeless

Don McLeese, a noted and respected local editorialist, wrote, "The principal for opposition to the homeless ban is simple: It criminalizes economic class rather than public offense."[31]

This was my response to Mr. Earle.

House The Homeless, Inc.
P.O. BO 2312
Austin, Texas 78768-2312
   August 19, 1997

District Attorney Ronnie Earl is right. We do all share a commitment to the quality of life in our community. However, it is important that this quality of life be extended to all of our citizens not just those who are safe in their homes. Even the visibly homeless citizens of Austin, who have lived here an average of 7 years, deserve to feel safe. They too are tax paying citizens as this is a sales tax state. Do they not deserve to be safe from repeated, unjust, selective arrest for the crime of sleeping?

Mr. Earl claims that, "the ordinance does not punish persons for being homeless." How does he explain that of the 2,000+ persons arrested, all were homeless? When City Council Members passed the ordinance they referred to it repeatedly as the Homeless Ban, and one Assistant City Manager was caught on tape espousing, "make no mistake, our goal is to run these people out of town!"

Mr. Earl states that the ordinance merely punishes certain conduct (*i.e.* living in public places). It's been repeatedly asserted that "we're not punishing the person, we're only punishing the behavior." With 42% of the visibly homeless working every week, then why are they still homeless? They are still homeless because it takes twice the minimum wage to get a one bedroom apartment in Austin. A person could work a full time job at McDonalds and a full time job at Wendy's and still not make enough to rent a one bedroom apartment. They are still homeless because we, the employers, don't pay a fair wage for the labor they provide. How can we then make criminals out of them for sleeping in public when their "behavior" (sleeping in public) is a direct consequence of our unwillingness to pay a fair wage?

Some people say that there are plenty of places offering help and that they could easily get off the streets, but I think that even Ronnie Early using New Math would be hard pressed to show how 5,000 people can sleep in only 400 beds.

Mr. Earl asserts that in a "safer climate" created by this ordinance, people will feel more compassionate toward the needs of the homeless. As we turn otherwise law abiding citizens into criminals for sleeping, how likely is it that people are going to feel compassionate and want to help them? After one and a half years of arresting "criminal sleepers" and returning them to the street, still with no decent paying jobs and no housing, "the duty to care" has not been embraced in any real sense.

Thousands of people both visible and invisible still remain homeless while this bad and clearly unconstitutional law remains in place. With over 3,000 police hours spent arresting criminal sleepers since its inception, does Mr. Earl really believe that people feel that this is the best use of our limited police resources? Or do people really feel safer as a result? In a special report to City Council, it was admitted that people arrested under this ordinance are only driven deeper into the woods. Between 1985 and 1995, 12 to 14 million people have experienced homelessness. What happens when the woods of America fill up? What laws will we pass then?

For those of you who stayed long enough to see the end of the second day of the City Council Hearings on the "No Camping Homeless Ban," then you witnessed a small miracle in Austin. In the last hour of the two-day hearings, people began to listen. People with fixed positions unequivocally supporting the ban went to the dais and wavered. They still felt affronted and confronted by homeless people trashing out their parks and they still wanted that to stop. But for the first time, they acknowledged that these homeless people were just that . . . people . . . people who had fallen on hard times.

People who if they could afford a home would not be defecating or changing their clothes in the woods. They would not be trashing the parks but rather using trash pick up. And the sleep that they experienced would not be violently disrupted by a police officer lording six feet over them, waving a drawn billy club and arresting them for criminal sleeping.

I'm sorry that Mr. Earl who seems so interested in this subject was unable to share in that Council experience where no one felt threatened and all positions were heard. It was a moment of realization that this is an Austin problem about the quality of life for all its citizens.

Richard R. Troxell

President – House the Homeless Inc.

At the end of the day, the ordinance was not repealed. No vote was ever taken. In fact, it remains in force even today. In response to Mayor Kirk Watson and his handling of the situation, I was inspired to write the following, which I read to the citizens of Austin during "Citizens Communication."

Richard R. Troxell

Smart Growth

Camelot
House The Homeless, Inc.
P.O. Box 2312
Austin, Texas 78768-2312
476-4383
La Croissance Intelligent
(Smart Growth)

And it came to pass that a new King was to rule the small kingdom. It was said that he was "The Great Unifier." And the people rejoiced. And it was said that his energy was only surpassed by his grand vision for the kingdom.

And by and by it came to pass that multitudes of travelers migrated to the great city in search of untold fortunes. Magnificent monuments of commerce were constructed and the kingdom prospered. The people found happiness and contentment. The land became known as Camelot. And the King reveled in each new challenge with each bringing an endless number of decisions and each outcome advancing the welfare of the kingdom. But it came to be known, that not all of the King's subjects were faring as well, nor were they all sharing equally in abject happiness. For even though the King was a kind and generous King, each decision designed to advance the welfare of Camelot brought with it more and more hard choices. Still, the King's vision was strong and his course was clear. So even though small sacrifices had to be made at the expense of some of the poorer subjects, these were but small sacrifices and besides. . . were they not for the good of the many? And so it went for many years. And peace and prosperity reined in the land and among the King's courtiers. Until one day, at a great ribbon cutting ceremony, a small child stepped in front of the King and faced him squarely saying only, "Please Sire, my village is in trouble and my people need your help." The King stopped immediately and asked who had brought this trouble? The boy responded by saying, "It is they Sire, The Weight of the Many 'Good' Deeds." The King stood quite still pondering the boy's words for a very long time. Finally, he spoke and said, "Of course we want to help you, but there are two things. First, the Weight of the Many Good Deeds are too important to just be interfered with even for the benefit of your whole village. For we must remember, the vision is much greater than thee or me.

164

And secondly, I will surely come for you when I have finished cutting this ribbon and all of Camelot is built."

The boy's heart was laden with sadness and yet he bowed respectfully and said, "I will take your word Sire, but I fear it will be too late upon its coming." Feeling abandoned and betrayed, the boy returned to his village known as "The Land Beyond Hope."

Much time passed and Camelot flourished and the people rejoiced. And the King had always meant to keep his promise, but there was always something else to be done. Until one day, a sound began. It was a low-pitched sound that came from far off. But soon, it began to grow. And it grew and it grew and the sound became a moan and the moan turned into a groan and the groan slid into a wail and the people became quite alarmed. And they sought discourse with the King's courtiers and begged for the King's council and for his action. Finally, the King realized the wail was coming from the village that rests in the outer most woods of the kingdom. . . from where the small boy had lived, in the Land Beyond Hope.

The King called for his Calvary and signaled for his greatest steed to be saddled and with great pomp and pageantry he set out with great deliberation and his best army.

They rode for three days and three nights without stop. On the morning of the fourth day, they crested a hill and looked upon a vast wasteland of death and destruction. Men, women and children . . . all were dead. The King, still mounted atop his steed, was suddenly overwhelmed with despair and raised both fists to the heavens shaking them violently as he cursed the "Forces" in unbridled anguish.

With tears rolling across his face, The King was caused to look down. And there standing before him, was the same small boy who had stood before him so many years before. But the boy's eyes were now sunken deep within his head and he had grown no bigger than when they had first met so many years before. He had only grown into a frail and broken young man. The King, beseeching the boy, implored him, "What hath wrought this destruction? Tell me, Tell me!

And then the boy, ever so slowly, raised his head. Finally, his focus rested with that of the King and their eyes met. Quietly he spoke. . . "With respect Sire, it is the Aftermath." "The Aftermath?!" queried the King incredulously, "The Aftermath?" his voice rising. "Yes Sire, the aftermath of when we benefit the many and neglect the needs of the few."

Richard R. Troxell

President

House the Homeless, Inc.
December 3, 1998

* Note. At the Council meeting where this was read, the mayor rushed through a multi-million dollar development project that would make the people living in Austin's homeless shelter...well... homeless.

The mayor was quoted as saying, "Each member of this council understands that this is not a perfect situation." At the same time, city council member Beverly Griffith said that, "Giving the public only one week to comprehend the deal's many moving parts was just not enough. The Computer Science Corporation, CSC proposal, has come on to the council agenda with virtually no community input." Without any public discussion the city cooked a deal giving Computer Sciences Corporation a 99 year lease on three city properties that included the one serving Austin's homeless citizens. The deal was to give the city a lake front city hall location and bring in 3,500 new downtown employees. The city did get the city hall, but it was more like three hundred employees and the deal that "had be to made that week" which also brought the construction of two CSC buildings twelve years ago, finds the one which was the home of the homeless, still with a dirt floor on the ground level and the current homeless shelter which was to be on 3.5 acres, ending up on a quarter of a city block...smart growth.[32]

Proposed City of Austin Procedures Regarding the "No Camping" Ordinance

There are two important additions to this open-ended chapter in the lives of the homeless: 1) All references to "sleeping" were struck from the ordinance. 2) House the Homeless created a 9-point procedure for enforcement of the No Camping Ordinance, the 9-point procedure reads as follows:

1. Establishes Standardized Police Protocol for dealing with homeless citizens.

2. Requires Police sensitivity training on homeless issues (Academy and In-Service).

3. Requires any police officer, upon observing, but prior to approaching a person suspected of violating the No Camping Ordinance, to call the Salvation Army or other emergency shelter facility and determine that there is a specific bed available for that particular individual. Inability to identify a specific available bed will result in no interaction involving COA Police Officers and Austin's citizenry with regard to the No Camping Ordinance.

4. Establishes that a person can only be warned to stop life sustaining activities such as found in the No Camping Ordinance if there are emergency shelter beds available.

5. Requires the COA Police Department to maintain a separate log (time and place) of all inquires made to establish bed availability.

6. Requires COA Police Officers to escort or direct the individual to the facility upon locating an available bed.

7. Requires that in the event that existing warrants or other circumstances result in an arrest of an individual, all personal belongings will be protected, preserved, and returned to the individual upon release. A single point of contact and a COA police officer will be made responsible for all protected property items. The arrested individual will be given a comprehensive inventoried list of belongings taken and held and will be provided in writing the contact name, phone number, and procedure for the return of said belongings. Claim forms for damaged or missing items will also be provided at the time the inventory list is provided.

8. Requires that documents appear in both English and Spanish.

9. Establishes a 3-person advisory/oversight committee consisting of a City official, an ACLU attorney, and a representative from the Austin Area

167

Homeless Coalition to ensure appropriate implementation of these agreed upon procedures.

Revised 9/21/99

12/01/05

When I wrote these simple procedures, we felt it was possible that the police department would easily adopt it. It seemed so incredibly fair. The procedures would require that a police officer who saw someone camping in public would check on availability of temporary housing before issuing a ticket. If resources were available, the person would be directed to them. If the individual was later seen camping during the same 24 hour period and had not taken advantage of the alternative opportunity, they would be ticketed. If no available bed existed, they were not to be bothered. The police would then record the encounter. This would give the City Council, et al, the information and statistics to properly assess the general situation/ need throughout the city. The procedures were never implemented. Some say it involved too much common sense.

Guys celebrating No Camping victory. Photo from *Austin American Statesman*.

The Sweet Taste of Victory!

On Tuesday May 16, 2000, Magistrate Jim Coronado, in the 299th Judicial District Court of Travis County, issued a Final Ruling in the "No Camping" case — City of Austin vs. Christopher Standage. The judge ruled that the ordinance was constitutional. However, he also wrote that:

"The Petitioners have shown on behalf of their Class of Homeless, that the portion of the ordinance which relates to sleeping in public, or making preparations to sleep including the laying down of bedding in a public place, is a violation of due process. And the ordinance is so vague as to promote discriminatory enforcement as it fails to provide any standard for an officer to discern whether one is camping in public or taking an innocent nap in a public place."

Sweet honey in the rock! After five years, twelve pre-trial hearings, countless No Camping cases, three public hearings, hundreds of letters, a thousand phone calls, thousands of wasted man/woman hours, we won!

In response to the ruling, the Austin City Council, much to its chagrin, voted to strike the words "sleeping" and the reference to "making preparations to sleep, including the laying down of bedding for the purpose of sleeping."[33]

In response to the court ruling, the Austin City Council issued Ordinance #0000928-40 which was approved by the City Attorney, Andrew Martin, attested to by the City Clerk Shirley Brown, and signed into law by Mayor Kirk Watson!

The draft Ordinance below reflects the debate, the controversy it created.

Ordinance #0000928-40

An Ordinance Amending Section 10-1-13 © Of The City Code Regarding Camping In Public Places.

Be It Ordained By The City Council Of The City Of Austin:

Part 1. Section 12-1-13 of the City Code is amended to read as follows:

(A) Except in designated areas, it shall be unlawful for any person to camp in any public area.

(B) In this section [As used herein], the term public area means [shall mean] an outdoor area to which the public has access and includes, but is not limited to, streets, highways, parks, parking lots, alleyways, pedestrian ways, and the common areas of schools, hospitals, apartment houses, office buildings, transport facilities, and shops.

(C) In [For purposes of] this section, the term "camp" [CAMP] means to use a public area for living accommodation purposes such as, but not limited to, the following:

[(1) Sleeping, or making preparations to sleep, including the laying down of bedding for the purpose of sleeping;]

(1) [(2)] Storing personal belongings;

(2) [(3)] Making a camp [any] fire;

(3) [(4)] Using any tents or shelter or other structure or vehicle for a living accommodation [sleeping];

(4) [(5)] Carrying on cooking activities; or

95) [(6)] Doing any digging or earth breaking.

(D) The activities listed in subsection [division] (C) of this section shall constitute camping when it reasonably appears, in light of all the circumstances, that the participants, in conducting these activities, are in fact using the area for living accommodation purposes regardless of the intent of the participants or the nature of any other acuities in which they may also be engaging.

(E) It shall be an affirmative defense to prosecution that a person is the person who owns the property or has secured the permission of the property owner to camp in a public area.

(F) This section does not apply to permitted camping or cooking in a city park in compliance with park regulations.

Part1. The Council waives the requirements of Sections 2-2-3 and 2-2-7 of the City Code for this ordinance.

Part 2. This ordinance takes effect on October 9, 2000

Passed And Approved

September 28, 2000   Kirk Watson

　　　Mayor

Approved: Andrew Martin Attest: Shirley A. Brown

City Attorney   City Clerk

This meant it was no longer illegal to sleep in one's vehicle. This meant that preparing to sleep and actually sleeping (except in the park after curfew) was now legal in the City of Austin.

Appearing on the front page of the Metro section, filling half the page were dozens of members of HTH hooting, hollering, and jumping up and down in jubilation. It was still illegal to "camp," but the police had always said they would not pursue us into the woods, and we were not about to camp in downtown Austin.

We thought that surely we could finally get back to the business of working on the root causes of homelessness and stop wasting time on such foolishness.

From the perspective of House the Homeless, the victory was important on several levels. First, the guys felt they had done nothing wrong, so there was no justification for punishment. Second, they could stop wasting all of their time sitting in jail, and go back to work. Third, it was important that the issue of homelessness remain visible, front and center. If "the forces that be," had been able to sweep people out of sight, everyone would feel that the problem of homelessness itself was somehow resolved, and that would be the end of the community response to this life shattering phenomenon called homelessness.

The Taste Turns Sour

In September 2003, I began to receive complaints that homeless people were still being ticketed for camping when, in fact, they were merely sleeping. Homeless people at bus stops who slept while waiting for the bus were issued tickets for "Camping." People just setting their bags down in front of a police officer received a "No Camping" ticket.

House the Homeless held a meeting of about 40 homeless people who discussed the issue. After the meeting, we reduced everyone's concerns to writing and delivered them to the City of Austin. Specifically, we called for a suspension of the issuance of all "No Camping" tickets when people were merely sleeping. We called for a letter to be issued by the police stating that sleeping is legal anywhere in the City of Austin other than in a park after curfew or unless it blocks a passageway or on private property without permission. We called for police to retrain themselves about the legality of sleeping, about the associated issuance of tickets with the use of the offensive word "transient," and about the routine failure to properly note a mailing address on tickets. We submitted our demands along with about eight clear-cut examples of improperly issued tickets. We received a response that basically blew us off and said that improper issuance of "No Camping" tickets would of course be improper and, if the city were presented with any significant evidence of such activity, it would make an appropriate response.

My response was to use the Open Records Act to secure all of the recent "No Camping" tickets from cases that had not already been sent to offsite storage. I received 453 tickets.

Indicted!

I found irrefutable evidence in 193 of the tickets where "Camping In a Public Area" was the noted violation, that in the section marked "Comments," the officer had written qualifying comments that showed the individuals were in fact "sleeping" and *not* camping. For example, on a ticket issued at 500 East 5th St., in the Comments section was the notation: "sleeping on cardboard." Another ticket also issued at a downtown intersection stated "sleeping and using backpack as pillow." Furthermore, the tickets contained the word "transient" in the mailing address instead of the address for the Austin Resource Center for the Homeless (ARCH) or the Salvation Army where the ticketed people had expressly stated they were receiving their mail. We sent copies of our complete findings to the Mayor, the City Manager, all of City Council, the Police Chief, and the media who apparently couldn't have cared less. I also made a dramatic presentation before City Council during Citizen's Communication where I waved the stack of 453 tickets.

Blinded By the Light (At the End Of the Tunnel)

In early October 2002, writing on behalf of Police Chief Stan Knee, Assistant Chief Jim Fealy wrote to me as President of House the Homeless, that, the COA Police Department is preparing to re-educate its officers regarding the No Camping Ordinance and enforcement policy; will make it clear to officers that "sleeping" is not in violation of the ordinance; is preparing to make a short training film designed to ensure that officers understand the ordinance; and recognizes that utilizing mailing addresses such as the Salvation Army, etc. would assist the formal communications between homeless citizens and the police and the court system. Unfortunately, there was no reference to the repeated use of the defacing term "transient."

A few days later, the Senior Chief of the City of Austin Law Department wrote, "If a case is filed that refers only to sleeping, without sufficient evidence to support a conviction for camping, then the citation would be dismissed."[34]

Though this victory was sweet, time has worn on, and we have stopped fooling ourselves into believing that we have achieved the last word. The drive to criminalize homelessness will never stop, but then neither will we. We have no choice. We are targets running for our lives. Our only hope is to *end homelessness*. We just need enough breathing room to achieve the means to make that happen.

In August, 2003, three homeless guys received tickets for Camping on the old wood train trestle behind the old Austin Music Hall, where I was to have met Bruce Springsteen. The trestle is a classic turn of the century structure, where one might easily find Snidely Whiplash wringing his hands in anticipation and twirling each end of his handlebar mustache while awaiting the train that will decide the fate of the beautiful maiden who is tied to the tracks. No doubt, the gal has long since met her fate. So had the trestle. Long after the railroad stopped using it, the City of Austin voted not to preserve it but rather let Mother Nature and the law of entropy, take its course. Nevertheless, the guys had slept there and gotten "No Camping" tickets. The issue and note in the comments section on the ticket were different this time. The city was changing its tactics. The ordinance specifically stated "Storing Personal Items in violation of the No Camping Ordinance." This was a new, clever, never-ending attempt to use the ordinance to drive homeless people from the streets of Austin.

House the Homeless had gotten Legal Aid to help us, with the assistance of Robert Doggett, defend ourselves.

Our guys move around every day. Not all of their belongings (sleeping gear) will fit into any small storage space that may be afforded them. If there is no sleeping availability at the Salvation Army or the Homeless Resource Center, they find a place and lie down to sleep for the night. Whatever belongings they have with them are laid down with them until they stop sleeping in the morning, gather their things, bedroll, etc. and leave. I contended that this was a "short term event" and had nothing to do with the "storage" of belongings. I reasoned that *the laying down of bedding (not illegal and temporary), is to storing personal items (illegal and long term), as sleeping (not illegal and temporary), is to camping (illegal and long term).* Again, I became a witness.

This time, however, I became an expert witness to *nothing.* Every day at noon instead of eating lunch, I choose to reduce my stress by taking a daily run on Austin's Hike and Bike trail. For months, on my way to the trail, I moved halfway across the new footbridge that now stands parallel to the old trestle. At this halfway point, I leaned toward the rail and stretched first one and then the other calf muscle holding the position for 30 seconds. In this therapeutic ritual, I always faced south. In so doing, my gaze fell upon the exact spot where Mike Orem, Mike Hawkins, and their two buddies were to have camped. I did not see them on the morning before they were charged with camping, nor had I seen them on the morning of the day after they received the no camping ticket citing the "Storage Of Personal Items." Therefore, they could not have been there very long...probably just long enough to sleep overnight.

It took a jury of six women just nine minutes to leave the courtroom select a jury foreman, and return with a verdict of not guilty!

Troxell — Obstruction of sidewalk. Photo by Alan Pogue.

And So It Goes

Police officers continue to issue tickets with varying approaches. We had tickets issued in March of 2005 for Camping On a Sidewalk. We had tickets issued for Blocking a Sidewalk when it measured 18' 2" wide. Of course, it was physically impossible for one person to block passage on such a wide expanse. The obviousness of this was not lost on the court. The two foot by three foot picture I presented was of three people lying head-to-toe, head-to-toe, head-to-toe, perpendicular to the sidewalk, with me still having room to walk by unimpeded. After presenting the photo before City Council the three signs out-lawing sidewalk blocking were removed the next day.

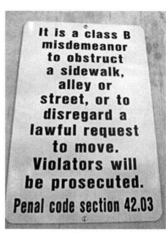

We continue to defend against these tickets and for the most part, the court just throws them out. But it is a serious hassle and continues to be a waste of tax payers' money and of the ticketed victims time. To this end, we continue to collect evidence in a police harassment suit that undoubtedly the City will insist that we bring against them.

The City of Austin has since passed a *No Sit / No Lie Ordinance* for the downtown area with a fine of between $200 and $500 for violations. In January 2010, House theHomeless conducted a health survey that exposed the fact that 48% of the people experiencing homelessness in Austin have disabilities that are so severe as to keep them from working. Once again, House the Homeless is in a pitched battle protesting these oppressive fines issued to people sitting down in response to their disabilities. The City's action is unconscionable and in all likelilhood in violation of the Americans with Disabilities Act. Through an Open Records Request, we've also learned that of the 807 convictions under the ordinance in 2009, 96% were issued to people experiencing homelessness. Clearly, this is *selective enforcement* and *targeting*. House the Homeless continues to collect evidence in a police harassment law suit that undoubetly the City will cause us to bring against them for their actions.

FIVE:

PROJECT FRESH START

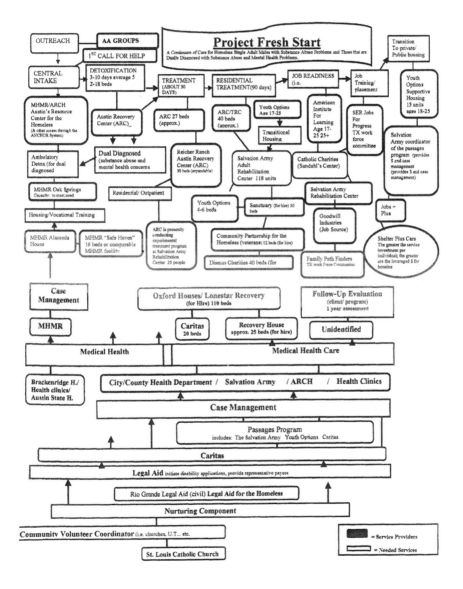

An Integrated Approach to Solving Homelessness

These many years of hard struggle for dignity and fairness drew heavily on our time and resources. However, we never lost sight of our goal, which is to *end homelessness*. Some point to the words found in the *Bible* and say that is not possible, "the poor will always be with us." Perhaps. I certainly will not argue with that thought. But homelessness is something else.

As a young man growing up in Middle America, I was never aware of homelessness. I did however have some sense of poverty having lived in both North and South Carolina. Later living in Maryland, I would zip in and out of neighborhoods in Washington D.C. on my bicycle engaging in something I refer to as "ride-by culture absorption." I saw run-down apartment buildings; I saw housing authority buildings in every state of disrepair. I saw all forms of drug sales and prostitution and drunks, but people were not homeless as far as I could tell. It never became apparent from the countless conversations that I had with folks sitting on their stoops that anyone was homeless. I knew that people thought I was out of place and that, as a white boy in their neighborhood, I was probably crazy, but safe enough to speak with, and I made friends. I made many friends. I learned that one could always find a cheap motel or go stay at the Young Men's Christian Association, YMCA. Through those relationships, I learned a lot about things generally. Today, we see this thing we call homelessness, and we do not seem to see those same facilities. We no longer see cheap motels, and the YMCAs are almost all gone in terms of a place to stay. In fact, they have changed their name to simply the "Y."

All sorts of events occurred to create the phenomenon of homelessness we see today. Double digit inflation attacked family incomes forcing both parents to work...not just one. We saw the end of the Vietnam War with soldiers returning home, broken and then discarded. We saw low wages and double-digit inflation create financial pressures that led to a record number of divorces. We saw the creation of latch key kids — kids, who have to come home unsupervised, so that their parents or their single parent could put food on the table. We saw a loss of millions of cheap motels that converted to condominiums or were torn down to make parking lots in the 1980s. We saw almost all the YMCAs close their doors and no longer offer cheap overnight housing. We saw the close of our mental health institutions as a result of the abuses we committed against our mentally ill. We saw the loss of the high-rise apartments where we used to house our poor families.

So now, as Americans, we have come to know homelessness. But our homelessness is different from the rest of the world because it is contrasted by our unabashed and seemingly endless wealth. We have people who have lost their apartments and are now couch hopping, moving from one friend's couch to the next after a few weeks or a few days. We have people who have lost their jobs, packed what little they have left, and then chase jobs while living out of their cars. We have battered women who have fled in the middle of the night with really nothing other than their children. They too are living in cars and women's shelters. We have veterans who have served our country well in Vietnam, Desert Storm, the Gulf War, Iraq and in Afghanistan killing in the name of God and Country, returning to their home only to find they have none. Others were so traumatized, like myself, that they vomited it all up and wandered the country aimlessly for years confused, in pain, and abandoned. In World War II and the Korean War, the condition was called Shell Shocked. In Vietnam, it was called Post Traumatic Stress Disorder, PTSD, and it went untreated or self-treated. It was a senseless war in which soldiers, myself included, were left unsupported at every turn in Vietnam and again when we returned home. The ones that it did not maim or kill, it made crazy and homeless for many years. Some are still that way.

When the courts flung open the doors of our mental health institutions, and people with very serious mental health concerns were let out, they found our streets. Today, the social safety net has been shredded and the flow of social services dollars has dwindled to a trickle. Only the most severely afflicted with schizophrenia, bipolar disorder, and major/chronic depression find help, but even that is a rarity. So now these overlapping events have all added up to make this thing we call homelessness. We speak of it and perceive of it in terms of being one big impossible bolus that sticks in our collective throat and, as a nation, we can hardly begin to digest the concept.

I have come to realize that homelessness is this huge unwieldy conglomerate made up of regular folks and their multitude of collective adverse experiences. We have single men, single women, children, women with children, men with children (fairly rare), disintegrated whole families, battered women, veterans, people with mental health problems, and people with substance abuse problems. In addition, we have people who are dually diagnosed with both mental health problems and substance abuse problems.

As Founder and Director of Legal Aid for the Homeless for Texas Rio Grande Legal Aid, it is my job to operate a legal outreach office in the local homeless resource center. It is known as ARCH, Austin's Resource Center for the Homeless. There, I see the disabled homeless. These are the truly broken ones. I see people who are living on the streets of America who are experiencing severe mental health problems and self-medicating with some memory deadening substance, usually alcohol, but anything will do.

It occurred to me in 1997 that if we were going to achieve our goal of ending homelessness then we needed to interject a different perspective/ approach into the dynamic. We needed a *Fresh Start*.

I believed that what we needed was to identify the needs of homeless people and the resources to meet those needs. I figured the way to increase resources was to create a business model to address this litany of human concerns. It seemed reasonable to me that if we could create a pragmatic business approach to solving homelessness for the most devastated faction of the many that make up homelessness, then we could devise a pragmatic approach for each of the other factions. Therefore, I focused on my folks, people who were experiencing homelessness and were also dually diagnosed with both substance abuse and mental health problems.

I knew that if we were going to convince legislatures and foundations that our course of action was worthy of funding, we would need to take a totally new approach. Our practice had been to fund individual organizations to provide a particular service. For example, a funder would be asked for funds for 200 people to get GEDs (high school equivalency diplomas). The funder then put out a Request For Proposals, RFP, and would then make a contract with the organization offering the best sounding deal (lowest cost) that met their stated goal. The winning organization would provide the service by enrolling the 200 people in the GED process. The organization would then meet an outcome requirement of 80% graduation success, and everyone would be happy. The problem was identified, quantified, outcome measures were set and reached and hands were shaken. However, should the *measure* be the need for a GED, or even getting it, or should the true measure be that of *exiting people from the streets?*

To jump start Project Fresh Start, I suggested that we think in terms of funding an entire process. I envisioned an entire process where people enter at a starting point, move through a seamless *Continuum of Care*, and continue to get whatever service they need from inter-connected service providers until they exit on the other end of the continuum having become empowered, employed and/or stabilized. For each continuum, we should identify each and every "need" required to aid an individual in passing through the continuum and come out on the other side of homelessness.

We should identify everywhere in the community that a need could be met. Then we would create a visible pathway, a roadmap for the individual to follow.

We would measure success not only in terms of what a social service entity produces relative to its projected promises, but also in terms of the ultimate success of the individual relative to their achieving stability and/ or self-reliance. The goal of "stability" would be for the disabled, and self-reliance would include employment. The goal was not necessarily to create new programs, but rather to tie together the productive ones that already exist in a cohesive fashion.

We would create an entire system where case managers would guide participants through a holistic recovery process, not just pointing participants to various resources but to a whole continuum of recovery.

The process encompassed no less than twenty-three separate core operations, run by twenty-three separate organizations. Each single operational element was perceived to be crucial to the ultimate success of any single service through which the individual would pass along the continuum. The failure of any one single element could be expected to result in the overall failure of any individual being able to pass through the process. We already saw that unlinked services were not helping people exit the streets, even if an individual component met its funding goals. So there were often segments of achievement, such as securing the GED, but over all failure in terms of people not exiting the street.

I determined that there must be a single oversight entity or Managed Service Organization, MSO (as it became known) that would hire a Network Manager who would ensure total program continuity.

Too often, for example, a person might reach the 4th stage of development only to find no transition bed available forcing him to return to the streets. While he waited for that bed to become available, he would, in all likelihood, succumb again to the pressures of his addiction or economics. As a result, all the invested effort, all the people hours, all of the confidence building, and all of the taxpayer investment would be lost to one more failure in a life which had been built upon failures.

I designed the MSO to operate through a Network Manager who would see to it that each separate "need" category was coupled with a specific organization that was capable of producing what was required to meet that need. This would be done through a competitive bid process. The Network Manager would ensure that the services provided by each entity remained at a constant level. This would ensure that a predetermined number of clients could pass through the continuum without experiencing any gaps in services. In other words, the Network Manager would make sure that no one going through the continuum would be stymied due to a lack or delay of services, or due to the lack of funds to acquire those services. Of course, the Network Manager would also be charged with maintaining coordination and harmonious interaction among the various service providers.

Note: At the bottom of the flow chart you will see the legend, which shows that the boxed headings are the NEEDS and the encircled entities are those service providers in the community that might be able to meet that particular need.

As designed, people would enter on the top left hand side at the "Need" identified as "outreach." This is known as a single point of entry or, SPOE. From here, people would pass into detoxification and substance abuse treatment and then move toward jobs and housing either to the right or down the left side of the chart if they had mental health concerns.

A critical element of the continuum is the Nurturing Component. In the 1980s when social engineers were asked by funders how much a project would cost, we, as social engineers, would look at our slide rules and then at the funders and tell them, "It will cost exactly $1.00." The funders would reach into their pockets, cock their heads to one side or the other, count the amount visible and declare in a clear and unwavering voice, "Well, I only have eighty-five cents." We would insist that it would cost $1.00, and they would respond, "Eighty-five cents, take it or leave it." We always took it. Then we discarded one or two things: Follow Up Care/Evaluations or the Nurturing Component or both. These were hard choices, and we made bad decisions. We took the money and operated our under-funded compromised programs. Programs failed, funders lost faith, and our friends who were struggling fell by the wayside one more time.

The Nurturing Component can be as formal as organized religion or it can be an AA buddy, but whatever it is to the individual, everyone needs a support system. When you have lost everything including your family ties, you need someone to lean on. Ironically, today faith-based initiatives are being called essential elements to any program.

With the help of my Ameri-Corps assistant and close friend, Katie Grau, we packaged Project Fresh Start into a booklet. We then set out to garner letters for support of the paradigm shift of how we deliver social services in my community of Austin, Texas (Anywhere USA). We secured the support of the Austin Area Homeless Task Force, Mayor Kirk Watson, Texas House of Representatives Jeff Wentworth, State Representative Sherri Greenberg, State Representative Elliot Naishtat, State Representative Terry Keel, and State Representative Glenn Maxey. With the help of my friend Howard Jones at the Salvation Army Rehabilitation Center, we set up a group meeting of all of the parties and all of the organizations identified in Project Fresh Start.

The presentation to the assembled 23 service organizations was dramatic, and it went without a hitch. It included a tour of the South Congress Salvation Army transitional housing/rehabilitation facilities. The participants were thrilled with the gathering and the concept of our project. I was most pleased, but walked away with a feeling that remains with me today. Something occurred in that room that was fully unexpected.

I thought that the gathering would be a pleasant reunion for the providers that we had assembled. Therefore, we made it a social event with drinks and pastries, etc. What occurred was more dramatic than I had expected. Folks knew this provider or that one. They knew a provider with a service closely associated with a service that they were providing, but for the most part, they were strangers! The level of association and coordination of services that we envisioned was more desperately needed than ever I had imagined. Baby steps.

Together, we set out to create a model project. I determined that a twenty-person trial project would be ideal. Twenty was not unwieldy, and it was large enough to convince funders of a successful approach.

The Service Needs Included:
- ✓ *Central Intake*
- ✓ *Detoxification (level I)*
- ✓ *Ambulatory Detoxification*
- ✓ *Treatment – Inpatient (level II and III)*
- ✓ *Treatment – Outpatient (level II)*
- ✓ *Treatment – Outpatient (level IV)*
- ✓ *Mental Health Services*
- ✓ *Transitional Housing*
- ✓ *Job Readiness*
- ✓ *Job Training/Placement*
- ✓ *Transition to Private/Public Housing*

✓ *Nurturing Component*
✓ *Medical Health Care*
✓ *Legal Services*
✓ *Case Management*
✓ *Network Management*

Governor George W. Bush Backs Project Fresh Start

When I mapped out the community of Austin for Project Fresh Start, I did so believing that there were limited resources available and that the major problem was that there were a few gaps in services. I was more than a little astonished to learn that it was not possible to put 20 people through the process! The services just did not exist. There was no continuum. We patched together the continuum as best we could.

I brought in my good friend and colleague David Evans from Austin Travis County Mental Health Mental Retardation, MHMR, to provide mental health services. MHMR, now known as Austin Travis County Integral Care, did this using money from their existing budget. They eventually also served as the MSO. However, there was no getting around the fact that we did not have the jobs component. This was amazing. We had all of these people, homeless and out of work, and there existed no job opportunities for them.

Traditional avenues of funding would require a tremendous amount of time, and we were feeling the urgency of the need to move forward now. I learned that the Governor had "discretionary funds" that could be used for appropriate special projects. I set out to meet with the staff of Governor George W. Bush. Six months later, after endless phone calls and meetings, Albert Hawkins, Governor Bush's Chief Financial Officer, cut the check.

As far as I know, the House the Homeless Project Fresh Start is the only homeless organization/project to receive such funding from the Governor's Office. I am convinced that we were funded because Mr. Bush could relate to the need for jobs and the opportunities that would be provided. Our proposal presented both. After we got the money, the good folks at Easter Seals stepped up and became our jobs provider.

Success!!

We successfully put 18 of the 20 original people through our program! This was big. The program was heralded as a unique success worthy of replication. We received the Community Collaboration (Legacy) Award. This was presented by City Search, the United Way, and the Austin Chamber of Commerce! We were beaming for weeks!

Project Fresh Start is unique because it calls for a paradigm shift in how organizations get funding. Each Board of Directors would have to yield the organizations' individual project outcomes to the collective benefit of the community. Outcomes would no longer be based on producing individual units of service, but would be based on the outcome of ending homelessness for an individual. We realized that this would not happen overnight. It would require "political will," both top-down and bottom-up.

During the months that followed, I monitored the success of Project Fresh Start. I kept in touch with the guys. I watched them struggle. Emotionally it was very hard. The transition was extreme. We were moving people from an abjectly homeless state to a fully housed, reintegrated, stable state.

There are people in our society who are disabled and are unable to work. There are other people who have worked extremely hard, but have created no work record; homemakers fall into this category. The community of America has chosen to assist these folks with financial support known as Supplemental Security Income, SSI, of $674.00 per month. This means that $674 is what they have every month to rent their apartment, buy food, use for transportation, purchase clothing, spend on toiletries, and use on health care items. Given the cost of living, the only way these people could be housed was to subsidize housing where taxpayers foot the bill, or by doubling or tripling people up with strangers.

Soon Project Fresh Start's success fell from eighteen to thirteen. In nine months, we had nine people remaining in housing. In a year's time, we had lost almost everyone. This told us that we, as a nation, would end up subsidizing workers. They would have to rely on housing supports and food stamps because their wages did not stretch far enough to get them into, and then allow them to keep, basic rental housing.

According to the U.S. Department of Labor, the current Federal Minimum Wage, FMW is $7.25 per hour. Until 2009, it was $5.15 and had been that amount since 1997! According to the last several U.S. Conference of Mayors' reports, minimum wage workers cannot move into or afford to keep a one-bedroom apartment anywhere, with very few exceptions, in this country.

Destined to Fail

So that meant that Project Fresh Start was no good. It was a ruse, flawed. Here we were coordinating all of these heretofore-uncoordinated services of all the social service agencies in the most cohesive, productive, cost effective manner possible. We had gotten down trodden people engaged, brushed off, detoxified, job trained, placed in jobs and into housing only to realize that they were destined to fail as *the wage, set by the federal government, would not sustain them.* This was a powerful epiphany. The same was true for the folks receiving disability benefits. The dollar amount was/is just too little to sustain people in housing. The disability stipend is about *half* that of the Federal Minimum Wage.

Edward Forrest Dutcher

Edward Forrest Dutcher is better known to his friends as "Dutch." His mid 30s look belies his true age of 45. His towering height of 6'5," his shortly cropped strawberry blond hair and his indefatigable attitude combine to give him a boyish look. In spite of spending years of living in and out of homelessness, he retains a youthful build which hovers between lanky and muscular by holding onto his life long dream of operating his own furniture moving business.

While he has never achieved his dream, he keeps it in his sights. On Mondays, Tuesdays and Wednesdays, he works at Austin Affordable Furniture, a family furniture store where he clocks 30 hours per week at $7.50 per hour. On Thursdays, Fridays and Saturdays he works at another small company that is a home furniture moving business. This brings his weekly work hours to 60 where he is paid on a commission basis. Some weeks there is no work.

At present, he is once again renting a motel room on a weekly basis for $185.00 per week plus a $10.00 deposit. This comes to $850.00 per month. When the work is inconsistent, Dutch has to rent on a daily basis, which then costs $30.00 to $35.00 per day or as much as $1,000 per month. So when he can least afford it, the rent goes up. He has wanted to get an apartment, which would drop the rent to the range of $600 or even $550 per month but this would require a deposit of $550 plus first and last months' rent.

Dutch struggles to save enough money for a used van that would launch his own moving business. Instead, all of his energy goes to basic survival and supporting other people's businesses.

National Recognition

In 1997, the work of House the Homeless caught the attention of Michael Stoops, national organizer for the National Coalition for the Homeless. I was invited to Washington DC to receive the Beverly "Ma" Curtis Award for formerly homeless individuals who reach back. I was awe struck with their dedication to the same core issues that I had learned to embrace.

The National Coalition for the Homeless believes in and advocates for Housing Security in the form of safe, decent, affordable housing for everyone. Today, they continue to support the National Housing Trust Fund.

They believe in Health Care Security-Universal Health Care and NCH promotes the Single Payer system.

They believe in Human and Civil Rights.

And lastly, they call for Income Security...Livable Incomes for people who *cannot* work, and they now promote the Universal Living Wage for those who *can* work.

SIX:

THE UNIVERSAL LIVING WAGE

Photo of Frederick Gentry by Alan Pogue.

Dedication:

For Thomas Michael Sawyer and so many others.

There is an enlarged picture on my office wall of Thomas Michael Sawyer, the first man to receive a No Camping ticket in Austin. He has his back to the camera. The photo is black and white. It is fairly grainy. Tom is pushing a shopping cart loaded down with three very large black trash bags. It is obvious even to the casual observer that the bags are filled with cans. The bags are stuffed to the point of bursting. Even empty, they must yield a notable weight as he is bent slightly forward, his shoulders are scrunched, and his knit shirt has come un-tucked in his effort to push the cart forward.

My attention is drawn to this picture repeatedly. My thoughts are drawn to it certainly because Tom is now deceased and I lament his loss, but I also see in that picture of Tom, not a bum, as so many would describe him, but rather I see Tom, the worker. There is no supervisor, no one to watch him, no one to direct him. He is self-motivated. Like countless others, he would get up before the sun and continue to work well after the sun went down. Tom's work ethic was intact. He went to work in that fashion everyday for just a saw buck and then to "Church Under the Bridge" on Sundays, but he found himself working outside the system like so many others. And I find myself asking why? What's gone wrong with this picture?

The Case For a Universal Living Wage

Jerold Waltman Professor of political science at Baylor University author of the *Case for a Living Wage* and author of this book's Forward, sets the stage for our thinking about a Living Wage. He simply states that, "A citizen's pay for a full time job should provide enough so that 1) no one will be forced to live below a decent level...and (such that) 2) the degree of economic inequality is not too great."

He goes on to suggest that there are a couple of approaches to determining the living wage. One is to set the wage at or above some established poverty level and the other is to set it at a percentage of some variable.[35] We choose the latter and common sense dictates that we use the cost of housing as the base of our formula.

The Yardstick

Imagine, if you will, our society as a horizontal yardstick divided into three one-foot lengths. Imagine that the yardstick represents our socio-economic structure. It is comprised of three, one-foot sections. In the foot on the right my beautiful seventeen-year-old daughter, Colleen (Now 20, I can hardly believe it.), is represented. She, like her friends, is in school. Her task is to learn. At present, this is the sum total of her job. Neither she nor any of her friends are expected to make any significant financial contribution to society at this stage of their lives. In fact, from the day they enter kindergarten until they are 18, they cost us as taxpayers a considerable amount of money. We construct and maintain learning institutions, so they will be equipped to complete their task of being good students and ultimately good productive workers. Loving my daughter as I do, Colleen is not financially contributing anything to the system and that is OK. That is not her job. Her job is to major in art, minor in business, take French, actually learn to speak the language and tell me to whom to write the checks. (Between 17 and 20 the majors are changing, but you get the idea.)

On the left side of the yardstick is another one-foot section. In this section are Colleen's grandparents. They are in their mid-seventies and entitled to retire. They have worked hard all of their lives and for their remaining years will reap the fruits of their labors. They will cease working and instead rely on their savings and Social Security for the rest of their lives. People in this foot are no longer expected to make substantial financial contributions into the system. That too is OK.

197

This just leaves the middle foot — the "worker foot" to not only sustain itself, but also the other two sections. That is a tremendous financial responsibility.

Starting now and continuing for the next five to thirty years, a dramatic shift will occur and an exceptional number of people will leave the "worker foot" as "baby boomers" and move toward retirement. Regardless, the "worker foot" will still continue to be expected to sustain both the "student foot" and the "retirement foot."

Within the worker foot are 10.1 million minimum wage workers.[36] Additionally, it is estimated that there are another 10 million undocumented workers in this foot.

These 20 million people are working at, or slightly above, an hourly wage of $7.25 per hour, a wage insufficient for them to move into and keep basic rental housing as individuals. The National Coalition for the Homeless points to this and states that again in 2010, 3.5 million people are expected to experience homelessness.[37] Folks are working, but their wage is not enough to sustain them in housing. Therefore, hard working minimum wage earners are falling out of the "worker foot" and experiencing homelessness. This does not bode well for our society as a whole. Between the aging workers shift of the "retirement foot" and good working people falling out of the "worker foot," and the continued drain of the "learning foot," there is a tremendous strain on each end of our yardstick. Some say the stick could break. Others say that it has already snapped and the evidence is the unbridled immigration that has poured into this country in recent years.

Undocumented Workers

President George W. Bush spoke about a guest worker program to fill the jobs "that Americans do not want." Well that's true. Americans do not want these jobs... at least not at the wage being paid. For someone coming from a country where $5.00 *a day* is "good" money, work at five, six or even seven dollars per hour is *very* good money. Especially if you are willing to live eight people in a room for seven to eight years so you can send 65% of your wages back home.

Conversely, for someone living in Austin, Texas where it takes a wage of $13.23 per hour to get into and keep basic rental housing, why would anyone accept a job that pays $7.25 per hour? They would not. So the minimum wage jobs that must be done are filled by people willing to risk their lives to enter this country, live one on top of another in deplorable conditions, and send a good portion of that wage back to *la familia*.

One thing is clear, undocumented workers and drug dealers are not pouring across our northern border. Why? Think about it. It's not because we have a better security system on our Canadian border. It's because the economy of our neighbors to our north is good. In the South, it is so bleak that people are willing to leave their families or risk death by selling drugs in an economy that holds little to no alternative or hope.

Solution. President Obama needs to create a Business Leadership Corps of 1,000 business leaders who are willing to go south of the border and immerse themselves in one-on-one, business/cultural relationships with a sister business and help blow life and alternatives into those economies. Our business ambassadors should be provided special financial incentives for their efforts. Tariff incentives should be explored and commerce, job expansion and employment opportunities at local living wages values encouraged.

At the same time, President Obama and our leaders to the south need commerce policies designed to deter corrupt practices and take steps here in the north to halt the growing drug market that North America has become. By building stable economies to the south that pay living wages, the undocumented worker issue here in the north will dissipate. Furthermore, new markets will open up for North American business, and maybe, just maybe, we can stave off ever encroaching drug wars that are migrating to the north.

Finally, if businesses in North America begin to pay fair living wages, i.e. enough to afford basic food, clothing and shelter, they will find that they have most of the local workers that they need.

The Federal Poverty Guideline

When examining the issue of homelessness as a product of poverty, one can look to the U.S. Government for perspective. In 1963, the U.S. Government established the Federal Poverty Guideline.[38] President Johnson was in office. He was from the South. He had seen poverty, so he knew the face of it when social engineers spoke about hunger in Appalachia. This is the impoverished region within the Blue Ridge Mountains including West Virginia. Pictures of starving children were shown on our airwaves and the "War on Poverty" commenced. As the "bread basket of the world," we declared that it was unacceptable that anyone go to bed hungry in America.

Of course, it was important to know how poor you had to be in order to be considered impoverished. So, a standard was created.

A woman at the Social Security Administration, Mrs. Molly Orshanski, took a small basket and filled it with the "food staples of life." She placed meat, then bread,(no doubt white)and then potatoes, into the basket. (Dr. Atkins is likely rolling over in his grave in anguish.) Nonetheless, she then placed the food in the basket, used a multiplier of three, and then multiplied this by the number of people in the household. Voila! They had created the Federal Poverty Guideline. This same standard is still in use today. The question arises how relevant the standard was/is in reality. In 1963, food made up 23% of the monthly family budget. Housing at that time made up 29% of the monthly family budget. Today, food makes up only 16% of the monthly family budget whereas housing makes up 37% to 50% or more.

Obviously, the most costly item that we all share is *housing*, not food. Logic dictates that if our lives are centered around housing, and if the majority of our living expenses are for housing, and if the lack of housing results in homelessness, then *the goal should be to make basic wages relate to our ability to afford basic rental housing.*

The Federal Minimum Wage

This brings us to the Federal Minimum Wage (FMW). In 1938 both halves of Congress established the FMW in response to the millions of men who wandered our country during The Great Depression looking for jobs at a wage that would sustain them. There were over 14 million people unemployed. The government determined that the minimum wage needed to be about fifty cents an hour. So it was set at twenty-five cents. [39]

In spite of starting a little light in the pocketbook, the minimum wage served this country fairly well until 1973 when double digit inflation struck as a result of an "energy crisis." I remember before 1973 being able to walk onto any construction site, embellish my capabilities, get hired, strap on a hammer, work a full, hard day and walk away with enough money at $1.60 per hour to rent a room, stash my stuff, get clean, rested and return to do it all over again the next day. However, by the 1990s the high tech boom hit America head on. The cost of everything inflated again. When the dust finally settled, the cost of just about everything settled back close to its original cost *except housing*. Landlords offered $1.00 move-in-specials, dispensed with security deposits, gave free microwaves, etc. to get people in, but the rents did not go down. As a result, the cost of rental housing in urban areas soared well out of reach of minimum wage workers.

When Congress "debated" an increase in the FMW, which they did every four or five years, they'd start by plucking a number out of the air. They'd start at a dollar or a dollar and a half over several years. They would wrangle over this for about a year and in the end, settle on something that is less than a dollar. The amount related to nothing. It was not based on need or affordability. It was simply plucked out of the air. Clearly, this represented our society's finely honed skills of science and logic coming together.

Housing

Housing is what we need in order not to be homeless. Clearly, housing is the antitheses of homelessness and visa versa. We as a capitalistic society have also said that we do not relish a society where the taxpayer is shouldering the bill for housing our nation's working poor. Because both halves of Congress have already determined that a FMW is the law of the land, legislators say why not just simply adjust the base amount slightly.

What needs to occur, however, is to *make the FMW relate to the local cost of housing throughout the United States.* This provides an incentive to work. Americans would seek those jobs that don't currently pay a living wage. Workers could be assured of housing *affordability,* and the economy would be stimulated by filling the housing needs (construction thereof) that minimum wage working people could then afford.

In 1997, I devised a single national formula, using existing government guidelines, that ensures if a person works a forty-hour week, then the wage they earn would enable them to afford basic rental housing, along with food, transportation, clothing and access to the emergency room wherever that work is done throughout the United States.

Wow! Who can disagree with this approach?

Besides, what is the alternative?

People are going to survive, and they will do it any way they can. In this society, money dictates everything. People will sell whatever they can to get by. Of course, at the lowest economic level, without minimally adequate wages, there are only two things readily available to sell: drugs and other people. This is not my vision for America, but it seems to be our reality. This does not bode well for us. We need to choose the viable work alternative instead.

America is the greatest nation on earth, the land of milk and honey, the land of opportunity, but not for all people working and living here. The system is failing them and squeezing them out. It is forcing people to make bad ethical decisions just to survive. The system is robbing them of their dignity and of their self-respect. It is driving them off the tax rolls and onto the tax dole...or worse.

Why would anyone work at a minimum wage job of 40 hours a week when it will not even get him/her into housing? With the "worker foot" shrinking, does it make any sense that we allow 3.5 million people to fall into homelessness in our country? Remember, the federal government says that 42% of the homeless are working at some point during the week. The work ethic is there; however, the wage is not.

Conservatively, we believe that with the passage of the Universal Living Wage, over 1,000,000 minimum wage workers will be able to work themselves off the streets of America.

How many more people would be able to get off our streets if there were a pathway...if the wages would ensure their ability to afford basic food, clothing, shelter, and access to health care? We think it is worth exploring.

It is an international reality. Migrant workers will continue to pour across our borders as long as their economies fail to provide them basic living wages in their own country.

When the ULW is passed, there will be a huge stream of income available for housing. Once the ULW goes into effect, we will put the difference between the FMW ($7.25 per hour) and its new level in any Fair Market Rent region throughout the United States into the pockets of millions of minimum wage workers, all of whom need the same thing...housing. For the first time, there will be millions of people with the financial ability to afford basic rental housing. Today, in 2010, that housing stock does not exist. There has been no financial incentive to build it. There will be plenty of financial incentives when the ULW is passed. The soundness of our logic is reflected in the endorsement of the ULW by the national construction company, HSR Construction, which resulted from a series of deliberate, formal discussions.

Some people have suggested that, upon the passage of the ULW, housing costs will soar, raising housing costs beyond the reach of renters, and cause unbridled inflation. This is problematic but not exactly accurate.

First, the cost of everything else has *already* inflated. The FMW, has not kept up. Because the ULW is indexed to the local cost of housing, if anyone is willing/able to work 40 hours then he/she will be able to afford basic rental housing *regardless of how expensive basic rents become.*

Second, we believe that, once established, the free market would continue to respond to this enormous pool of funds by building local housing. For the first time, there will be incentive in the market for corporate interests to apply pressure on the rental industry to keep rental prices in check. Failing that, because the federal government is already monitoring and establishing Fair Market Rents, and the FMW, it will be in position to respond to any unscrupulous market gougers in an appropriate fashion.

U.S. Fair Labor Standards Act, 1938

According to statistical surveys, minimum wage workers have spent almost 100% of past wage increases right back into the economy thus creating quick economic growth and job creation.[40]

As seen with the passage of the U.S. Fair Labor Standards Act in 1938[41] in response to The Great Depression, establishing a living wage similarly stimulates the overall demand for goods and services in the economy. Families become dramatically more credit worthy and can avail themselves of more goods and more services.[42] The overall demand for goods and services will increase demand for low wage workers as industry responds to this demand and stimulation.[43]

Paying a living wage will create new business as new revenue promotes commerce. Many economists argue that higher pay results in increased productivity by making jobs more desirable to both get and keep, thereby reducing recruitment, training and supervisory costs associated with high rates of turnover. Paying a living wage is good for the local economy because small local businesses rely on local dollars. Obviously, more money for city dwellers will mean more customers for municipal businesses. To a lesser extent, the same is true in rural America.

It has been suggested that paying living wages would prevent business from locating to one or another specific municipal district. However, because the ULW is uniform across the board nationwide and will affect people equally on a relative basis, that won't occur. It creates a level playing field. Additionally, businesses choose cities in large part because of quality of life issues and governmental considerations. A 1998 study issued by ICF Kaiser Economic Strategy Group, of San Rafael California, produced for the Greater Austin, Texas Chamber of Commerce entitled, *Next Century Economy*, states: "in order to maintain Austin's economic success and high standard of livability, the region should focus on the business already here as opposed to attracting new business." The report cited three elements of a "Sustainable Advantage Economy," including the need for, "a long term commitment to improve quality of life and to address social disparity issues as the economy develops."[44]

Tipping

The act of tipping is pervasive throughout our culture. Many businesses contend that they could not survive without the tipping dynamic. "**T**o **I**nsure **P**romptitude" is one suspected origin of the acronym TIP found on brass urns in coffee houses and local pubs in sixteenth century England.[45] The history of tipping in both Europe and the United States, where it took hold after the Civil War, is fascinating.

Over time, employers, employees and patrons have all organized both *for* and *against* tipping with great passion. In fact, tipping was outlawed in Washington, Mississippi, Arkansas, Iowa, South Carolina, Tennessee and Georgia only to be later reinstated in every state between 1913 and 1926. Tipping in the United States has become a multi-billion dollar source of income. There are 33 tipped service professions. Tipping in the restaurant industry alone now amounts to $25 billion dollars per year.[46]

Today, people tip because it is a social norm, an expression of gratitude, born out of economic compassion, and a way of ensuring future good service. It is generally believed that tipping improves the quality of service, and while marginally small, there is a statistically significant correlation between tipping and the quality of service.[47] Under the Fair Labor Standards Act of 1938, employers of people who earn a living based on tips, must pay tipped employees $2.13 per hour. This basic wage plus the tipped amount brings the overall wage up to the FMW level. The FMW is presently set at $7.25 per hour. Once the tip raises the wage to this level, the employer has met his/her obligation.

At the Universal Living Wage Campaign, we advocate adjusting the FMW using the ULW formula, which is based on existing government guidelines and ensures that anyone working a 40-hour week will be able to afford basic rental housing.

We may be tempted to suggest that the tip ratio should remain the same under the ULW as it is today. In other words: $2.13 per hour is 29% of $7.25. Keeping the same ratio, it could be suggested that the base tip amount should be 29% of whatever the new Universal Living Wage amount calculates out to be in each ULW region, throughout the United States. This would seem to be a reasonable approach. However, businessmen such as Jeff Trigger, past Managing Director of the renowned Driskill Hotel in Austin, Texas, suggested that it would be hard to justify asking employers to pay a higher amount of wages when a tipped employee in 2010 may make as much as $30,000 per year in tips. It may be hard to imagine, but under the law, these are minimum wage employees and the business must pay the base amount of $2.13 per hour so long as the patron provides a tip that brings the wage up to the current FMW of $7.25 per hour.

In response to this business concern, the ULW campaign looks to the original premise of the FMW: a person willing to work a 40-hour week job should be able to afford basic food, clothing, and shelter. Therefore, we believe that the current federal standard should continue to prevail. Thus, once an employer has brought the wage up to the new ULW amount in that particular Fair Market Rent Area, (as established by the US Department of Housing and Urban Development), *through either tips or wages*, then the employer will have met his/her financial and legal obligations to the employee as far as this initiative is concerned.

For example, in Austin, Texas, in 2010 the adjusted FMW using the Universal Living Wage would be $13.23 per hour. Under this new approach, an employer would continue to be obligated to pay no more than $2.13 per hour so long as tips provided by patrons produce a total hourly wage of $13.23.

There are some who feel that the entire "tipping process" generally lends itself to under reporting of income. Under the law, current enforcement standards of employers paying minimum wage will continue to prevail. It will continue to be the responsibility of the employee to accurately report all wage earnings to the IRS as required under law. *While tipping today is generally intended to show gratitude, some of us believe that tipping should be done away with as it leads to unpredictable budgeting practices which destabilizes our most vulnerable workers and shifts financial responsibility from the employers who benefit from the work to the restaurant patron.*

It is important to recognize that most employers are paying at or just above the FMW. However, when exploring changes to federal policy our thinking must be as expansive as possible. We must consider concerns from all quarters, especially the business community.

Teenage Workers

For some, there exists a perception that the typical minimum wage worker is a teenager working at a fast food restaurant who lives at home with his/her parents. However, according to the study, *The Sky Hasn't Fallen*, and the study, *America's Well Targeted Raise*, both produced by the Economic Policy Institute, teenage minimum wage workers account for only 7% of the total minimum wage workforce. About two-thirds of minimum wage workers are full time, over 20 years old, about two-thirds are women and about two-thirds do not live with their parents. Furthermore, the report confirms that 40% of them are the sole source of income for their household.[48]

Some suggest that teenagers and young adults will be hurt by the increase, i.e. they will be passed over for older employees. However, again, according to *The Sky Hasn't Fallen*, that didn't happen.

There is an argument that, because "so many" minimum wage workers are teenagers (clearly not the case as just evidenced), there should be a sub-minimum wage. However, according to the Bureau of Labor Statistics, only 5% of all fast food employers use the sub-minimum (training) wage structure. The sub-minimum wage was made possible by the 1989 minimum wage law. The vast majority of employers never even consider using it because it is so uncompetitive that employees won't consider working at such slave wages. They know that they need to be *wage competitive* right from the start and pay the full wage.[49]

The question arises as to what is the justification for paying teenagers who live with their parents at the ULW rate. Certainly, the goal of the Universal Living Wage is to set a wage at which all minimum wage workers are able to afford basic housing. We believe that wages should relate to a "unit of work." It does not matter if a black person, a white person, a male or female, an 86 year old or a 16 year old performs that work. If an employer believes that someone is capable of doing the job, and hires her/him, then a Universal Living Wage should be paid regardless of who performs that work. Again, we recognize an employer's discretion to hire and fire but obviously it should be at the ULW standard. I paid my daughter, Colleen, by the ULW standard. However, because she's a wee five feet tall, I do not hire her for every task. Additionally, if a few additional people benefit from the standard used to ensure housing millions of our nation's wage workers, then so be it.

Others Affected by the ULW

According to the report, *The Sky Hasn't Fallen*, the last minimum wage raise did increase earnings of low-wage workers, and this increase primarily benefited low-income families. Additionally, according to the report, *America's Well Targeted Raise*, also released by the Economic Policy Institute, 57% of the gains from the increase went to working families in the bottom 40% of the income scale.[50]

Job Loss

Some argue that the wage increase will lead to job loss. Once again, the increase in 1997 did not lead to job loss. *The Sky Hasn't Fallen* report ends with this: "given the statistically and economically insignificant (and mostly positive) employment effects of the change, it might be more useful if the next debate spends less time focusing on the cost of the increase and more on the benefits to low-income families." The report was supported by grants from the Rockefeller Foundation, and the Charles Steward Mott Foundation, and the U.S. Department of Labor.[51]

Ben Bernanke, during his first month of serving as the newly appointed Federal Reserve Chairman, testified before the House Financial Services Committee. Congressman Bernie Sanders asked Mr. Bernanke if Congress should raise the Federal Minimum Wage... "so that every worker in America who works 40 hours in a week escapes poverty?"

Mr. Bernanke responded: "I'm going to be an economist and give you the one hand, the other hand. On the minimum wage, it is actually a very controversial issue among economists. Clearly if you raise the minimum wage then those workers who retain their jobs will get higher income, and therefore it helps them. The concerns that some economists have raised about the minimum wage are first, is it as well targeted as it should be? This is, how much of the increase is going to teenage children of suburban families, for example? And, secondly, does it have any employment effects? That is, do higher wages lower employment of low-wage workers?" Mr. Bernanke then definitively declared, "My response is that I think it doesn't lower employment."[52]

According to authors Robert Pollin and Stephanie Luce, following a minimum wage increase, we may see unemployment numbers rise. *However,* they focus our attention on the fact that, many low-income people that are out of the labor market and who have stopped looking for work, tend to re-enter the job search market following a minimum wage increase. In so doing, the unemployment numbers seem to swell, giving the impression that there is an increase in the number of unemployed when in reality, they are just returning to the "offical" ranks of the unemployed job seekers where their numbers are again counted.[53]

Outsourcing

If we raise wages, will the low wage jobs become more vulnerable to being outsourced to countries where the labor is cheaper. The shocking common sense reality of it is that service jobs cannot be, nor will they be, outsourced. Minimum wage jobs are service jobs required to support the local community. While so many other blue and white-collar jobs can and are vulnerable to outsourcing, low wage jobs will remain in this country. Someone must stand in that cafeteria line and prepare and serve the food. Someone has to be present to wash the windows. Someone has to be here to pick up the toilet brush to clean urinals. Ditch digging is local. Laying rebar on a construction site is local. Selling retail and flipping burgers are all local. These jobs cannot be outsourced to India or China. Remember that, unlike in the past, when minimum wage jobs were stepping-stones to the next better paying jobs, people now are remaining in these low wage jobs for ten years and longer.[54]

As Professor Pollin and Dr. Luce pointed out, we have a "minimum wage family" in this country. If people are going to remain in these minimum wage jobs for an extended period of time, and these jobs cannot be outsourced, then indeed we must ensure that every eligible minimum wage worker is being paid a Universal Living Wage.

Inflation

One of the great fears about increasing the FMW is that it will cause the price of everything to go up. The reality of it is that wages are just one of many economic factors that create the cost of an item. Manufacturing, transportation, equipment, rent, warehousing, advertising, business location, income demographics of the community, employee recruitment, training expenses and wages all add together to create the cost of an item. The cost of goods does not automatically have to rise just because one small portion of their make-up increases. An example of the non-inflationary relationship between wages and the cost of goods can be found in the 1996 survey report entitled, *Think Again: A Wage and Price Survey of Denver Area Fast Food Restaurants*. This survey focused on four national fast food chains: Arby's, Burger King, McDonald's and Taco Bell. All are major employers of entry level, low-wage workers. It was concluded that higher prices did not necessarily accompany higher wages.

In fact: "Survey results indicated that higher starting salaries are coupled with only slightly higher, identical, and in many cases lower prices than those in stores that paid a lower starting wage."

For example, the lowest paid Arby's employees were found at a franchise charging the second highest price for a meal. Conversely, a Taco Bell store paying $1.50 per hour above other restaurants for starting wages simultaneously had the lowest food prices among the twelve other Taco Bell restaurants surveyed.

Overall, the study clearly showed that just because wages rise, there is not and does not have to be a corresponding increase in prices. It would appear that the rise in pricing is more a question of what the market will bear, what the consumer will tolerate.

This is not to say that there will not be economic pressures of an inflationary nature. We are talking about, in some cases, substantial increases to the current minimum wage to meet the bare minimum amount necessary to afford basic food, clothing, and shelter. Large employers of minimum wage workers may need to realize a little less profit. Similarly, small employers will need to learn to grow at a much more reasonable rate. While, at the same time, increased demand for goods will protect business' bottom line from being negatively affected by wage increases.

Let the "Free Economy" be Free

Over and over again, a select few businesses repeat: *There should be a free economy…let the free economy decide the wage rate.*

I am more than a little bit concerned about a "free economy" that, for the most part, is based on the taxpayer subsidizing business with six subsidies: Food Stamps, TANF (Temporary Aid to Needy Families), the HUD Section 8 Housing Subsidy, the Earned Income Tax Credit, General Assistance and Tips. Patrons of many businesses are expected to bring the minimum wage of $2.13 per hour up to $7.25 per hour by paying tips in the restaurant industry. Count them…as many as six subsidies. These are all subsidies that the taxpayer and patrons are expected to pay because business has not been asked to value its workers on the same level as it values the other components of doing business.

Why don't we respect worker value? Today, business watches from the sidelines or lobbies the Federal Government to set a FMW below that minimum amount necessary to afford the most basic level of housing. Until 2009, Congress had not raised the minimum wage since 1997, and business continued to hide behind Congress and state that $5.15 per hour was all they were required to pay.[55]

Between 1997 and the ten years that followed without a minimum wage increase, there were dramatic changes in the market place. There had been both the high tech boom…and the bust. Housing costs skyrocketed in our urban centers and continued to climb. Congress had abandoned both the business community and low wage workers by not making an adjustment until 2009. The earning power of the minimum wage worker had dropped to its lowest level since 1962.

Without Congressional guidance on the FMW, the market had been very *free*— free falling that is. Many employers having felt the pressures of market forces responded by paying $6.00 or even $7.00 an hour to minimum wage workers. However, this occurred in cities where minimum life sustaining costs were double that which has been established by our own government standards.[56]

Nevertheless, employers did not respond appropriately. They did not say to their employee, "Gee, Sally, are you able to pay all of your bills? Are you stealing to get by, Sam? Are you doubled up with strangers, Margaret? Are you selling drugs to make ends meet?"

No, that did not occur. For the most part, without the appropriate guidance from Congress, business failed its employees and, as a result, left itself in a destabilized condition. As a result, business continues to face exorbitant retraining costs and a failure rate at unacceptable levels.

We live in a consumer driven society. Everyone is exposed to the televised version of the number of cars, resort homes and sail boats that the successful are expected to own. We have come to believe that if we open a business and employ people, all of the successful trappings of business should instantly be ours. Perhaps, we will have to learn that it is not all instant success. Operating a small business or a non-profit business is hard work. We are suggesting that the 64% failure rate of all small businesses after only 4 years may often be related to the fact that we continue to create destabilized work forces by paying our workers less than the minimum amount needed to afford the necessities of life. If we are to have a more stable business community, if more businesses are to succeed, if our full time minimum wage workers are to sustain themselves and stay off the dole, then we as a society will need to roll our sleeves up just a little higher, businesses will need to become fully engaged community partners, and we, as consumers, will need to pay a little fairer share.

The Effect of the ULW on Housing

The ULW Ten Year Plan supports the Bringing America Home Act, an umbrella bill that calls for National Health Care, the National Affordable Housing Trust Fund and Livable Incomes, which include the ULW for people who are *able* to work. We also call for fixing the Supplemental Security Income program and other supports for people who are *unable* to work. We recognize that the federal government is not likely to provide a *Livable Income* standard for people who *are not* working before it creates a *Living Wage* standard for people who *are* working. The soundness of our logic seems to be reflected in the national endorsement by the Spina Bifida Association of America. From our perspective, the FMW is their glass ceiling. As a society, we must raise the economic floor of the minimum wage workers to a level that allows them to afford basic rental housing, and then we can argue from a moral perspective that those persons on fixed incomes should also be supported with income that allows them to afford and maintain housing without risk of becoming homeless. Why the distinction? Passage of the Universal Living Wage returns to the employer full responsibility for paying workers a *fair wage for a fair day's work*. On the other hand, stipends and supports place the responsibility, both moral and economic, fully on the shoulders of the American tax payer (as it should). We may have to lead and show the way before we as a society fulfill our obligations to our fellow human beings.

The Universal Living Wage Formula

The Universal Living Wage Formula is a simple, three-pronged formula.

✓ Work a 40 hour week

✓ Spend no more than 30% of one's income on housing.

✓ Index the minimum wage to the local cost of housing.

Let us take a brief look at each of these prongs that make up the concepts behind the mathematical formula.

Work a 40 Hour Week

First, we are talking about wages and the standard government work week (40 hours). While we speak in terms of being able to afford housing on a monthly basis, it is important to understand that just as the FMW is an *hourly wage*, the ULW would also be an hourly wage. What we are saying is that if one puts 40 units of work wage together, four times a month (4 weeks in a month), that wage would be sufficient for a person to afford basic rental housing no matter where that person works throughout the United States. This may require that a part time worker of 20 hours per week secure a second part time job of an additional 20 hours to accumulate 40 units of work, etc.

Spend No More Than 30% of One's Income on Housing

The United States Department of Housing and Urban Development, HUD, is a Department of the U.S. Government that deals with housing issues. It was established in the 1970s. It uses this 30% standard as a guideline in creating its Section 8 Housing Voucher Program.[57]

Additionally, America's banking institutions use the same guideline. If you were to apply to purchase a home, and the bank determined that in so doing you would be spending more than 30% of your monthly household budget on your mortgage payment, they would not assign you a note and give you a mortgage. They have similarly determined that the 30% standard is most appropriate for determining a reasonable margin of financial safety.

Index The Minimum Wage To The Local Cost Of Housing

The U.S. Federal Government established the Federal Poverty Guideline as a poverty standard and currently uses food costs as the basis for it. Food, however, is a flexible commodity. Housing is not, making housing or the lack of it, the true target/need required to attack poverty.

The housing that we are referring to is the most basic rental housing available. Again, we are suggesting a minimum wage that would enable an individual to rent an *efficiency* apartment. An efficiency apartment is one step below a one-bedroom apartment. In an efficiency apartment, you would find a single room that might allow for a "Murphy" foldout bed or a couch and serve as the kitchen, living room, and bedroom. You might find space for a hot plate, and you would share a bathroom down the hall. This is the sparsest of conditions.

HUD has a voucher rental program where it subsidizes landlords. This is called the HUD Section 8 Voucher Rental Program.[58] Allow me to explain the program. Suppose a one-bedroom apartment rents for $600.00 in your area. However, suppose people in your area needing a one-bedroom apartment cannot afford to pay more than $400.00. The federal government steps in and provides a $200.00 housing voucher that the tenant passes through to the landlord. This is a win-win situation for both the landlord and the tenant. However, the taxpayer is required to pick up the tab.

In order for the federal government to determine what value to attach to the voucher, it has designed a program called the HUD Fair Market Rents, FMRs, where it goes around the country and determines what one would need to pay to rent an efficiency, one bedroom, two bedroom, three bedroom, and four bedroom apartments in any particular area.[59] HUD does this by using a sophisticated formula which helps them review these amounts yearly *although it does not necessarily make annual adjustments*. There is also a two-year time delay before factoring in new housing starts in the equation. HUD Fair Market Rent Areas are approximately the size of counties and are often exactly that, counties.

FMR Standard

FMRs are gross rent estimates; they include shelter rent and the cost of utilities, except telephone. HUD sets FMRs to assure that a sufficient supply of rental housing is available to program participants. To accomplish this objective, FMRs must be both high enough to permit a selection of units and neighborhoods and low enough to serve as many families as possible. The level at which FMRs are set is expressed as a percentile point within the rent distribution of standard quality rental housing units. As of April 2010, the current definition used is the 40th or 50th percent of standard quality rental housing units rent. These percentiles are drawn from the distribution of rents of units which are occupied by recent movers (renter households who moved into their unit within the past 15 months). Newly built units less than two-years-old are excluded, and adjustments have been made to correct for the below market rents of public housing units included in the data base.

By combining these three existing government guidelines: 1. work 40 hours in a week; 2. spend no more than 30% of one's income on housing; 3. index the minimum to the local cost of housing, we create a mathematical formula, which ensures that if a person works a 40-hour week, their earnings would be enough for them to afford basic rental housing wherever that work is done throughout the United States.

We have stated that we want a full time worker to be able to afford basic rental housing. This will position him/her so that they can then pursue either additional education or the American Dream or both.

One Size Does Not Fit All

In advocating for fixing the Federal Minimum Wage, there are those that would use the existing methodology of selecting a *single wage amount* for the entire country. For example, some have suggested a $10.00 per hour wage for the entire country. To select such a wage would be inappropriately excessive and, therefore, damaging to business and yet insufficient at the same time. When looking at the HUD Section 8 figures, we see that efficiency apartments in New York City cost approximately $846.00 per month. Under the ULW formula, we can see that one would need to earn a wage of $16.27 to rent this efficiency apartment. At the same time, using the same HUD formula and calculations, we see that in Mansfield, Ohio efficiency apartments rent for $395.00 per month and would require a wage of only $7.60 per hour.

So, if we had selected the single national wage amount of $10.00 per hour, we would not have gotten one minimum wage worker off the streets of New York City. At the same time, we would have destroyed small businesses in Mansfield, Ohio with $10.00 per hour wages when people only need $7.60 per hour to be housed, fed and clothed. One size does not fit all. This formula ensures that wages relate to the need to afford basic rental housing where that work is done…no more…no less.

In part, it may have been the cost of this housing differential that added to Congress's inability to increase the FMW between 1997 and 2007. Even a modest increase would be inappropriately high in much of rural America.

Established Practice

The U.S. Military takes local housing costs into account when establishing pay rates. The U.S. government uses what it calls the Base Allowance for Housing (BAH) to provide uniformed service members accurate and equitable housing compensation based on housing costs in local civilian housing markets when government quarters are not provided. The total BAH is based on *geographic duty location*, pay grade, and dependency status.

On January 1, 1998, the Defense Finance and Accounting System introduced BAH to replace the Variable Housing Allowance (VHA) and Basic Allowance for Quarters (BAQ) programs because "the old VHA/BAQ housing allowance system was unable to keep up with rising housing costs," and members were being forced to pay higher out-of-pocket costs than originally intended. With BAH, pay increases are indexed to housing cost growth instead of pay raises generally, thus protecting members from any further erosion of housing benefits over time.

The BAH is calculated by "computing…local price data of rentals, average utilities and insurance."[60]

Local Wage Versus State Wage

Similarly, we suggest that it is appropriate to use rental calculations relative to local housing costs in areas about the size of counties. As stated, the federal government refers to these as HUD Fair Market Rent Areas. In the 1990s when we entered the high tech boom, the entire country did not benefit from the success. However, many urban areas did. Financial success hit many of our urban centers, and housing costs soared. In the urban centers like Austin, Texas, an efficiency apartment rents for $688.00 according to HUD. This requires a living wage of $13.23. At the same time, in cities unaffected by high-tech growth such as in Abilene, Texas, it would cost only $485.00 per month to rent the same apartment requiring a wage of only $9.35 per hour. *Therefore, it can readily be seen that even within one state there is a dramatic difference in rental costs, resulting in the need for greatly varied and customized wages.* In this fashion, we have gotten the worker the very base amount necessary to survive without unduly or unfairly impacting business. Not damaging business interests is critical to the success of economic adjustment.

National Formula Versus Local Initiatives

There are well over 100 local living wage campaigns at this point. Several have been successful at increasing the minimum wage (130 ordinances passed as of 2007, according to the Brennan Center for Justice), but what about the scores of communities that cannot spearhead campaigns to fight economic forces that stand in opposition? What about America's rural communities? Do these workers not also deserve a roof over their heads? Most local living wage campaigns target and positively affect city workers, county workers and sometimes those that contract with them. However, if we doubled, no tripled, or even quadrupled, all of the workers affected under these campaigns, we would not see income equity reached in 2000 years. Even in Louisiana where several thousand workers may be affected, the numbers pale in comparison to the need. In fact, there are 10.1 million minimum wage workers nationwide. When you factor in that according to the National Coalition for the Homeless there are 3.5 million people experiencing homelessness, we conservatively estimate there to be *over* 10 million minimum wage workers. This jives with the 2000 Census. By employing the Universal Living Wage formula, we can begin to move all of these workers along a wage continuum that approaches self-reliance.

Additionally, we see local initiatives as being vulnerable to attacks and repeal. For example, in 1996, the Houston, Texas, Living Wage effort to raise the minimum wage to $6.50 per hour was stopped cold in the last week of the campaign. Moneyed interests poured over 1 million dollars into creating misinformation and then handily defeated the initiative.

With that said, there are serious concerns in the business community about local living wage campaigns. It has been suggested that local campaigns that draw circles around geographic areas are potentially damaging to small businesses. In fact, this was the basis of resistance to a living wage initiative in San Antonio, Texas, where it was feared that large business could and would pull up stakes and relocate just outside of the newly proposed wage boundary or that businesses would be drawn away from the region. The President of the San Antonio Restaurant Association was quoted as saying, "We need to work with businesses to get businesses in San Antonio. Let us say for instance that Houston does not have a living wage and San

216

Antonio does, and the PGA (Professional Golf Association) says, 'I can go to Houston and get these incentives to come, and I'm not forced to pay this living wage.' So what is going to happen? Where are they going to go? They are going to go to Houston. On the other hand, the Federal Minimum Wage establishes a balance. It is all industries. It is nationwide. So there's a balance . . ."[61] What this business leader is trying to say is that he can deal with a level playing field where all wages are raised relative to their local economies. What he sees as untenable is a situation where a local/isolated wage increase allows a business to simply cross the line and operate at an unfair advantage.

In 2003, other efforts were thwarted. In Suffolk, New York, a legislative victory was reversed after only four months. Even the Louisiana initiative came under extreme legal attack and serious efforts to repeal it. The Brennan Center for Justice represented folks involved in living wage campaigns. They reported a case, "New Orleans Campaign for a Living Wage v. City of New Orleans, 02-CD-0995" that made it to the Louisiana State Supreme court in 2002. In that case the present wage law, the uniform application of the FMW, was upheld. Continuing in this constricted, localized fashion will result in decades of anguished struggle with only mixed results.

With annual homeless memorials being held in cities all across America, we feel that time is of the essence. We see that our minimum wage workers are being tossed into the streets. We recognize that we must quickly end their homelessness and prevent others from joining them. As a result, we believe that, more important than using living wages as an organizing tool, we are charged with a moral imperative to end the condition of homelessness now. We believe that, in the final analysis, a strong single federal law is the answer to ensuring continuity, stability and timeliness.

Finally, there have been successful efforts to create state laws that "prevent exceeding the federal minimum wage in private and/or public contracts." Thus far, at least ten states have enacted preemption statues in recent years to ban local minimum wage laws: Louisiana, Arizona, Colorado, Florida, Georgia, Missouri, South Carolina, Oregon, Utah and Texas. Oregon and Florida have passed legislation to increase their minimum wage while both still have laws that prohibit "political subdivisions" from passing wage related laws. Therefore, if for no other reasons than fairness, equity and creating a level playing field for businesses, we must fix the minimum wage at the federal level. We must remember that the Federal Minimum Wage was created through the Fair Labor Standards Act, and enacted by *both* halves of Congress in 1938.[62] We must now make sure that it continues to reflect a uniform national standard.

ULW Effect on Business and Tax Payers

Wherever there are workers and employers, there exists a symbiotic relationship, which is bordered by a delicate framework. The employer needs the employee for their labor and the employee needs to make at least a minimal living through the employment. While the need is mutual, the power balance is not, and therefore, workers must hope that the employer will embrace the principals of the Universal Living Wage formula. This formula ensures that if an employee works a standard number of hours, that employee should, because of the work, be able to afford the basic life-sustaining necessities (food, clothing, shelter, and access to health care). This is consistent with the United Nation's document, the Universal Declaration of Human Rights, which identifies these life-sustaining necessities as "definitive components of the right to a minimum standard of living and dignity for every (nation) state."

Living Wages Are Good For Business

When workers make more money, they also have more money to spend. In fact, minimum wage workers have spent almost 100% of past wage increases. Increased personal income inevitably promotes commerce and stimulates local and nationwide economies. By protecting and stabilizing the very foundation of enterprises, the employees themselves, we can equally protect and stabilize businesses everywhere.

Support Trades

As stated previously, there are presently 10.1 million minimum wage workers in the United States.[63] These employees comprise our nation's pool of workers, which, for the most part, provide support for our principal businesses.

Minimum wage jobs are basically support jobs. These low paying jobs are found in businesses such as the restaurant industry, janitorial, construction labor, landscaping, laundry, etc. They support principal businesses that pay well above the minimum wage. Minimum wage businesses hire people based on the need to meet the support/service requirements of principal businesses. If Intel moves to town, it does not make the decision to do so based on minimum wage salary scales because it does not generally employ workers at that low wage level. On the other hand, when Intel builds its offices, it may contract employees such as construction laborers and landscapers who are minimum wage "support" workers. Once the facility is built, the core business will also need laundry services, restaurants, janitors, receptionists, etc.

The pool of minimum wage workers includes:

Restaurant Workers	Theater Attendants
Construction Laborers	Farm Workers
Dry Cleaner Operators	Receptionists
Janitors	Nurses Aides
Day Care Aides	Maids
Store Clerks	Poultry Processors
Hotel Workers	Child Caretakers
Bank Tellers	Home Care Aides

Garage Attendants	Landscape Workers
Retail Salespersons	Data Entry Keyers
Car Washers	Elder Care Aides
Manicurists	Security Guards
Ambulance Drivers	Infant Care Takers

The original minimum wage idea came in response to the legions of unemployed, underemployed, and low-wage workers roaming the country following the 1930s Depression just as they are today. It was decided that, in order to stimulate businesses and the economy, these workers needed to be economically stabilized. In exchange for a full day's work, a man needed to be guaranteed a wage sufficient to secure basic food, clothing, and shelter. The absence of an adequate wage resulted in high employee turnover, increased absenteeism and an increase in internal employee theft.

High Turnover and Retraining Cost Savings

Henry Ford, the father of the American automobile, was facing exorbitant retraining costs due to high employee turnover. He was being forced to replace every employee four times per year. He found that absenteeism was at an equally unacceptable level. To address this concern, he almost doubled the daily wage of his workers to $5.00/day.

The immediate result was:

1) Significant reduction in employee turnover,

2) Significant reduction in retraining costs,

3) Significant reduction in unscheduled absenteeism, and

4) Almost complete stoppage of internal theft (roughly 50% of the theft in today's retail world is committed by a business' own employees).[64]

Furthermore,

5) Ford created a true economic stimulus because his workers put discretionary funds right back into his company as purchasing consumers.[65] In other words, they bought the very cars they were making by using their new found wages.

All of these results are possible today with the adoption of the Universal Living Wage.

The ULW will dramatically reduce employee turnover. Such reduction of turnover means a significant reduction in retraining costs. This results in huge business savings.

The ULW will significantly decrease unscheduled absenteeism. Again, this will result in financial savings. This will help businesses avoid having higher salaried employees, or even the small business employers/owners avoid having to temporarily step into these low wage positions. Business can thereby stop wasting money to pay substitutes at a much higher dollar amount while they perform someone else's lower paying job leaving their own work undone.

To illustrate these effects, examine the findings of Michael Reich of the University of California. He reviewed a quality standards program initiated in April 2000 in the San Francisco International Airport. The $5.25 starting wage had been increased to $10.00 per hour plus health benefits, or to $11.25 per hour without health benefits. (The industry wage average had been $6.00 per hour.) Turnover dropped from 110% to 25%. Additionally, employers reported that skills, morale and performance improved while absenteeism and grievances dropped.[66]

The reduction of employee turnover by paying higher wages has been further demonstrated by the practices of the New York worker-owned home healthcare facility, The Cooperative Home Care Associates. They employ 450 employees and are paying $7.65/hour, which was 20% above the area average at the time. They also provide health benefits, training, and compensation for travel time for employees to see clients. As a result, they experienced a job turnover rate of less than 20% as opposed to the industry level of 60%.[67]

Further illustrating the point, Vice President Artie Nation, speaking for Mirage Hotels, credits the low turnover in his casino hotels of only 70% (as opposed to an industry high of 300%) as being the result of better wages and training.[68]

Enactment of the ULW means stabilized, loyal employees who feel respected for their work contribution. This results in substantial reduction in the number one dollar drain in the retail industry, *internal employee theft*. The two largest retail employers in the world, McDonalds and Wal-Mart, would greatly benefit from this dynamic. Employees tend not to steal from people who show them respect and support their economic needs by paying them living wages.[69]

It is also important to note that, when employers are forced to hire emergency temporary workers, they must pay for the service. Moreover, as stated, any new employee means more down time in training that new individual. The savings here are notable.

Work Opportunity Tax Credit

In an effort to help business replace employees who have left their employ and help train new replacement employees in the food industry, Congress passed legislation that provides $2,400 under a law called the Work Opportunity Tax Credit. Every time an employee leaves a business, that business can claim a retraining stipend, and this can be repeated as often as every 400 hours per replaced employee.[70]

Why would any business want to do such a thing so often as every 400 hours? Well imagine this: if an employee were to leave, the business can then go out and hire a replacement worker. Along with the new employee, the business receives a $2,400 retraining stipend to teach the new employee to operate the cash register, etc. Good deal for everyone, right? But what if the employer has transformed the cash register from a numbered instrument to a pictured instrument so that rather than having to key in data, the new employee can just push a picture of a hamburger or a picture of French fries? The employer then keeps the balance of the retraining stipend. (Sound familiar?)

In 1997, the subsidy under this program was $385 million. *Potential* savings are significant:

If you take 2,080 hours (number of hours worked in a year by an employee working 40 hours per week) and divide that by 400 hours (the minimum work hours for a single employee necessary for the business to be eligible for the subsidy) this will equal a 5.2 potential turnover rate (Henry Ford was facing a turnover rate of 4.0). In modern times, this is the same turnover rate experienced at the Greeley Beef Slaughter House supplying ConAgra.[71]

Potential benefit to businesses 5.2 x $2,400 retraining subsidy = $12,480 per employee slot per year. $12,480 x 4.5 million minimum wage workers in the fast food industry[72] equals a *Potential* savings of $56,160,000,000. Hopefully, this is an exaggerated projection, but the point is that if treating employees well and paying living wages reduces the turn-over rate, then there is significant potential savings to the American tax payer.

On the other hand, I can think of at least one major employer who uses a picture register approach and seems to make working there harder and harder as their employees close in on the 400 hour mark.

Stability Leads to Better Financing for Business and Families

New small businesses are more likely to receive bank loans and support from the Small Business Association (SBA) by being able to produce solid business plans . . . plans that show that they are providing adequate budgeting to support all aspects of their business in a sustainable fashion. This includes manufacturing, advertisement, geographic considerations, warehousing, transportation, employee training, and wages.

According to Professor Robert Pollin and Dr. Stephanie Luce in the analytical book, *The Living Wage-Building a Fair Economy:* "Family reliance on non-health related subsidies will fall by 16.1%, and the family will become dramatically more credit worthy . . . thus being able to avail themselves of more goods and services, which in turn will serve to stimulate the local economy when earning a living wage."[73] Furthermore, according to Beth Schulman, author of *The Betrayal of Work: How Low-Wage Jobs Fail 30 Million Americans and Their Families*, these minimum wage jobs are no longer the employment/economic stepping stones of the past, but rather the economic job *plateaus* at which people/families are stagnating for as many as ten years.[74]

According to the report, *The Sky Hasn't Fallen*,[75] the 1997 minimum wage raise did increase earnings of low-wage workers, and this increase primarily benefited low-income families. Additionally, according to the report, *America's Well Targeted Raise*, also released by the Economic Policy Institute, 57% of the gains from the increase went to working families in the bottom 40% of the income scale.

Tax Savings

It is our belief that if businesses paid fair, living wages then the tax burden, otherwise shouldered by tax payers, would be dramatically reduced. In other words, where businesses have fallen short in paying a wage sufficient to cover the costs of life's basic necessities, individuals are being forced to fortify their income with subsidies such as food stamps, TANF, and general assistance.

While we tend to think of minimum wage workers as individuals, we find that they are often attempting to sustain more than just themselves on the minimum wage. Economics Professor Robert Pollin, in his book, *The Living Wage/Building a Fair Economy* suggests that there exists a prototypical U.S. minimum wage family. This family comprises four people: two children, and two adults, one of whom is working at the minimum wage.[76] Because the minimum wage falls short of economic sustainability, a significant amount of government subsidies are required to support this family. With the enactment of the ULW, it is conservatively estimated that a potential tax savings of $10.7 billion per year can be realized.

A savings of 10.7 billion dollars per year in food stamp and welfare savings could be realized based on: a four-person family consisting of one minimum wage worker, one spouse, and two children.

According to the 2000 census there are: 10.1 million minimum wage workers.[77] 65% of these include one or more members of a household who work and yet must be subsidized with $1,627 per family through food stamps, EITC, and Medi Cal.[78]

10.1 mil x .65=6.565 mil

$1,627 (savings per family) x 6.565 mil

= $10,681,255,000 Potential Tax Savings w/ Passage of the ULW

This is a gross estimate and based on California state and federal subsidies in 1997. This shows that if our nation were to subsidize all four person minimum wage families where we support a full time worker as is done in California, the cost to tax payers would be $10,681,255,000. Why should we as tax payers pay this subsidy if business is the one benefitting from the employees' labor?

Self-Sufficiency Models and the Dynamic Nature of the ULW

There is an approach to economic family stability that costs out exactly how much it takes to afford basic living by calculating one light bulb and one roll of toilet paper at a time. Using this data proponents calculate how much a worker must earn per hour in order to afford their household items and expenses. This is the Self-Sufficiency Standard.

Wider Opportunities for Women, WOW, devised the Self-Sufficiency Standard. The Standard sets out precisely how much money working adults require to meet all basic needs without governmental subsidies. The Self-Sufficiency Standard assumes that all adults in the household are working and includes the costs associated with working full time. Thirty-seven states have completed calculations including Texas which was the last one tabulated in 1997.

The Universal Living Wage can be seen as an economic mechanism for *achieving* this Self-Sufficiency Standard. However, not only does the ULW establish a *pathway* to achieve the Standard, it does so through incremental steps using existing governmental guidelines.

Similar to this Standard, the ULW assumes full time workers in the calculation. Also similar to the Standard, the ULW considers local housing costs. The Standard then painstakingly looks at a plethora of other ancillary costs and takes into account that their costs inflate at various rates. The ULW also takes into account these other costs. Two-thirds of the total wage is available to meet monthly budgets beyond housing costs (rent or mortgage).

The ULW formula sets the FMW level so that individual workers will be able to afford an efficiency apartment. This will prevent economic-based homelessness for all of our nation's 10.1 million minimum wage workers. Then, because the formula is "dynamic," members within each Fair Market Rent region can (at prescribed times) vote to move the community along the formula continuum.

In other words, every full time worker is initially assured of reaching economic viability at an efficiency apartment level. Subsequently, with the ULW formula, each community (through local elections) will have the ability to extend that economic viability to the next housing level. For example, by using the same ULW formula, and then by merely substituting the HUD Fair Market Rent amount for a *one*-bedroom apartment instead of the *efficiency* apartment, we then produce a wage that provides economic viability for all workers who need a one-bedroom apartment. This would be appropriate where a community has determined that a single working mother with a child should not be allowed to remain homeless due to inadequate wages. There are federal restrictions for certain financial support programs that prevent a person with a child from living in an efficiency apartment, and for good reason.

As a practical matter, it is not recommended that the FMW exceed the amount needed to afford one person an efficiency apartment except in those cases where 51% of the registered voters in a FMR area (usually county size in nature) vote to raise the scale so that, for example, a single woman with child, working full time, is not left homeless.

The ULW formula produces similar economic levels to those of the Self-Sufficiency Standard. However, the ULW identifies the vehicle (the Federal Minimum Wage) and lays out the staged pathway (over ten years) and the methodology for actually reaching the economic viability.

Comparing Three Living Wage Standards

The Living Wage standards presented here come from three different groups among many. They attempt to arrive at a better method of measuring the basic needs of families and individuals. The comparisons were created by the Delaware Housing Coalition, DHC, 2001-2002. DHC is a stellar statewide organization researching and fighting for safe, decent, affordable housing for all people in the state of Delaware. The three standards compared include one promoted by the National Priorities Project, the Economic Policy Institute and the Universal Living Wage.

Standard 1: National Priorities Project

The National Priorities Project (NPP) developed a conservative family budget from a detailed methodology that can be obtained from NPP. The NPP Living Wage for a family of three in Delaware is $14.38 and $15.88 for a family of four.

Standard 2: Economic Policy Institute

The EPI Living Wage for Delaware is even more detailed and painstaking, with account made for variations in cost by county, as well as the age and sex of family members. The methodology was developed and applied in the publications *How Much is Enough and Hardships in America*, Economic Policy Institute. The EPI Living Wage Standard for Delaware is the highest of the three, with a Living Wage for a family of three ranging from $15.23 to $15.92. The range for a family of four goes from $17.56 to $20.74.

Standard 3: House the Homeless (Universal Living Wage Standard)

The Final Living Wage standard is based on the fair market rent (FMR). It comes up with a range from $11.71 to $13.98 in Delaware, assuming the family of four would be able to live in a two-bedroom unit. (Including the very real possibility of needing a three-bedroom unit for the family of four increased the upper range of the Living Wage to $18.96).

Conclusion of Delaware Housing Coalition's Search into the Best Formula for Determining a Living Wage[79]

"The Universal Living Wage makes a simple and powerful argument. Housing is the heaviest household burden, and the poorest people in a community should be able to make enough working full-time to afford the very cheapest housing. The advocates of a Universal Living Wage promote the passage of new federal minimum wage based on, at the very least, the efficiency apartment FMR. This argument has the appeal of being a wage that is not tied to any particular sector of the labor force (e.g. public employees) and it takes as its primary consideration: the homeless of our community." Ken Smith DHC Executive Director.

Side by side comparison of Wage Proposals in 2007

Below is a side by side comparison of three wage proposals considered and promoted in and outside of Congress in 2007. This is followed by a comparative comment by myself.

Proposal/Formula	Wage Determinant	Methodology
Kennedy bill	Minimum wage: Fixed amount set by law since 1938	Proposal was to increase the minimum wage to $7.25 over 2 years.
Kennedy/Gutierrez bill	Sets the "living wage" at the federal poverty level (FPL) for a family of four.	($17,050/year) in 2007
Universal Living Wage	Working 40 hours/week, person would spend no more than 30% of their income on housing. Indexes the wage level to the FMR levels set by HUD. Takes FMR for i.e., a one bedroom unit, divides that	Varies with each locality.

	figure by .3, multiplies it by 12, and then divides it by 2,080 to determine hourly wage.	
Clinton bill	Provides that the ongoing minimum wage rises in proportion to a percentage of Congressional raises.	Raises the current federal minimum wage by $2.00 per hour as the starting point.
Self-Sufficiency Formula	Calculates how much money working adults need to meet their basic needs (including paying taxes) without subsidies of any kind, related to family size and composition and geographic location.	Varies with each locality. Expectation is that it will be used to evaluate the impact of proposed policy changes, such as restructuring subsidy programs, changing co-payment schedules, etc.; assesses the ability of various jobs, occupations and sectors to provide self-sufficiency wages; understands the interactive effects of taxes and tax credits; targets education and job training investments, etc.

Chart prepared by Mary Ann Gleason former Executive Director of the National Coalition for the Homeless.

Note: Senator Ted Kennedy's bill picked an unrelated number out of the political air. The day it was passed, it did not get one minimum wage worker off the streets of the very city where it was passed into law.

The Senator Kennedy/ Gutierrez's bill based their wage on the Federal Poverty Guideline, which uses food as its core need and standard. I have already shown how inappropriate food is as a measure of need in this country. It is the lack of the ability *to afford basic rental housing* and other monthly expenses upon which the self-sufficiency models are based. Again, the self-sufficiency models are very thorough in identifying *"need,"* but have no *vehicle* for achieving their goal.

The Universal Living Wage, on the other hand, indexes the wage to the local cost of housing throughout the United States using existing government guidelines. It uses the existing Federal Minimum Wage as the vehicle to achieve its goal of enabling over 1,000,000 minimum wage workers to work themselves off the streets of America and prevent economic homelessness for all 10.1 million minimum wage workers.

Kenneth Wayne Staggs

Kenneth Wayne Staggs was born in Fort Worth, Texas. He just "celebrated" his fifty-fifth birthday on the 26th of May. His father died in 1980 and his mother passed in 2003 from complications of diabetes.

Kenneth's life work has been with his hands where he has taken his love for wood and hammered out a productive life of carpentry and more refined cabinet making. He has kept at this work for 35 years. At $15.00 per hour and by living in Fort Worth in Texas, he had just barely managed to hold on to a house that he had purchased in more flush years.

Today, instead of a hammer he now holds a cane in his right hand. When he sits down which is fairly often, his left pants leg rides up to expose a substantial leg brace. This is the residual of a job injury that cost him his job and his home. Living in a world that lacks paid leave, sick days, and any kind of health benefits and far too little income to create any kind of savings, Kenneth's fall from the scaffolding at J.C. Penny didn't stop until he landed with a resounding thud at the local homeless shelter.

He is forced to accept food stamps, which he receives in the amount of $200 a month. He has not yet filed a claim for workers' compensation which, of course, will be opposed. He continues to live at the homeless shelter, but has taken this opportunity to reflect on his life, and he's "found Jesus." He shares his spiritual readings with others..."nothing too serious, just enough to help them lighten their load," he says. He grins, and is not hurt in the least by his gentle look and his long, shoulder length brown hair that pleasantly frames his face and is laced with single strands of silver.

Kenneth is struggling with his physical recovery at Disability Assisted Resources (DAR). He intends to return to carpentry upon his recovery. He is hopeful that the market and the wages will pick up so he can again start all over.

Richard R. Troxell

The Universal Living Wage Campaign

The mission of House the Homeless is to end homelessness, as it exists today.

In 2008, the National Coalition for the Homeless[80] had a bill before the U.S. Congress, HR4347, calling for a three-pronged solution for ending homeless. First, was *national health care*, second prong was *affordable housing*, and the third was the creation of *livable incomes*. This third piece included providing livable incomes for the disabled homeless and for the working homeless. *The Universal Living Wage is about dealing with the financial needs of the working homeless.*

In 1997, activists in Austin, Texas set out to create a living wage campaign. After searching intently for a logical standard for setting the living wage, I devised the Housing Model referred to here as the Universal Living Wage formula. Our group of activists were bolstered by the strong ethical standard mirrored in the formula and, in 1998, traveled to Boston, Massachusetts to meet with other local living wage coalitions. Our intent was to learn from the other campaigns and to offer the housing model as a national model for a national campaign. We carried the formula as if in a small box to be guarded and as a treasure that we were going to bestow upon others. There were dozens of other living wage campaigns and there had been one municipal living wage victory at that point. However, none of them was using any kind of standard for establishing the new wage amounts they were promoting. They were using the current federal policy of picking a wage amount out of the air. The only difference was that they were picking a bigger number than the United States Congress.

We walked away from the conference undeterred, but convinced by arguments at the conference that, before we launched and won a *national campaign*, we should first make in-roads by winning small municipal campaigns.

So for years, we marked time with our local campaign in Austin. As we inched forward, we kept an eye on the other living wage campaigns around the country. I realized, however, that even with the victories won around the country there were glaring problems. First, the victories affected very few people. The affected numbers usually amounted only to a few hundred people who worked for city or county governments. These effected people already had jobs and merely received nominal wage increases. Second, even as wage increases were extended to subcontractors of the municipalities,

232

it became obvious that there was a clouded enforcement issue requiring intense and constant scrutiny. Third, local living wage victories were constantly being reversed in our court system. Fourth, we felt that people in jobs outside city or county government and those in suburban and rural America were also entitled to living wages; but at this rate, it would be literally thousands of years before income equity would reach across all of America, if then. There are now ten states that have passed laws that prevent localities (other than government entities) from establishing a local living wage above the federal minimum wage!

These combined observations reinforced my initial conclusion that we needed a national campaign. Congress had resolved this issue in 1938 with the creation of the Fair Labor Standards Act and the creation of the Federal Minimum Wage. We needed to update the mechanism designed to address this issue. By 1997, I had been elected to the Board of Directors of the National Coalition for the Homeless, NCH, and had begun working in earnest to ensure that the ULW formula and campaign be made part of their Five Year Strategic Plan. NCH having voted the ULW into the Strategic Plan in 2001, NCH also voted to pay its staff employees a Universal Living Wage!

Finally, on tax day, April 15, 2001, four years after devising the formula, we went on line with the ULW Campaign at www.UniversalLivingWage. org.

Our Secret Weapon

The first phase of the campaign was simple and straight forward. We worked to build awareness and a national/local grassroots movement. The campaign focused on four basic groups for support: Religious, Union, Non-Profit, and Business. It made sense that, because these groups were already organized and represented the target population, we start with them. Jo Ann Koepke is the secret weapon of the campaign. Every day, sitting in her wheelchair, with the use of her one good arm, she searches the internet and transcribes contact information that she then e-mails to me.

Jo Ann was born December 28, 1947, in Hoskins, Nebraska, population 200. She is quick to point out that 200 may be an inflated number but, having lived in a farm outside of town, she is not exactly sure. There were ten children in her family, five brothers and four sisters. Her beloved brother Gary passed away in 2004. She received a BA in 1984 and an M.A. from Norwich University in Women's Studies in 1990. She was able to get her master's degree as she had time on her hands — she had been relegated to her wheelchair in 1983 as a result of physical abuse in her 10-year marriage. The details remain sketchy, but she tells me it's all interrelated.

When I met Jo Ann, it was October 19, 1992. She had tracked me down from a newspaper article when she had read about Diane Briesh Malloy, the homeless woman I had found in Town Lake. Jo Ann had told me that she had deeply identified with Diane. She stated definitively, "It could have been me." The more I learned about Jo Ann the more I agreed.

At that time, Jo Ann was literally one paycheck away from being homeless. In fact, she had been homeless at two points in her life already. She was telemarketing and earning just enough to pay rent, pay her phone bill and have $30 for food — nothing else…a totally subsistence existence. Jo Ann started volunteering for House the Homeless almost immediately. It may have been that first day in fact. That is sort of her way. Once I got to know more about her, I helped her apply for disability benefits. As it turned out, the first job that she had gotten after securing her master's degree had been at a women's center. She had a good work record before she lost the job, so she qualifies for $1,584 per month, almost triple what SSI disability recipients with no work record receive — $674.00 per month.

In January 1995, Jo Ann convinced me that she/we (House the Homeless) should *adopt* a homeless child. With her guidance and oversight, we adopted Babirye Joweria and Jo Ann became a "mum" as Babirye calls her. By age 12, Babirye had lost five brothers and sisters to malaria. Her mother had been murdered in Uganda's civil war, a horror she was forced to witness. Her father had died of AIDS. She is from the African village of Buganda in Uganda.

Our connection originated through the Christian Children's Fund. At one point, we sent her money for seeds which she successfully planted and grew into mature crops. With those earnings, she bought a cow. The cow gave birth to a calf. Babirye then became the most propertied woman in her village. She created beautiful/simple batik paintings of her village and people. Jo Ann sold her art here in America with the help of a Women's Co-Op in Babirye's village. She wrote one of the eulogies for one of our Homeless Memorials, which I later shared at Citizens Communication before the Austin City Council. All of us with House the Homeless are proud parents. Her art hangs in Jo Ann's home, as well as in mine. Babirye is 27 now. She is working for an accounting company writing software. She has also adopted a daughter, Hanif.

Jo Ann has now encouraged House the Homeless to adopt our newest member, Kayaga Rebecca, who is from the same village as Babirye.

Jo Ann continues to help our ULW campaign almost daily by finding and forwarding contact names from the internet. Some days this is more difficult than others. She suffers from fibromyalgia, severe grand mal seizures, and lupus. Her companion and protector is Peace Rose, her sweet, fluffy calico cat who makes a fuss about pawing Jo Ann in special ways when Jo Ann is about to have a seizure. Jo Ann then straps on the crash helmet that I got her and braces for the impending trauma. Three or four days later, when she surfaces from the fuzzy postictal period of confusion following the seizure, she rolls her wheelchair back to her computer and sends me some more contacts. Jo Ann embodies the heart and spirit of who we are and what the campaign is all about.

Who Are We?

We are the disabled, the damaged and forgotten reaching back and out to others whose lives mirror our own. We are the survivors of "Alice's Restaurant." We are the veterans trying desperately to crawl off the battlefield. We are the unionists fighting for our fellow workers be they employed or not. We are believers who pray in a thousand different ways. We are the squeaky wheels. We are the working poor and the unemployed united for economic justice and are willing to fight our way through hell's kitchen to get a seat at the table. We are the industrious. We are willing to work until our fingernails crack and the tips of our fingers bleed. We are the believers. We believe in equality and opportunity. We believe in dignity and above all, fairness. Lastly, we are hopeful. We are hopeful that with hard, dogged determination that we can change things for the better...not just for ourselves, but for all.

James Hawkins

James Hawkins was born in Pasadena, CA in 1956. His life was in sales. He sold cars, musical instruments and, for 13 years, he sold saws for Industrial Carbide. When the market shifted, so did James. He worked as an Intake Coordinator for a Health Center and even as a short order cook. In fact, his last fulltime job in 2001 was as a short order cook for Sizzler Restaurant in San Diego, CA. At the time, he shared a single house with four other people for $1900 per month plus utilities of $240. His share of rent and utilities came to $535.00. He was not able to save any money, but he was able to make ends meet...or so he thought. In reality, each month he slowly slipped a little further behind on his bills. He began to realize that, even with sharing the house costs with three other people, he was in over his head. He had been unable to land a better paying job, so when an opportunity came to leave San Diego (a friend liquidating his business needed a driver), James took it. He ended up in Austin, Texas. He immediately got a job as a short order cook, and he and his friend shared a two-bedroom apartment for $750.00. Just as his friend's savings gave out so did James' health.

At age 46 he underwent open heart surgery. A stent was put in to try to get more blood to his heart. Having worked hard his whole life, James became despondent as the lack of oxygen to his heart rendered him weaker and weaker. Unfortunately, the operation was far from successful. Apparently, the stent was put in the wrong place, and additional corrective surgery cannot be performed as the situation has been described as inoperable. James was found to be presumptively disabled and received his first monthly check of $674.00. With the employment portion of his life truncated, James' despondency is verging on panic as he realizes that there is no way he can be sheltered and feed himself in Austin, Texas for the paltry sum of $674.00.

Supporters of the ULW

Most nights, we produce a mailing to 35 of the potential contacts that Jo Ann has gathered. We introduce them to the ULW, send them a list of others who have signed in support, and provide a blank endorsement for them to sign and return to us. The rate of return is 1 in 35. As of today, 1,706 businesses, unions, non-profits, and faith-based organizations have returned signed endorsements. This means we have sent out more than 59,000 personalized letters. This has resulted in organizational endorsements in every state in the Union including Alaska, Hawaii, Washington DC and Puerto Rico. With endorsements like Education Austin, a teachers' union of 5,000 members in Texas, IBEW all across America, Local 1000 of the Service Employees International Union, SEIU in California and its 10,000 members, the Communication Workers of America, CWA with 650,000 members, we now boast that there are millions of registered voters endorsing the campaign.

Campaign Kits

When organizations express interest in the campaign with their endorsement, we ask if they would like a "Campaign Kit" to advance the cause. We raise the funds to send a kit that typically has within it:

✓ Cover letter explaining the kit.

✓ Leaflet that we call the National "Bullet Page" that states the goals and benefits of the initiative.

✓ "Bullet Page" in Spanish.

✓ Skit that two people can perform either on radio or during Citizens' Communication at local city council meetings.

✓ Prepared radio announcement that is to be adjusted to the local area presenting it.

✓ Suggested Press Release.

✓ Editorial that can be adjusted to each locale.

✓ Petition so individuals can endorse the campaign. This is used in tabling activities.

✓ Suggested "Union Letter" that can go out to local unions in an effort to interest them in the campaign.

✓ Sample Public Service Announcement.

✓ 2 sample Congressional Leader Letters.

✓ Copy of the Endorsement for new organizations to sign.

✓ The most recent endorsement pages identifying all businesses, unions, non- profits, and faith-based groups that have endorsed the campaign. (This is listed by state throughout the U.S.)

✓ Suggested "Next Steps" paper that helps the local campaign get started.

✓ 20 bumper stickers.

✓ 20 red and white ULW flash signs.

✓ 5 business cards.

✓ 20 ULW buttons to use when on delegations.

✓ 40-100 small handouts prepared by the CWA identifying goals and benefits of the ULW (known as "push cards").

✓ A six foot banner (upon request).

✓ 5 Universal Living Wage pens.

There are now 88 different cities that have ULW warriors possessing campaign kits. The campaign continues to grow.

SEVEN:

WHERE DO WE GO FROM HERE?

National Days of Action

Tax Day

On Tax Day, April 15th, Americans line up, sometimes for miles, with our car windows rolled down and wait anxiously to hand our tax returns to a man or woman in an orange vest holding a reinforced, wire rimmed, white plastic, portable U.S. Postal mailbox. TV cameras roll for the 5 o'clock and the 10 o'clock news as the media chronicles this completely American ritual year in and year out.

The "Living Wage Warriors," members of the Universal Living Wage Campaign, are right there with their red and white flash signs, passing out leaflets and soaking up precious media coverage. Our leaflets make the point that *if all employers paid a ULW to their minimum wage workers, the need for tax subsidies such as food stamps would be greatly reduced.* In the leaflet distributed in Texas, we point to the University of Texas as an example. A number of years back, we found that UT (one of the wealthiest universities in the world) paid their support staff so little that 230 of them were being subsidized by you and me with our taxes. They had to receive food stamps to subsidize their salaries just so they could eat adequately. We believe it is a moral issue that anyone who works a forty-hour week should be paid enough to afford basic rental housing and enough to eat. In 2006, we flew banners at 86 "actions" across the nation that declared:

> Reduce Your Taxes!...
> with a
> www.UniversalLivingWage.org

We posted photos of these protests on our website. This simple action creates high visibility, is a simple, yet dynamic, event and hopefully makes a clear statement. The tax day action is also a great local organizing tool around wage issues.

Bridge the Economic Gap Day

A considerable number of people in this country struggle on a daily basis to make economic ends meet. They share a growing sense that there is a "gap" between the "haves" and the "have-nots." More and more people now recognize that this gap is increasing the ranks of homelessness. We also believe that the ULW can act as the "bridge" between employed laborers who are unionized, and unemployed minimum wage workers who are either homeless or on the verge of becoming homeless. We believe that growing recognition of this situation will help the nation move toward our goal of fixing the Federal Minimum Wage with a ULW, and simultaneously attract new workers into our unions.

The Action!

On Labor Day Plus 1 (the first day following the national holiday of rest, recognizing our nation's workers, Labor Day), we return to work, and during rush hour, gather on our nation's bridges and fly banners:

> Bridge the Economic Gap!
> with a
> www.UniversalLivingWage.org

We also fly our local union and organizational banners in support of living wages. Our website continues to display stories about the need for a ULW and the need to join with unions to create a stronger work place.

Again, this simple action exposes the issue directly to thousands of motorists at each strategically selected bridge. It also draws media attention and enables us to advance the cause of the ULW.

At Last…The Beginning!

I am writing this section of the book from Inks Lake State Park. I am here with my dog, Hummer. It is not what you think. At 120 pounds, this German Sheppard/Rottweiler mix came with his name. Apparently, he would hum as he suckled his mother. Now he strongly resembles the overgrown motor vehicle.

It is Sept 9th 2005. We have been here for three days trying to decompress from the first Universal Living Wage-National Day of Action. We stood on the bridges of America and flew the banner:

"Bridge the Economic Gap" with a www.UniversalLivingWage.org.

Our hope was to raise awareness about the campaign and draw folks to the website.

For four years, we had been "cold" writing organizations and introducing them to the Universal Living Wage and inviting them to sign an official letter of endorsement.

Three months ago, we appealed to those endorsing entities and asked them to send us money. That's right…raw hard cash. Nickels, pennies, and dimes — we would take anything! We priced out our banners and found a vendor willing to do them for $135.00 each. We ordered thirty banners. I was fairly sure that a good response from our endorsers might bring a call for between 16 and 23 banners. I sent out an initial letter and a "call for leadership." I explained that Bridge the Economic Gap Day would be a great local/national organizing event that would require very little work on their part. We would send our endorsers and participants blank press releases in which they could tout their own organizations and their own local living wage issues. On top of that, we offered to send them the banner for free, and encouraged them to fly their own organizational banner. This was a great deal!

We split up calling the endorsement list among four of us with some folks at the National Coalition for the Homeless calling our union supporters. The response was strong and immediate. *In just two weeks*, we had 27 "Bridge Captains" identified. These leaders were willing to receive the banner and act as the point person on the bridge. We decided to first line up as many bridge captains as possible and then re-contact them later to work out details and bridge logistics.

At the end of three weeks, we had 39 Bridge Captains and commitments in 32 states! It seemed remotely possible that the impossible could be attained. My friend, Michael Stoops, national organizer and once acting Executive Director of NCH, said that we would need more than just folks on just 20 bridges to get media attention. I believed him. But it occurred to me that the hook might be having a Bridge Action *on at least one bridge in every state in America.* I could hardly allow myself to imagine such a thing, let alone voice my hopes. The date of the event was the day after Labor Day — "Labor Day Plus 1" — September 6, 2005. On this day, everyone returns to work after a three-day weekend and the highways are full. It was now early August and time was running out. I made a tactical decision. As soon as we got one commitment in a state, we would stop calling organizations in that state and move on to the next state. If there was time (and energy) left, we would later go back to the top of the list and call for second and third Bridge Captains in each state.

How does the expression go? "Nothing succeeds like success"…but it damn sure can break the bank. Being successful was going to cost a lot of money. If the campaign's moral premise had not resonated with J.D. Moore, our banner vendor, we would still be talking about what might have been. We placed a second order for banners. When we finally placed the third order, J.D. was selling banners to us at $110.00 each! These double thick vinyl 4 ft. by 10 ft. banners included red, white, and black lettering with our logo, double stitched with 10 grommets. Wow! J.D. made the price low enough for us to succeed.

Another bright point in the financial component came from my good neighbor Tom Holmes. I road my bicycle into his driveway following a good hard ride. Hard bike riding gave me time to focus on the campaign. Tom was unloading his SUV. We exchanged pleasantries. Tommie asked, "How's it going?" Tom is a 69-year-old West Texas "boy" born and raised. He was a geologist and a Texas oilman in days gone by.

When a Texan asks, "How's it going?" It is like a southern gal saying, "Ya'll come by and visit us." Only a Yankee would actually drop in. Having been mostly raised in the East; when Tom asked, "How's it going?" I did not hesitate to tell him. In fact, I've been corralling him in his driveway for sixteen years. His views have afforded me invaluable guidance in terms of how to couch arguments to reach a variety of perspectives.

Just watching his face scrunch up often told me what I needed to know. At this particular moment, with no real purpose of thought, I began by lamenting the downside of success. I explained my efforts to get banners out into the nation and how I was pleasantly surprised that there had been a widespread call from organizations wanting to participate and requesting banners. I explained that our coffers were all but depleted, and yet we still needed to purchase boxes, postage, and hopefully more banners. But my focus this day was on the need to afford a national newswire press release.

I had already sent the "fill in the blank" media releases for organizations to adapt and get the word out locally, but I was convinced that in order for news assignment editors to become focused on our event, we would need to approach them top-down as well as bottom-up. A national news blast would cost close to $600.00. In spite of having already spent close to $20,000 on this initiative, it was painfully evident that a mere $600.00 was now beyond our reach.

Through years of discussion, Tom and I came to a couple of points of mutual understanding. The first being that neither one of us wanted to see homeless people living in our parks and sleeping in the doorways of our businesses. The second major point of agreement was that rather than further burden taxpayers with the problem, those that could, should work themselves off the streets. Finally, we both felt that *somebody* needed to take action and do *something*. I guess Tom saw me as somebody who was trying to do something. He briefly excused himself saying he was going to get his checkbook, and saying, "I guess I can help you with a little something." He returned with a check. I felt pleased, genuinely pleased, and of course validated. Tom and I had come a long way together. Humbled, I thanked him profusely. Tom said, "Who knows, I might get on one of those bridges." I slipped the check into my pocket and said goodnight. I felt good.

It was not until the next morning when I pulled out the check and prepared to endorse it when I saw the amount. The check was for $1,000.00!

The Bridge Draws Near

In the meantime, the phone calling had become more intense. Every time one of us got a commitment, we would call all the other volunteers so that they could stop their calling in that state and move on. The line-up of callers was small. It consisted of Diane, Monica (Jillessie), Anna, Kelly, Jo Ann, and me. I kept the callers to just a handful of folks because this after all was our database! From the very beginning, we had promised our endorsers that we would neither buy, sell, trade, nor give away their personal information. I trusted those few good folks to ensure that we honored that commitment.

Anna with NCH was a student. However, she was attending Harvard, so it was understood that she was bright. In spite of the fact that most of our union endorsers were on August vacation, she pulled in 16 commitments.

Diane, was/is on disability with a brain injury, but she works very hard at volunteering. Unfortunately, she became sick during this period and her work became very uneven. But, determined as always, she added a great deal to this push. Jo Ann was having problems. She was experiencing an upsurge in the frequency of her grand mal seizures. Jo Ann was also suffering longer postictal periods. Following a seizure her thinking would remain muddled and confused for several days. I could only encourage her to rest during these times.

Jillessie, or "Monica" as she identified herself to the folks she called, was/is a doctor who felt she needed social service experience, so she came to volunteer with us. She had worked with us previously during the 6th printing of our Plastic Pocket Guide, an eight paneled, fold down laminated and scored social service reference card. It took serious "people skills" to work her way through each of 150 social service organizations, speak to each executive director, get them to agree to participate and reduce their many services down to seven to nine words. She also proved to be a dogged advocate on the phone for Bridge the Economic Gap Day.

In the third week of August, we boasted 64 commitments and had 44 states covered. Our 1300 + endorsements reflected an uneven disbursement of endorsements from across the country, but we had at least five endorsements in every state. (We would have had six, but Nebraska proved to be difficult, so we remained at five.) Of course, in some states such as California and Texas we had over 100 endorsing organizations each.

Due to my full time job, my calling was limited to two fifteen minute breaks and my lunch hour. However, at the end of my regular work day, I was able to catch Central Standard Time endorsers still in their offices along with the entire west coast.

By the last week in August, we had 79 bridge actions and 47 states. We were only short Nebraska, Delaware, and Hawaii. Otherwise, we were extremely close to reaching our national dream of one bridge in every state. We were all feeling an increasing building pressure to reach this goal. My Aunt Sylvia lives in Nebraska and is a retired employee of the Columbian Mission. I resisted the urge to make the contact as they had not previously endorsed us, but I sure thought about it.

In Hawaii, I was negotiating with a representative of the AFL-CIO, but he did not have the final authority to join the "Action." However, he was to be on a three-day trip with the man who did. The stress factor was high, as this "wait and see" period would stretch over the weekend with only one week before the National Day of Action remaining.

The prospects in Delaware were very bleak with a bullpen of only six organizations. I called my friend and former NCH member, Ken Smith. He is now the Director of the Delaware Housing Coalition. For almost three years, we had been discussing a possible endorsement. His Board of Directors, several of whom were bankers, had consistently resisted the endorsement. Ken, whom I have only met over the telephone, is quite bright. He is obviously a hard worker who examines all the facts and works to present them evenly. He is both patient and thorough. As seen earlier in the book, he had displayed an in-depth comparison of two "self-sufficiency" models and the Universal Living Wage on their Coalition website. The analysis showed that, while all three wage models reflected competitive wage values, only the Universal Living Wage had a "vehicle" to actually reach the intended economic goals. Nonetheless, the coalition had resisted endorsing the ULW until that Friday afternoon on August 25, 2005. Yes! Later that afternoon, Nebraska got on board, and a Health Clinic in Hawaii made a commitment to commandeer a bridge. We had done it! We had a Bridge Captain in all 50 states! *Sweet Honey in the Rock!!*

Of course, in the final week before the event, Utah and Rhode Island unraveled. My friend Noreen Snowcross, the Executive Director of the Rhode Island Coalition for the Homeless, had resigned and the program had not yet regained its sea legs. The idea of one more project seemed overwhelming to them. Many repeated calls to the acting Director, Leigh Pagnazzi, over several days finally resulted in a recommitment.

All the while, we were madly calling and e-mailing each of the Bridge Captains. We did this repeatedly seeking their bridge locations, so we could post them on the website in an effort to get them more support on their bridge. It was at this moment in my life that I understood the true meaning of the phrase, "herding cats." As dribs and drabs of information came in, we would rush it to Kathi Kimbriel — friend, author, massage therapist, and our webmaster extraordinaire. The pressure was on.

Then, in the homestretch, Jo Ann had another seizure. She was OK, but clearly, she would be out for the duration of this initiative. It was Monica's birth "week," and so she would be taking it off. Anna had gone back to Harvard, and I was trying to help arrange emergency responses to victims of Katrina, 250,000 who would end up in Texas, 22,000 of whom would make it to Austin.

The national press release went out on August 30th and we sent out our first fax to local media. In preparation of the "birth" day of the Bridge the Economic Gap Day, I had decided to have three bridges covered in

Austin. There would eventually be eight bridges covered in Texas when I revised the number in Austin to five saturating the North/South highways entering and leaving the city.

It was about this time that my friend Andrea Ball with the *Austin American Statesman* called. After four years, she was going to write a multipage expose on the campaign, the initiative, and the National Day of Action. The conversation started well enough… "I have good news… and I have bad news," she said. I sat down. The good news is "the bleeding has stopped, the baby arrived a little early (two months), and we're both OK. Without as much as a deep breath, she added, "The bad news is, I will continue to be recuperating [and this is where her voice got small] and won't be writing the story." I was shocked. My wife, fifteen years earlier had "complications" with the birth of our daughter. I will never, ever forget how that had put the entire universe in perspective for me. Simply put, I had been to Vietnam, but this terrified me. I never told Sylvia, and I had hoped I never showed it, but in that instant, all that fear came flooding back. After all, everything we do, all of it…absolutely all of it, is about family…and friends.

After Andrea had convinced me that she really was OK, which is not always so easy to tell as she wisecracks a lot, my heart sank. I knew that whoever covered the story; it would not be the same. However, she was OK and that was the important thing.

Three days before our National Day of Action, Debbie, one of our homeless gals said, "So Tuesday's the big day, huh? I guess you're scared?" "Well no, actually, I'm just excited," I said. Nevertheless, for three days I carried those words with me. What was there to be scared of? Failure? No, it was not that. Sure, I did not want failure for the guys, but *it is as much about the struggle as anything is*. Max had taught me that. Folks had already lost everything, so we may as well experience life to the fullest…then the phone call came. Rudy Anderson, with North Texas Jobs with Justice, called. The group had met. They "would not be doing the action." They were afraid. Apparently, someone had gotten hurt on a bridge action of some kind. I talked with Rudy discussing every possible safety precaution I could imagine. He went back to his people with several suggestions. The group would not budge. I told him I understood. I did actually. Debbie's words came back to haunt me for the three remaining days. For three nights in a row, I woke up sweating when in a repeated dream that one of the guys took a header off the bridge. He flew forty feet into five lanes of traffic. I continued to stress the need for safety with the Bridge Captains and advised them to select bridges with wide sidewalks, very wide sidewalks. I actually prayed that everyone would be safe. I never spoke of the dream.

September 6, 2005 — Happy Birthday!

On September 6th, the National Day of Action, we hit the bridges. We marched down the streets of Austin with 20 homeless guys carrying our banners 8 blocks to the 12th and 13th Street bridges over IH35. With our banner measuring 10 feet in length and our sidewalk periodically narrowing to as little as four feet, we kept opening and closing the banner over and over again like an accordion. We flashed our now famous red and white Universal Living Wage yard signs at every intersection showing the drivers our message, bolstering our commitment to the cause. There wasn't much foot traffic but, in as much as our path traveled past the Salvation Army, there were a few folks. Jose Segerro spoke very little English but very rapid Spanish to every Hispanic person we passed along the way. His stream of urgent, insistent Spanish words would be received with vacant blank stares as he rapidly told of our mission. Finally, some of their faces would come alive. In recognition, two of our would be advocates grunted out, "¡Huelga!" This means "strike." This was not exactly correct, but Jose would acknowledge the response with, "Si, Si" and a hearty slap on the back. Then we were one person more, our struggle was one person stronger. We felt good. We were united.

As we approached Interstate Highway 35, the ambient noise grew more intense. Of course, this meant my cell phone had to ring. It was Claire Osborne from the *Austin American Statesman*. She had been handed the story that Andrea Ball could not cover. Bad timing. I could not hear her. She had some prior knowledge of our general campaign, but very little understanding of what our Bridge the Economic Gap Day was about. Then she posed "The Question" …how much would the new wage be? I told her, "enough to ensure that a person working 40 hours in a week could afford basic food, clothing, shelter, and have access to health care wherever that work is done throughout the United States." She said, "I know, but how much?" I said it is different in every state… in every county…and this is a National Action. I could barely hear her, but she came back with, "OK, but how much? How much for Austin?" We had continued to march to our twin sets of four-lane highway and the overpass, the noise was over powering the conversation. The noise made thinking almost impossible. I was resolute, however, "Enough to afford the bare minimum necessities of life…just enough to survive." I could no longer hear her. I shouted that into the phone, said I was sorry and hung up. I wondered if I would be sorry. I hoped for the best, but I feared we would be reduced to a damning sound bite. As we mounted the overpass, we were greeted with a glorious sight…traffic that stretched north and south as far as the eye could see. It was crawling along at 10 to 15 miles per hour…a steady stream. Eight lanes of audience! We unfurled our first banner where traffic was heading from north to south. Five, 3 oz. weights at the bottom, kept the banner from flying back in our faces. We looped the ropes holding the banners around the bridge guard rails several times and held the loose ends. State law did not permit us to tie the banners to the bridge. We had also prepared 8 foot galvanized aluminum poles with drill holes and attachment wires to extend the banner above the guardrail if the police attempted to forbid us from dangling the banners over the bridge railing. When we unfurled our second banner, a roar of approval went up from our Hispanic friends. This banner displayed our message:

"Llenar el Vacio Economic" con el www.UniversalLivingWage.org.

On the black asphalt the temperature rose to well over 120 degrees. My wife Sylvia and daughter Colleen showed up with an igloo of ice and bottles of water. The guys were extremely grateful, but we cautioned them not to hold the bottled water over the bridge guardrails. We did not want any missiles rocketing down onto anyone's windshields. Suddenly, my dreams flashed back. I had a flash of vertigo as I looked at the eight lanes of traffic below. I steadied myself.

Other folks joined us from the Texas State Employees Union along with two "survivors" from Louisiana and hurricane Katrina whom I had spoken with the day before.

I then helped set up folks with banners facing south before I went two hundred yards further south to the 11th St. bridge where the whole scenario was repeated. I recharged the Bridge Captains there with the need for safety about both projectiles and crossing the overpass only at the end of the bridge.

Things started to get festive with all the honking and shouting. People really began to feel very good about themselves. They felt empowered and powerful. There were "affecting" their world. Sometimes the sheer power of 3/4 tons of steel moving through "their action" took on a role of lesser importance. The police came through. They cautioned my wife not to stop and disperse water in the middle of traffic...go figure. The officer then stopped to tell some of the guys to hold the ropes where the police had observed that they had tied it to the railing. The officer slowly drove away shaking his head and silently assuring himself that we were all miscreants.

Bam! In the middle of my interview with *Rumbo* (the Hispanic newspaper), there was a two car accident of significance at the parallel frontage road and our overpass road on the 12th Street bridge. Collectively, it all seemed like a bit too much was happening.

A "Bridge Over Troubled Waters"

After helping a disabled person exit one of the two damaged vehicles that was seeping gasoline, I headed over to MoPac. This highway with six to eight lanes is just as impressive as IH35, the one I had just left. The traffic was just as packed but moving steady at about 20 miles per hour. But, as I drove the highway toward the overpass, the feeling was much different. Strands of multi-colored balloons waved gently from each side of the banner high above us on the overpass. As people left town and headed toward the bridge, the landscape opened up the way Texas does. There were several smiling faces shining from the bridge and greeting people with long, gentle, wide sweeping waves. It was an incredibly pleasant experience. Here folks from the *Austin Advocate* (the homeless newspaper) including my friend Valerie Romness had assembled. They too had an attorney. Michelle Clark from Texas Rio Grande Legal Aid had joined them for support. As it turned out, there was no need. Their overpass itself was minimally traveled boasting very wide sidewalks and framed with a yellow striped buffer lane that further protected them from the road. They felt great. It was an excellent action. I stayed there in that oasis for only ten to fifteen minutes before I headed to our fourth bridge...the Lamar and Riverside Bridge.

Get Down!

The Lamar Street Bridge was the "party" bridge. This bridge is a pedestrian bridge that spans Town Lake and runs parallel to Lamar St. It then terminates at the juncture of Lamar and Riverside with an expansive intersection and very wide sidewalks. To this location, I had sent Saint Edwards (my alma mater) Universal Living Wage Warriors, University of

Texas School of Social Worker students, and AmeriCorps*VISTAs (on their first day). Lots of folks from the Gray Panthers, including my friend Alison Dieter, joined us, as did folks from the local NAACP. One of the additional banners that we flew here was a quote from the Reverend Dr. Martin Luther King, Jr. "There is nothing but shortsightedness to prevent us from guaranteeing a livable income for every American Family." We also flew another Hispanic Universal Living Wage banner as members of Casa Marienella joined us. There were children, laughing, singing and making their own wage chants. Members of Veterans for Peace joined us, as did regular folks just passing by. Because there was a lot of foot traffic, we gave out hundreds of "push" cards printed by the Communication Workers of America, (CWA) that extolled the goals and benefits of the campaign and outlined the Formula.

One of our two bridge captains here included Susan Blau, who heads up Saint Edwards University Universal Living Wage Warriors, whose husband, Fritz, owns and operates Motorblade Postering. As a small business, they have always supported the work of House the Homeless and the Living Wage campaign in particular.

The other bridge captain was the lovely Sara Hickman, song writer, singer, motivator, and close friend. She came with a parcel of other friends, her two children, and great enthusiasm. Collectively, they sang songs, rapped chants, and shared the moment.

Time was running out, so I raced to our fifth and last bridge where I found folks happily rolling up banners and collecting their signs. These were the young activists. The bridge captain Mary Hancock had been part of the very successful national movement to get Taco Bell to pay field workers more for picking tomatoes. Several gals from Code pink and my friend Deb Russell also joined us. They reported having a great, warm response from motorists who had waved and honked their horns in support of the ULW!

For those of us who could, we all then headed to Pease Park where our friends from Mobile Loaves and Fishes met all of our many factions from all of the bridges with open arms. We shared hot dogs, cold drinks, bridge stories, and our dreams for a kinder, gentler world where economic justice is the norm, not the exception. I closed with a few thoughts and the observation that all across the nation, folks just like us had been on bridges, sharing similar experiences, and the same dream. It felt good. It felt really good. We all felt it…hope.

From my hammock in Inks Lake, Texas, I can see Hummer out in the water harassing some ducks, the sky is turquoise blue and for the moment, all seems calm and everything seems possible.

See You On a Bridge — a Few Final Thoughts

We started with 87 commitments for bridge "actions." For one reason or another, fourteen groups were unable to get on a bridge, all told fifty-two groups were able to do an action. Forty-six requested to keep the banner for next year. Thirty-three groups committed to join us in April on Tax Day with eight more needing only to get Board approval. We recorded seventeen newspaper and magazine articles including numerous photos and one article written completely in Spanish.

Oh yes, the conversation with Claire Osborne from the Austin American Statesman resulted in no major exposé, and a misquote of the wage in Austin, but a spectacular aerial photo made up for everything. Andrea Ball's baby was born at less than two pounds. He did just fine, thank you. We, the irreverent ones, referred to him as "porky." Sylvia and Colleen were neither ticketed nor arrested for distributing water in the middle of the roadway, and no one took a "header" off a bridge...any bridge.

For our first national/grassroots Day of Action, it was a monumental success. In fact, I was astonished at how successful it was. However, we should not have been.

The signals are all there. People will continue to support this movement in ever-increasing numbers until we achieve a Universal Living Wage because it is based on a moral principle.

Further Reflections

Money makes the world go round. However, in most households, we do not discuss the family wealth, and we do not teach our children about it. When we, as a compassionate nation, rushed into Louisiana, wrapped our arms around 22,000 Katrina survivors, and brought them to Austin and Houston, TX, etc., we gave little to no thought to the economic consequences. Once here, we literally asked Louisiana folks, "Do you intend to get a job?" If the answer was, "Yes," we then gave them free housing along with other help for six months. Never once did we recognize that once they were transplanted to a different economy, the very same federal minimum wage of $5.15 per hour was no longer going to house them as it had done in Louisiana. In Austin and Houston, etc., for many of them, it was going to ensure their roles as the new homeless.

The bottom line is that it is about economics. We live in a capitalistic system. We exist by buying and selling things. Without that, you cannot exist here. If one wishes to survive, one must participate. *One must sell something.* Poor people have little to sell except drugs and each other. That is a very bleak scenario. That does not bode well for us as a nation. We must create other options. We must create opportunity.

The Universal Living Wage offers opportunity and hope. It tells me that as a worker, if I get a job, I can be totally independent. It tells me that if I work my 40 hours, I do not have to be on the dole. I do not have to stand in line waiting for a hand out that's all too meager. It tells me that wherever I travel throughout America, all I have to do to ensure a roof over my head, is to work hard and save 40 hours' worth of wage. It tells me I can get my dignity back. It tells me that I don't have to rely on local government to raise tax dollars to build a homeless shelter where somebody is telling me when to get up, what I will be eating, and when I will go to bed (without my spouse next to me).

The Universal Living Wage tells me that there is hope for confronting poverty and its economic roots. It tells me that, once this nation embraces the basic moral premise of the ULW, that there will be hope to confront poverty for minimum wage workers worldwide. As a worker, it tells me that once this nation embraces the Universal Living Wage, nations from all over the world will take specific steps to set their own standards and devise their own formulas. I have no doubt that once we embrace this moral work ethic, this component of poverty will yield.

Let's Get To Work Forum and Initiative

On May 21, 2009, with House the Homeless, Inc. in the lead, the Texas Homeless Network and the Ending Community Homelessness Organization hosted the *Let's Get to Work Forum and Initiative.* The forum, comprised of elected officials, employment and human service experts from Texas and across the U.S., discussed how other communities have attempted to develop pathways to employment and housing for persons experiencing homelessness.

The forum, sanctioned by Austin's Mayor Will Wynn and Travis County Commissioner Judge Sam Biscoe, featured a panel of local employment experts that discussed and explored the "Ready, Willing and Able" employment programs that are operating in Pennsylvania and New York. The Corpus Christi Economic Development Corporation was also invited to discuss their use of local tax revenue to award development grants to business job initiatives.

These local experts evolved into a Task Force and Implementing Committee whose focus has been to create *pathways* to exit homelessness through employment. These pathways enable individuals that are experiencing homelessness to pursue job training that results in fair wage jobs through cooperating local employers, thus creating true self-reliance for the workers.

Program participants will enter the "pathway" through existing transitional supportive housing programs or by applying to the program directly. Program funding will *match* the Federal Minimum Wage of $7.25 per hour thereby creating a living wage.

House the Homeless, Inc. and Mobile Loaves and Fishes are co-chairing the Task Force and Implementation Committee, which includes local employment and human service experts. Additional committee members include staff from the Texas Workforce Commission and Work Force Solutions among many, many others.

An Oversight Committee will monitor the implementation, operation and effectiveness of the proposed program. This modest model, involving twenty hand-selected participants, once proven to be practical and effective, will be replicated throughout the state of Texas.

Program Justification

On Tuesday August 19th, 2008, the University of Texas School of Social Work presented its preliminary findings on their "Solicitation" (panhandling) Report. They interviewed 103 individuals asking them why they were standing on our street corners and asking for money. They found that 51% of those surveyed wanted job training and 52% were looking for work and their over-riding common theme was that they were "soliciting for daily survival."

In the Unsheltered Homeless Count Survey, conducted in Austin in May 2007, over 200 respondents were interviewed. When asked as to the cause of their homelessness, 100 said it was because of being "unable to pay either their rent or mortgage." Another 118 said it was "due to unemployment."

In a third survey, this time conducted by the City of Houston Health & Human Services Department, 345 persons were interviewed. When asked their reason for their street solicitation, 250 or 72.5% stated it was to gain "income for survival." When asked if they enjoyed street solicitation 280 or 81.2% said, No."

When asked what would be required for them to stop street solicitation, 196 or 56.8% responded with "employment."

The fourth survey was conducted by House the Homeless Inc. in Austin in November 2007. 526 people experiencing homelessness were successfully interviewed. Nearly 38% said they were working on some level at the time of the interview. When asked if they would work a 40 hour week job, if they were sure it would pay them enough to afford basic food, clothing, shelter, (in other words a Living Wage), 468 or 90.7% said they would work 40 hours for a living wage.

In a subsequent survey conducted January 1, 2009 by House the Homeless, 429 people experiencing homeless were interviewed. Of those responding, (out of eleven, options), "job loss" ranked 1st at 150 and "insufficient income" ranked 2nd (unduplicated) with 94 as to the cause of their homelessness. Some might say these two causes could be combined under "insufficient income" for a total of 244 (or *over half* of those interviewed).[81]

Also in this survey, we compiled a list of 20 jobs that are being taught at the Austin Community College. We then asked, "If you could earn a living wage (enough to pay for food, clothing, shelter (including utilities) by doing one of these jobs, would you accept training? Yes—317 and No —38.

We then asked them to rank their top three employment training choices. Their response:

112-truck driver	34-small engine electrician
38- tow-truck operator	109-landscaping
64-bus driver	29-phlebotomy (draw blood)
41-small engine mechanic	61-heating and air conditioning
52-computer tech repair	36-nurses aid
25-TV/VCR/DVD repair	15-accounting
51-welder	37-administrative assistant
18-outboard motor repair	17-wedding planner
44-solar panel installer	33-upholstery
35-auto body repair	30-dental assistant

The surveys, coupled with the *Let's Get to Work Forum*, provide the justification and the framework for the creation of *pathways* to assist people experiencing homelessness to go through job training and end up in living wage jobs.

This program utilizes and involves city, state, federal, in-kind dollars and participants that include businesses, non-profits, educational, faith-based, and affected persons to improve our community in devising a replicable *Initiative*. Hopefully, this initiative will demonstrate the benefits of the ULW to the Federal Government. However, it is an *artificial* wage program and is only a signal for the Federal Government to tweak the Federal Minimum Wage and evolve it into the Universal Living Wage.

On the other hand, by continuing to increase the minimum wage by an amount less than that necessary to reach the Federal Poverty Line, we only assure minimum wage workers eternal poverty.

The choice is ours.

Let's go to work. Visit our website at www.UniversalLivingWage.com or www.UniversalLivingWage.org.

Have your organization, business, nonprofit or union endorse on line today.

See you on a Bridge!
In Unity, There is Strength
Richard

Epilogue

Now, five years after starting this book and after several hundred attempts at finding a publisher, I found Susan Bright, poet and publisher of Plain View Press. She graciously offered to publish our book declaring it to be, "too important not to publish."

I've had to bury my best dog, Hummer, and forever say goodbye to my good friend, neighbor, and west Texas sounding-board, Tomie (Tom) Holmes. Sadness is just a part of life. But if you're lucky, it ultimately yields a treasure chest of good warm memories. Christopher Standage our redheaded long time "No Camping" champion, was found dead in his trailer on land that had simply been given to him. He had just returned from his annual pilgrimage to his beloved Kerrville Folk Festival when in the biggest heat wave in recent Texas history, he simply laid down and moved on. He was a good soldier of peace.

Our beloved people's champion, Senator Paul Wellstone who was the first national legislator to agree to carry the ULW bill, died in an airplane crash before the bill became a reality. I vividly remember standing in his office listening to the political support he would require in order for him to carry the bill, when my I noticed a photo in his office. He was in Sudan, Africa. I too had been there. I particularly remember the city of Shendi where my thermometer had long ceased functioning at 120 degrees yet locals sat around drinking hot tea in a very casual manner while my friend Eric and I could barely move. When I inquired about the photo, I learned that the Senator had helped orchestrate an air-lift of the Falashas, the Black Jews, from Sudan to Israel. As it turned out, the air-lift had followed an overland trek of these survivors of the Diaspora, from the Simian Mountains in Ethiopia where my best friend Eric and I had first traveled in search of their very existence back in 1982. Small world.

I was sure that such an incredible connection/coincidence meant that somehow our paths were destined to have crossed again around the effort to pass the Universal Living Wage in Congress. Not true. Within a year, he was killed in a small plane crash... our dream yet unrealized. This was a huge loss of a man who was an American moral compass.

Congresswoman Julia Carson out of Illinois, then stepped up to the plate and introduced the National Coalition for the Homeless, Bring America Home Act intended to end homelessness in America and that called for a "Sense of Congress" about a Universal Living Wage. She later died as well.

Today, Congressman Keith Ellison from Minnesota has come forward and agreed to carry the Bring America Home Act but with a full Universal Living Wage bill as an intact component this time.

And of course, Senator Edward Kennedy has also passed on. He was lovingly known as "the lion" from when his voice would roar in the United States Senate calling for justice and the raising of the FMW. He was responsible for many increases of the FMW throughout the years. Similarly, he was responsible for the three step increases that moved us, after a long 10 years, from $5.15/hour to $5.85/hour on July 24, 2007, then to $6.55/hour on July 24, 2008, and finally to $7.25/hour on July 24, 2009 where it rests today with the workers still in poverty. A great man but a failed approach.

President Barack Obama

One a Final note. On March 2nd, 2010, while addressing an audience in Savannah Georgia, President Barrack Obama called for living wage jobs! In so doing, he became the first sitting president in history to do so. He was quoted in the New York Times as saying,

"When it comes to domestic policy, I have no more important job as President than seeing to it that every American who wants to work and is able to work, can find a job that pays a living wage."

The President went on to say, "That was my focus last year and that is my focus this year, to lay a foundation for economic growth that will create jobs."[82]

Before you could say "Holy Wage Batman!", House the Homeless had a banner made, and I gathered 50+ of my closest friends for a photo op. We saw this as the *bat signal* with the president of the United States saying, Living Wage Jobs, who's with me? We took our photo with a wide angle lens and our usual share of problems and made a 20" by 30" post card. We sent the post card with a letter that simply read:

Dear President Obama,

We are citizens of Austin, Texas, comprised of people who are homeless, formerly homeless and others who are fully engaged in fighting to end homelessness. We read of your speech on March 2, 2010 as reported in the New York Times when you basically said that everyone should have a job that pays a living wage.

Banner sign to President Obama. Photo by Alan Pogue.

We are at-the-ready to assist you in whatever it takes to make living wage jobs a reality in America. We await your directive. Thank you for your leadership.

> *In Unity, There is Strength*
> *Richard R. Troxell*
> *President, House the Homeless*

How cool is that? We're *an army in waiting*! Tell us what to do and we'll do it. And of course, because it was a post card, we scrawled across it, "Wish You Were Here!"

While we struggle to correct the wage issue at the *Federal level*, people in our municipalities and across our nation are *desperate* for economic relief. Aside from the 100 plus local living wage campaigns, organizations like House the Homeless, are now promoting *living wage jobs programs* all across America, and, oh yes, we continue to wage battle against *Economic Injustice!*

Appendix:

National and International Endorsers of
The Universal Living Wage Campaign

International
Communications Workers Of America, International
Nonviolence International
Centre for Social Justice- Ontario, Canada
The Big Issue in Scotland- United Kingdom

National
American Federation of Teachers AFT
CCW/AFTEF Center for the Child care Workforce/ The AFTE Foundation
Center for Community Change
Center for Economic and Policy Research
Central Conference of American Rabbis
Church Women United
Citizens Policies Institute
Citizens Policy Institute
Coalition on Human Needs
Communication Workers of America, National
Community Family Life Services, Inc.
Community for Creative Non-Violence (CCNV)
Community IT Innovators, Inc.
Co-op America
Friends of the Earth
Gray Panthers
Green Party of the United States
Homeless Children's Playtime Project
Housing Assistance Council
IBEW National
Jobs with Justice
Labor Council for Latin America
NAACP
National Alliance of HUD Tenants
National Association of Social Workers
National Coalition for Asian Pacific American Community Development
National Coalition for the Homeless
National Community Reinvestment Coalition
National Council for Urban Peace and Justice
National Council of Churches/ Economic/Social/Justice Program
National Health Care
National Law Center on Homelessness & Poverty
National Low Income Housing Coalition
National Network for Children
National Network for Youth
National Organization for Women (NOW)

National Priorities Project
National Rural Housing Coalition
Network: A National Catholic Social Justice Lobby
North American Street Newspaper Association
Pax Christi
Physicians for Social Responsibility
Presbyterian Church (USA)
Religious/Labor Coalition
SEIU
Spina Bifida Assoc. of America
The Coalition on Human Needs
The Salvation Army-WDC
Union of American Hebrew Congregations
United Methodist Church Board of Church and Society
Universalist Service Committee
Washington DC Bureau of the Rainbow/PUSH Coalition
Washington Legal Clinic for the Homeless
Women of Reform Judaism

State Endorsesrs of theUniversal Living Wage

Alaska
Alaska Mental Health Consumer Web Inc.
American Friends Service Committee
Anchorage Council of Building & Construction Trades
Beans Café Jim
Catholic Social Services
IUOE Local 302
Laborers International Union of North American Local #942
MSMiaN & Sons
Sheet Metal Workers Union Local #23
The Alaska State Coalition on Housing and Homelessness
The Brother Francis Shelter
YWMCA of Anchorage
Msmian & Sons

Alabama
Alabama Appleseed Center for Law & Justice Inc.
Alabama Arise
Alabama Coalition Against Hunger
Birmingham Health Care
Christian Service Mission
CWA Local 3902
Franklin Primary Health Center, Inc.
Greater Birmingham Ministries
Habitat for Humanity Baldwin
Housing First
Metropolitan Birmingham Services for the Homeless

Montgomery Community Action, Inc.
New Futures
Safeplace, Inc.
UAW Local 1155-Birmingham
UAW Local 1413
UBCJA/SCIW #2401

Arkansas
Arkansas Foodbank Network
Central Arkansas Building & Construction Trades
Central Arkansas Labor Council
Central Arkansas Library System
City Life News & Publishing Co.
College Station CDC
I.B.E.W. Local Union 295
IBEW Local Union 700
Moody Chapel - African/Methodist/Episcopal Church
Painters Local Union #424
Plumbers and Pipefitters Local 155
The Arkansas Hunger Coalition
The Kings Outreach
Watershed Human Development Ctr.

Arizona
AFSC Arizona Area Program
Arizona Coalition to End Homelessness
Arizona Homeless Center
Border Links
City Life News and Publishing Company
Communication Workers & American Local 7050
Community Housing Partnership
Community Information and Referral
CWA AFL-CIO Arizona State Council Ronda Graff
Habitat for Humanity Valley of the Sun
IATSE Local 875
IBEW Local Union 518
Interfaith Coalition for the Homeless, Inc.
Ken Cole Sustainable Living Center   Bed Ridden
Northern Arizona Veterans for Peace "Bud Day" Chapter 108
People Experiencing Homelessness
Phoenix Consortium for the Homeless
PPEP Microbusiness & Housing Dev. Corp.
Prescott Area Habitat for Humanity
Primavera Foundation
Professional Musicians of Arizona, AFM #586
Project Aware Men's Shelter
Save the Family Foundation of AZ
Southwest Center for Economic Integrity

Spirit of Service, Inc.
The Brewster Center Domestic Violence Services, Inc.
Unite Here 631
WHEAT

California
AFSC Farm Labor/Project Cam Pesino
AFSC Pann Valley Institute
AFSC San Diego
AFSC Stockton, CA
Amalgamated Transit Union 1225
American Apparel
BeeBright
Beyond Shelter
Building & Construction Trades Council, San Mateo County
Building Opportunities for Self-Sufficiency
C.E.O. Women
California Affordable Housing Law Project
CareLink-CMC(HCH)
Carpenters Local 1789
Church of Theater Arts
Coalition for Humane Immigration Rights of L.A.
Coalition of California Welfare Rights Organizations, Inc
Community Homeless Alliance Ministry
Community Technology Alliance
Contra Costa Homeless Ombudsperson
CorpWatch
CWA 9510
CWA Local 9503
Drawbridge
Drywall-Lathers Local 9083
Ecumenical Ministry in the Haight Ashbury
Fair Housing Council of San Diego
Global Exchange
Green Building Pages
Greg Braendel at Career Dreams Inc.
Gubb & Barshay LLP
Haight Ashbury Clinic
Half Moon Bay Mutual Benefit Center
Health Care for the Homeless
Home and Community, Inc.
Homeless Health Care Los Angeles
Housing America
Housing California
Housing Rights Committee of San Francisco
IAM Local 1173
IATSE #122
IATSE Local B-192
IBEW Local Union 11

IBEW 551
IBEW Local 100
IBEW Local 18
IBEW Local 234
IBEW Local 595
IBEW Local 428
Imperial County Building Trades Council
International Alliance of Stage Employees (IATSE) Local 905
Interfaith Committee for Worker Justice
International Brotherhood of Electrical Workers 617
Kasper Organics
Kate's Caring Gifts
Kern Inyo & Mono Building Trades
Korean Immigrant Workers Advocates Southern CA
L.U.L.A.C. 147
Laborers Local Union 886
Lamp Community
Lighthouse Church- Fort Bragg
Living Wage Coalition of Sonoma County
Los Amigos of Orange Co.
Los Angeles Alliance for a New Economy
Los Angeles Coalition to End Hunger & Homelessness
Los Angeles Youth Network
Mazon: A Jewish Response to Hunger
Monterey Bay Central Labor Council, AFL-CIO
Moonridge Realty
Motion Picture Machine Operators, IATSE Local 169
Ms. Lefkowitz's Jewish Law II Class Period B6
NABET-CWA Local 53 (59053)
New Native, Inc.
North Bay Labor Council, AFL-CIO
Northeast Valley Health Corp
OneDance: The People's Summit
OPEIU Local #3
Open Circle
Orange County Community Housing Corporation
Orange County Interfaith Coalition for Social Justice
Organic Attire
Partners in Urban Transformation
Peoples Self-Help Housing Corporation
Plumbers, Steamfitters & Refrigeration Fitters UA Local Union 393
Project Censored
Religious Witness with Homeless People
Resources for Independent Living
Rock the Vote
Roofers and Waterproofers Local #95
Sacramento Homeless Organizing Committee
Sacramento Housing Alliance
Sacramento Mutual Housing Association

San Diego Coalition for Homeless
San Francisco Hillel
San Francisco League of Urban Gardeners
San Mateo County Central Labor Council
Santa Cruz County Coalition for a Living Wage
Seavile Employees International Union Local 434B
SEIU 434B
SEIU- Local 121 RN
SEIU Local 347
Service Center for Independent Living
Shelter for Homeless Women and Children
Shelter, Inc. of Contra Costa County
Sign Display Local #510 AFL-CIO
Sonoma, Mendocino, and Lake Counties Building and Construction Trades Council
Teamsters Local 601
TEAMX, Inc./SWEATX
Tenant Associations Coalition of San Francisco
The Affordable Housing Network of Santa Clara County, CA
The Civil Service Div. of CSEA Local 1000 SEIU AFL-CIO, CLC (California State Employees Association
The Coalition on Homelessness, SF
The East Oakland CDC
The East Oakland CDC
The Higgins Foundation
The Housing Rights Committee of SF
The Southern California Association of Non-Profit Housing
The Write Way
Tides Foundation
U.S. Mexico Border Program
UFCW Local 1167
UFCW Local 1428
UFCW Local 1442
UFCW Local 1442
UFCW Local 770
Unite Here Local 11
United Brotherhood of Carpenters Local #743
United Farm Workers
United Here! Local 681
United Taxicab Workers
Veterans For Peace Chapter 71, Sonoma County
Veterans Speakers Alliance/VFP Chapter 69
Voice4Change
Western Regional Advocacy Project (WRAP)
Women For Orange County
Women of Color Resource Center
www.GrassrootsHost.com
Catholic Charities of San Jose
New Society Publishers

Colorado
Access Housing
American Friends Service Committee- Colorado
Authentic Alternatives, Inc.
Colorado Coalition for the Homeless
Colorado College Community Kitchen
Colorado Fiscal Policy Institute
Colorado Jobs With Justice
Colorado Yurt Company
CWA District 7
CWA District 8
Denver Homeless Voice
Denver Urban Ministries
Earthlinks
Epilogue Book Company
Global Girlfriend
I.B.E.W. Local 68
IBEW 667
IBEW Local 969
Men's Health at Denver Health Medical
Mercy Housing, Inc
Samaritan House
Sheet Metal Workers I.A. Local #9
St. Francis Center
Stout Street Clinic
Suicide Risk Response Services, Prof. LLC
The Cofax Community Network
The Greeley Transitional House, Inc.
The Uptown Partnership, Inc.
The Women's Crisis Center/ Violence Prevention Institute
Urban Peak
Warren Village
Wyncia Scrap Bags

Connecticut
AFSCME
AFT Local 1547
American Federation of Musicians Local 400
American Federation of Teachers Local 5049
Connecticut AFL-CIO
CSEA, SEIU Local 2001
CT Coalition to End Homelessness
CT Health Care Associates, NUHHCE, AISME
Flavours of Life, Ltd.
Greater Hartford Labor Council
IATSE Local 74
IATSE Local 84
Mutual Housing Assoc/S. Central
Roofers Local 9

District of Columbia
American Federation of Teachers AFT
Capital Area Food Bank
CCW/AFTEF Center for the Child care Workforce/ The AFTE Foundation
Center for Community Change
Center for Economic and Policy Research
Central Conference of American Rabbis
Church Women United
Citizens Policies Institute
Citizens Policy Institute
Communication Workers of America, National
Community Family Life Services
Community Family Life Services, Inc.
Community for Creative Non-Violence (CCNV)
Community IT Innovators, Inc.
Co-op America
CWA Local 2336
First Trinity Lutheran Church
Friends of the Earth
Homeless Children's Playtime Project
Housing Assistance Council
Jobs with Justice
Labor Council for Latin America
National Association of Social Workers
National Coalition for Asian Pacific American Community Development
National Coalition for the Homeless
National Community Reinvestment Coalition
National Council of Churches/ Economic/Social/Justice Program
National Law Center on Homelessness & Poverty
National Network for Children
National Network for Youth
National Organization for Women (NOW)
National Rural Housing Coalition
Network: A National Catholic Social Justice Lobby
Nonviolence International
Pax Christi
Physicians for Social Responsibility
Presbyterian Church (USA)
SEIU
Spina Bifida Assoc. of America
The Capital Area Foodbank
The Coalition on Human Needs
The Salvation Army-WDC
Union of American Hebrew Congregations
United Methodist Church Board of Church and Society
Washington DC Bureau of the Rainbow/PUSH Coalition
Washington Legal Clinic for the Homeless
NAACP

Delaware
Better Homes of Seaford, Inc.
Delaware Housing Coalition
Delaware Statewide Association of Tenants
Delaware State Homeless Coalition
Green Party of Delaware
IBEW Local 1238
Saint Paul Church

Florida
Alachva County Coalition for the Homeless and Hungry, Inc.
All Faiths Food Bank
American Federation of Musicians Local 427-721
American Veteran Newspaper, Inc.
Artisans' World Marketplace
Ascension Social Concerns
Benedict Haven
Better Way of Miami, Inc.
Brevard Federation of Teachers
Broward Coalition for the Homeless
Camillos Health Concern, Inc.
Central Florida Voters Congress
Charlotte County Homeless Coalition
Coalition for Family Safety
Coalition for the Homeless of Paseo County
Coalition for the Hungry and Homeless of Brevard County
Coalition to End Homelessness
Community Coalition for a Living Wage
Community Coalition on Homelessness
Community Empowerment Services
Connections Job Development Corp
CWA Local 3120
David J. Murphy, RHCF, Inc.
David Lawrence Center
Democratic Club of Greater Fort Myers, Florida
Diocese of Saint Augustine
Domestic Abuse Shelter Homes, Inc.
Florida Acorn
Florida Coalition for the Homeless
Florida Housing Coalition
Florida Impact
Florida Keys Outreach Coalition Inc.
Florida State Lawn Care
Friends Meeting of Ocala (Quakers)
Goldenrule Housing & CDC, Inc.
Good Samaritan Health Centers, Inc.
Habitat for Humanity of Key West & Lower Fl. Keys, Inc.
Habitat for Humanity of South Brevard
His Place Ministries

Homeless Coalition of Hillsborough Co.
Homeless Coalition of Palm Beach County, Inc.
Homeless News Wire
Homeless Voice/ Florida
Hunger and Homeless of Citrus County, Inc.
IATSE Local 631
IBEW 222
IBEW Local 728
International Association of Machinists & Aerospace Workers, Local Lodge 2777
KissMyLayOff.com
Local 780, I.A.T.S.E.
Miami Coalition for the Homeless
Mid-Florida Homeless Coalition
Naranja Princeton CDC
North Broward Hospital District Health Care for the Homeless
Office of Justice and Peace, Diocese of St. Augustine
Pizzazz MEPG
Plumbers and Pipefitters Local 592
Polk County Opportunity Council
Recovery of Choice
Safety Net Foundation, Inc.
South Florida Jobs with Justice
St. Joseph St. Vincent dePaul Society
St. Mathew House
St. Vincent dePaul
Street Smarts Coalition, Inc.
Suncoast Professional Firefighters & Paramedics Local 2546
Terra Sancta Press, Inc.
The Human Services Coalition of Dade County
The Salvation Army-Broward County
The Shelter
The South Florida Community Development Coalition
The Southwest Florida Coalition for the Homeless
The Tallahassee Coalition for the Homeless
The Tallehassee-Leon Shelter, Inc.
The Transition House, Inc.
United Community Dev. Inc.
United Community Development, Inc.
Urban University Seminary
Yettie's Outreach & Dev. Coop

Georgia
Agnus Scott College- Human Services Committee
Atlanta Jobs with Justice
Atlanta Labor Council
Atlanta Union Mission
Atlanta Women's Foundation
Berry College Young Democrats

Children's Restoration Network
Columbus Housing Initiative
Covenant House
Empty the Shelter
Georgia Citizens Coalition on Hunger
Georgia Coalition to End Homelessness, Inc.
Georgia Employee Federation
Georgia Human Rights Union
Georgia Law Center for the Homeless
Georgia Rural Urban Summit
Habitat for Humanity of Forsyth Co.
Heavenly Bound Homeless Coalition
IATSE Local 824
J.D. and Associates
Jerusalem House Inc.
Living Room
Macon Outreach at Mulberry
Mercy Housing South East
Metro Atlanta Task Force for the Homeless
Metropolitan Columbus Task Force for the Homeless
People, Inc.
Rachel's Daughters, Inc. of Georgia State Univ.
Residential Connection, Inc.
Roofers Local 136
South Central Georgia Task Force for the Homeless
The Redistribution Alternative
The Young Adult Guidance Center, Inc.
Tyler Place CDC of Atlanta
Valdosta Project Change
Women's Economic Development
Women's Policy Group

Hawaii
AFL-CIO
East Hawaii Coalition for the Homeless
Hawaii State AFL-CIO
Hawaii State Coalition Against Domestic Violence
Laborers Union, Local 368
Musicians' Association of Hawaii
Pacific Islanders United Methodist Church
Street Beat
Waikiki Health Center
Waimaha/ Sunflower Residents Association, Inc.

Iowa
Affordable Housing and Homeless Partnership of Polk County
Broadlawns Medical Center
Churches United Shelter

Community Action Agency of Siouxland
Ctrl Iowa Bldg & Const Trades Council   Local 33
CWA AFL-CIO Local 2093
I.B.E.W. Local 1362
I.B.E.W. Local 1379
IAMAW Local 1728
Iowa City Federation of Labor
Iowa Coalition Against Domestic Violence
Iowa Coalition for Housing and Homelessness
Iowa Community Action Association
Justice Committee, Sisters of Mercy, Cedar Rapids
Operating Engineer Local 234
Roofers Local no. 142
Service Employees International Union Local 199
YWCA of Fort Dodge

Idaho
Helping Hand, Inc.
ID Community Action Network
Idaho Women's Network
Saint Vincent DePaul
Silver Valley People's Action Coalition
The Idaho Food Bank
Woodworkers W364 IAMAW
Your Family, Friends, and Neighbors, Inc.
Interfaith Alliance of Idaho

Illinois
Housing Action IL
Automobile Mechanics Local 701
BCMW Community Services
Bethel New Life
Breakthrough Urban Ministries
Center for Women in Transition
Chiapas Media Project
Chicago Coalition for the Homeless
Chicago Health Outreach
Chicago Jobs With Justice
Chicago Uptown Ministry
Chicago Alliance to End Homelessness
Deborah's Place
DuPage County Green Party
Health Reach
Helping Hands of Springfield
Illinois Hunger Coalition
Illinois Maternal and Child Health Coalition
Interfaith Housing Center
Jewish Council on Urban Affairs
Kushtush Organic

La Casa Norte
Local Union 705
Metropolitan Housing Development Corporation
National Student Campaign Against Hunger & Homelessness
Nonviolent Choice Directory
Peoria Federation of Musicians, Local 26
Protestants for the Common Good
Roofers Local #32
Saint Vincent De Paul
San Jose Obrero Mission
SEIU Local 668
Sisters of Mercy, Chicago Regional
South Side Mission
St. James Church
SWAN, Inc.
The Chicago Alliance to End Homelessness
The Pollution Solution
Tri-County Musician's Union Local 88
UAW Local 2488
Unitarian Universalists for Social Justice
United Steelworkers of America 745
Will Feed Community Org.

Indiana
AFSCME Local 3733
Brothers' Keeper, Inc.
Central Indiana Jobs with Justice
Community Faith & Labor Coalition
CWA Local 4700
CWA Local 4900
Family and Children's Services, Inc
Haven House Services
Horizon House
I.B.E.W. Local 2249
IATSE #836
IBEW Local Union # 153
Indiana Coalition on Housing and Homeless Issues
International Union of BAC Local 4 IN/KY
King Park Area Development Corp
North Central Indiana AFL-CIO Central Labor Council
One Paycheck Away
Roofers Local no. 119
Saint Joseph Valley Project/Jobs with Justice
Scott County Welfare to Work Task Force
Southern Indiana Housing Initiative
St. Joseph Valley Project- Jobs with Justice
Stepping Stones for Veterans, Inc.
UAW Local 685
Vincent House, Inc.

Wabash Valley Central Labor Council
YWCA of St. Joseph County

Kansas
Central & Western KS BCTC
Homestead Affordable Housing
IBEW Local 661
Inter-Faith Ministries Wichita
Kansas Action Network
Kansas AFL-CIO
Kansas Communication Workers of America, CWA
Kansas National Organization for Women
Kansas NOW
Labor Federation
National Action Network KS Chapter
New Beginnings
Plumbers & Pipefitters Local Union 441
SEIU Local 513
The Lawrence Coalition of Homeless concerns
Tri-County Labor Council of Eastern Kansas AFL-CIO
United Steelworkers Local 307

Kentucky
Ashland-Tomcats.com
Central Leadership Team of The Sisters of Charity of Nazareth
Coalition for the Homeless
CWA Local 3310
Daniel Pitino Shelter
FAHE Inc.
Home Alternatives
Homeless and Housing Coalition of Kentucky
Kentucky Communication Workers of America
Kentucky Jobs with Justice
Laborers Local 576
Laborers Union 1392
Laborers Local 576
Lexington Living Wage Campaign
Louisville Professional Fire Fighters Local 345
Senator Ernesto Scorsone
The Northern Kentucky Housing and Homeless Coalition
The Partnership Center, Ltd.
Utility Workers union of America, Local 600
St John Center for Homeless Men

Louisiana
A Different Approach Handicraft, Inc.
Common Ground/Relief
I CAN! America
I CAN! America, LLC

IATSE # 298
IBEW Local 861
IBEW Local Union 130
National Policy & Advisory Council on Homelessness
Operation Enduring Independence
Iron Workers Local 710
SMILE Community Action Agency
Smile Community Action Agency, Inc.
Unity for the Homeless

Massachusetts
Arise for Social Justice
Berkshire County Committee on Homelessness
BHCHP Consumer Advisory Board
Boston Area Rape Crisis Center
Boston Health Care for the Homeless
Campaign on Contingent Work (CCW)
Carpenters Local Union 40
Center for Social Policy
Central Mass. Chapter of Physicians Financial Responsibility
Central Massachusetts Housing Alliance
Citizens' Housing & Planning Association, Inc. CHAPA
Community Action Committee Cape Cod and Islands
Community Change, Inc.
Community Teamwork, Inc.
Cottonfield, LLC
Center for Social Policy/Give Us Your Poor
Cutting EJ
CWA Local 1365
Eastern Massachusetts Jobs with Justice
First Church Shelter
Greater Boston Food Bank, Inc.
Hispanic Community Church
Homeless Empowerment Project
Homes for Families
Jewish Community Housing for the Elderly of Amherst
Jewish Community Housing for the Elderly, Boston
Lower Cape Cod CDC
Lynn Housing Authority
MA Association of Human Rights Relations Commission
MA Career Development Institute
MA Affordable Housing Alliance
MA Coalition for the Homeless
MA Alliance of HUD Tenants
Mia Pruett Gardening
NAFFE
National Consumer Advisory Board
National Alliance of HUD Tenants
North American Alliance for Fair Employment

North Star Asset Management
Our Bodies Ourselves
Project Hope
R Solutions at Work
R Solutions at Work, Inc.
Samaritan Inn Shelter
Somerville Homeless Coalition, Inc
Suki, Inc.
Teamsters Local Union # 404
The Center for Popular Economics
The Food Bank of Western Massachusetts
The North American Alliance for Fair Employment
The Unitarian Universalist Funding Program
The Unitarian Universalist Service Committee
Tri City Housing Task force of Homeless families
UFCW Local 1445
Unitarian Universalist Service Committee
United for a Fair Economy
United for a Fair Economy and Responsible Wealth
Urban Edge
Women of Means, Inc.

Maryland
AFT Maryland
Alliance Inc.
Andrene Spence Act Database
Aurora Energy, LLC
Baltimore County Coalition for the Homeless
Baltimore City Health Care for the Homeless
Calvert
CEASMC
Center for Poverty Solutions
Children's Health Outreach Project
Community Action
CWA Local 2105
District Council #51
Gimme Shelter Productions
Health Care for the Homeless
Homeless Persons Representation Project, Inc.
Local Union 1501 IBEW, AFL-CIO, CFL
Mayan Hands
Patuxent Friends Meeting
Peace Action
Project PLASE, Inc.
Public Justice Center
SEIU District 1199E-DC
Sisters of Mercy Institute Justice Team
Sisters of Mercy, Baltimore
South Baltimore Homeless Shelter, Inc.

Sprinkler Fitters Local Union 669
The Art Therapy Studio
The Coalition for Homeless Children and Families
The Development Training Institute
UBC Local 340
United Ministries, Inc.
UPAYM Crafts
Wild Boar Creek, LLC
Women's Housing Coalition

Maine
City of Portland Social Services
Hospitality House Inc.
IBEW Local 1768
Kids Can Make a Difference
OHI
Portland Organizing to Win Economic Rights (POWER)
Radio Free Maine
Rumford Group Homes, Inc.
Teamsters Local 340
The Michalowski Group
The Preble Street Resource Center Consumer Advocacy Project
United Association Local 716
York Cumberland Housing

Michigan
A.B. Heller, inc.
Affordable Living Services
All Saints Episcopal Church
Altrusa Teen SHARE
Battle Creek Homeless Council
Clothing Matters
Consumer Advocacy Project
Detroit Air Transport 141
Guild/Sugar Law Center
Homeless Action Network of Detroit
IBEW Local 219
IBEW Local 252
IBEW Local 557
IBEW Local 665
IBEW Local 979
IBEW Local Union #131
International Brotherhood of Electrical Workers, Local Union 498
Michigan Coalition Against Homelessness
Our Brother's Keeper
People's Progressive Network of Washenaw County
RESULTS Kalamazoo
Safe Horizons
Southeast Michigan Jobs with Justice

Southwestern Michigan CLC
The Homeless Action Network of Detroit
UAW Local 600
UAW Local 652
Underground Railroad
Universal Living Systems
Vista Center of Flint

Minnesota
Beth's Buttons for Social Change
BiCounty CAP, Inc.
Carpenters Local #851
Carver Committee for Emergency & Transitional Housing
Central Lutheran Church
Central MN Housing Partnership
Churches United for the Homeless
Community Home Ownership, Inc.
Community Psychologists of Minnesota
Congregations Concerned for Child Advocacy Network
Division of Indian Work
Duluth AFL-CIO Central Labor Body
Elim Transitional Housing, Inc.
ELLM
Fathers and Children Together
F-M Dorothy Day House of Hospitality, Inc.
Houston Co. Women's Resources
Humphrey Job Corp Center
I.A.T.S.E. Local 13 Minneapolis/St. Paul
I.B.E.W. Local Union 294
Integrated Community Solutions
Intercongregation Communities Assoc.
KOOTASCA Community Action
Lakes & Prairies Community Action Partnership
Lutheran Social Services
Metropolitan Interfaith Council on Affordable Housing
Millwright Local 548
Minneapolis Pipefitters Local 539
Minnesota Coalition for the Homeless
Minnesota Housing Partnership
Minnesota Librarians for Social Responsibility
Mission Lodge
New Foundations, Inc.
New Pathways, Inc.
Northern Cradle (FKA April's Shelter)
Partners for Affordable Housing
People Escaping Poverty Project
People Serving People, Inc.
Perspectives, Inc.
Peta Wakan Tipi Fire Lodge

Prism-People responding in Social Ministry
Prodigal House
R S Eden
Ramsey Action Program Inc.
Range Transitional Housing, Inc.
Refugee Children, Inc.
Residents for Affordable Housing
RISE, Inc.
Saint Stephen's Human Services
Sheet Metal Workers #10, Duluth Superior & Ivon Range area
Shelter House, Inc.
Simpson Housing Services
St. Anne's Place
St. Paul Area Council of Churches
St. Stephen's Housing
St. Stephen's Shelter
The Gail Eckhaff Transitional House
The Housing Coalition of St. Cloud Area
The Mid-Minnesota Women's Center
Theresa Living Center
Tri-County Action Program, Inc.
Tri-Valley Opportunities Council
Urban Coalition of Saint Paul
West Central MN Continuum of Care Regional Task Force
Women of Nations
Women's Advocate's Inc.
Women's Rural Advocacy Programs, Inc.
Women's Shelter, Inc.
YMCA
Prism-People Responding in Social Ministry
Residents for Affordable Housing
RS Eden
Southwest Minnesota Housing Partnership

Missouri
Adequate Housing For Missourians
Arkansas Communication Workers of America, CWA
Christian Times
Community Alternatives
Community Assistance Council
Fathers' Support Center, St. Louis
Feed My People, Inc.
Housing Comes First
IBEW Local 695
Missouri Association for Social Welfare (MASW)
Missouri Communication Workers of America
National Association for Human Rights
Sanctuary In The Ordinary
Social Concerns Office-Diocese of Jefferson City

St. Louis B & CTC
St. Louis Jobs with Justice
Susan Ray Consulting
The Missouri Coalition for the Homeless
Unitarian Universalist Social Action
Veterans for Peace, Inc. (National)
What's Up Magazine

Mississippi
ECDI Hope
IBEW Local 1028
Mississippi United Against Homelessness
MS Workers' Center for Human Rights
Multi-County Community Service
Quitman County Dev. Org. Inc.
Quitman Tri-County Federal Credit Union
Southeaster Development Opportunities
Yazoo County Fair/Civil League

Montana
AFM Local 498- Musicians of Western Montana
American Friend Service Committee Cooperative Health Center
Cooperative Health Center
Indian Peoples Action
Jeannette Raukin Peace Center
L.U. 768 IBEW
Montana Coalition Against Domestic and Sexual Violence
Montana Community Labor Alliance/Jobs With Justice
Montana Human Rights Network
Plumbers and Pipefitters Local 459
Raise Montana
The Nurturing Center
The Samaritan House, Inc.

North Carolina
Alamanca County Inter Agency Council of Homeless Assistance
Ashville-Buncombe Homeless Coalition
Beloved Community Center
Bladen Brunswick Columbus CED
Catherine's House
Center for Participatory Change
Christian Social Ministries Commission Epis. Diocese of NC
Community Care Development Corporation
Culture's Edge
CWA Local 3640
East Carolina Community Development Inc.
Faith Action International House
Forests of the World, LLC
Inter-Faith Council for Social Service

Inter-Faith Food Shelter
Nehemiah Community Development Corp. of NC
New Directions for Downtown, Inc.
News…from our Shoes
North Carolina Council of Churches
North Carolina Housing Coalition
Northwest Continuum of Care
River City Community Development Corporation
Second Harvest Food Bank
Sociologists without Borders
St. Francis UMC
The Advocacy for the Poor, Inc.
The Change
The Homeless Coalition
Triangle Jobs with Justice
Urban Ministries of Wake County
Vance, Granville, Warrenton, Franklin Continuum of Care
VOA-Willow Pond, Inc.
YWCA Central Carolinas
YWCA of Greensboro

North Dakota
Affordable Housing Development Inc.
Dakota Center for Independent Living
First Presbyterian Church, Grand Forks
Joannis HCH Clinic
Lakes & Prairies Community Action Partnership
Lutheran Social Services of ND
Self-Sufficiency Program
YWCA Clay County Transitional Housing
YWCA Shelter (Unique Boutique)

Nebraska
Community Humanitarian Resource Center
High Plains CDC
Holy Name Housing Corp
IBEW 1597
Nebraska Housing Developers Association
SE NE Coalition for the Homeless-Catholic Services

New Hampshire
AFSC-NH
AHEAD, Inc.
Christopher P. Williams Architects
Concord Firefighters IAFF Local 1045
IATSE Local #195 NH/Lowell MA
Monadnook Area Trans Shelter
Monadrock Area Housing Coalition SW Community Services
Nashua Soup Kitchen & Shelter, Inc.

New Hampshire Catholic Charities
New Hampshire Homeless
Seacoast Living Wage Campaign
The New Hampshire Coalition to End Homelessness
WREN

New Jersey
Alliance Against Homelessness of Bergen County, Inc.
Apostles' House
Brunswick and Raritan Housing Corporation
Camden County Council on Economic Opportunity, Inc.
Carpenters Local Union 1305
Civic League of Greater New Brunswick
CWA Local 1022
CWA Local 1023
Department of Health and Human Services of the City of Trenton, NJ
East Brunswick Community Housing Corp.
East Trenton Initiative
Elizabeth Coalition to House the Homeless
Eva's Kitchen & Sheltering Program, Inc.
Fair Housing Council of Northern New Jersey
Faith, Bricks & Mortar, Inc.
Family Promise
FISH Hospitality Program, Inc.
Home Front
Housing & Community Development Network of New Jersey
Interfaith Council
Interreligious Fellowship for the Homeless
Mi Casa
Middlesex County Comprehensive Emergency Assistance System Committee
Middlesex Interfaith Partners with the Homeless
Monmouth County Coalition for the Homeless
New Jersey Association on Correction
NJ Inst. For Social Justice
North Camden Land Trust
North Hudson Community Action Corp.
Princeton Community Housing
Project Live, Inc.
The Crisis Ministry of Princeton and Trenton
The York Street Project
Triple C. Housing, Inc.
Volunteers of America Delaware Valley
Women Rising, Inc.

New Mexico
American Friends Service Committee AFCA
Clothes Helping Kids Inc.
Community Against Violence, Inc.
Health Care for the Homeless

Helping Hands Inc.
IAMAW LL 1635
IATSE Local 423
MacNab Design
McKinley County Federation of United School Employees (MCFUSE) AFT Local #3313
New Mexico Voices for Children
NM Coalition to End Homelessness
South West New Mexico CLC
Taos County Economic Development Corp.
The Albuquerque Center for Peace and Justice
American Childrens' Charities, Inc.
Global Property Management Group Inc
IATSE, Local 720
IBEW Local 357
Laborers Local #872
Las Vegas Catholic Worker
Nevada Hispanic Services, Inc
Progressive Leadership Alliance of Nevada
Pulidor Foundation
Restart Incorporate

New York
Adirondack Vets House, Inc.
Agenda For Children Tomorrow
Albany Jobs with Justice
American Federation of Gov. Employees, Local 1151
ATPAM- Association of Theatrical Press Agents & Managers
Black Veterans for Social Justice, Inc.
Bridge Center of Schenectady, Inc.
Brooklyn Carpenters 926
Buffalo AFL-CIO Community Service
Buffalo Musicians Union Local # 90
Carpenters Local 608
Cattaraugus Alleghany Central Labor Council
Cayuga/Seneca Community Action Agency, Inc.
Center for Economic and Social Rights
Center for Urban Community Services
Charas/ El Bohio Cultural and Community Center NY
Citizen Soldier
Coalition for Economic Justice/ Buffalo Jobs with Justice
Coalition of North East New York Assoc. Inc.
Columbia County Habitat for Humanity
Concern for Independent Living
Cornell Coalition for the Homeless
CSEA Labor Local 670
CWA Local 1104
CWA Local 1105
CWA Local 1109
CWA Local 1168

Disabled in Action Metro
Dr. Usdi
Economic Security Campaign
Erasmus Neighborhood Federation
Eviction Intervention Services
Fellowship of Reconciliation
Fox House
Garden City Teachers Association
Greater NY Labor Religion Coalition
HandCrafting Justice
Harlem Independent Living Center
Help USA, Bronx/Northern Manhattan
Homeless Alliance of Western New York
Human Development Services of Westchester
Hunger Action Network
Hunger Action Network of NYS
IBEW, Local 1381
Lincoln Square Neighborhood Center, Inc.
Living Wage Warriors of Long Island
Local 1170 Communications Workers of America AFL-CIO
Long Island Center for Independent Living, Inc.
Long Island Housing Services, Inc.
Long Island Labor/ Religious Coalition
Long Island Progressive Coalition
Mercy United CWA 1133
Met Council on Jewish Poverty
Metropolitan Community United Methodist Church
Mid-Hudson Labor-Religion/ Jobs with Justice
Multi-Talents, Inc.
NABET-CWA Local 11
Nassau/Suffolk Coalition for the Homeless
Neighborhood Preservation Coalition of NYS, Inc.
New York Children's Health Project
New York Urban League
Opportunities for Chenango, Inc.
Orange County Housing Consortium
Parent Watch, Inc.
Patchogue-Medford Youth and Community Services
Physicians for Social Responsibility/New York City
Picture the Homeless
Poor Homeless Farmers
Providence House Inc.
Readio.com
Religious/Labor Coalition
Roofers Local #195
Salem African Methodist Episcopal Church
Sanitation Officers Association
Schenectady Community Action Program, Inc.
School of Social Welfare

Senses
Sharp Committee, Inc.
SICM Food Program
Southwestern Independent Living Center
Southside Community Mission
Southtowns Rural Preservation Co., Inc.
Southwestern Independent Living Center
St. Andrew's Episcopal Church
St. Augustine's Episcopal Church
Starline Baker
Statewide Emergency Network for Social and Economic Security
Street News
Suffolk Welfare Warriors
The Council of Churches of the City of New York
The Hudson/Catskill Central Labor Council (AFL-CIO)
The Interfaith Alliance of NYC, Inc.
The Oswego County Labor Council AFL-CIO
The United Evangelical Council of Christian Churches, Inc.
The Vestry of St. Augustine's Episcopal Church
Thorpe Family Residence, Inc.
Town of Greenburgh
True Vine Tabernacle of God, Inc.
United Brotherhood of Carpenters Local Union 20
United Tenants of Albany
United Veterans Beacon House
Unity House of Troy, Inc.
USW Local 4-00054
Utica Citizens in Action
Western NY Area Labor Federation AFL-CIO
Women of Reform Judaism
World Hunger Year
Wyandanch Homes and Property Development Corp.
YWCA of Jamestown

Ohio
ABCD, Inc.
ACCESS, Inc.
AFL-CIO
American Fed of Musicians Local 101-473
Amethyst, Inc.
Asbestos Workers Local #84
ATLO Beacon Education Association
Bethany House Services
Care Alliance
Coalition on Homelessness and Housing in Ohio
Columbiana County AFL-CIO Labor Council
Columbus Coalition of the Homeless
Columbus Health Care for the Homeless
Columbus NOW

Columbus, Ohio CBTU Chapter
Community Shelter Board
Corporation for Ohio Appalachian Development
CWA Local 4320
CWA Local 4501
D.A.W.G.
Day Laborers Organizing Committee
Dayton Building & Construction Trades Council
Defiance County Residential Housing, Inc.
Dennis Kucinich for President Campaign
Division 4, Brotherhood of Locomotive Engineers and Trainmen
East Side Catholic Center and Shelter
Family Crisis Network
First Friends Church
Focus Homeless Services
Founders Path
Friends of the Homeless, Inc.
GCC IBT of District Council 3
George Randt MD
Glaziers Local Union 847
Grace Place Catholic Workers
Greater Akron Committee for Better Housing
Greater Cincinnati Coalition for the Homeless
H.M. Life Opportunity Services
Habitat for Humanity Defiance Co.
Housing Network, Inc.
Intercommunity Justice and Peace Center
International Association of Machinist- Aerospace Workers Local #2535
International Association of Machinist- Aerospace Workers Local #2794
International Brotherhood of Electrical Workers #573
Ironworkers Local 172
Kinetic Independent Newspaper
Laborers International Local 1015
Laborers' Intern Union of N America
Legacy III
Lifeline for the Empowerment & Development of Consumers, Inc.
Lima/Allen Council on Community Affairs
Lima's Samaritan House
Local 101-473 American Federation of Musicians
Mid-Ohio AFLCIO
NAMI-4 County
New Home Development
North River Development Corporation
Northeast Ohio Coalition for Homelessness
Northwest Ohio Affordable Housing
Northwest Ohio Housing Coalition
Northwestern Ohio Building and Construction Trades Council
Power Inspires Progress
QDROS.com

Regional Council AFL-CIO (Allentown)
Roofers & Waterproofers Local #44
Roofers Local 75 Dayton, OH
Roofers Local Union #42
Shared Harvest Foodbank
Sources Community Network Services
The House of Refuge Missions, Inc.
The Other Place
The Women's Connection in Cincinnati
Tri-County Independent Living Center, Inc.
Unite HERE
United Here Local 10
United Steelworkers of America Local #979
USW Local 1042
USWA Local 2173
West Ohio Food Bank
Western Reserve Building and Construction Trades Council
Women for Racial and Economic Equality
Women Speak Out for Peace and Justice
Ohio Now
Universal Health Care Action Network

Oklahoma
AFGE Local 916
Deep Fork Community Action
International Union of Painters and Allied Trades #807
My Sister's Keeper
OK City Federation of Teachers, Local 2309, AFT
Oklahoma Communications Workers of America

Oregon
Alima Cosmetic, Inc.
Bend Area Habitat for Humanity
Central Oregon Jobs with Justice
Environmental Justice Action Group
Eugene-Springfield Solidarity Network/Jobs with Justice
Glad Rags
Hawthorne Auto Clinic, Inc.
IATSE Local 28
IBEW Local Union 48
Keepers! Inc.
Laborers Local 121
Machinists Union Local 63
Mid-Willamette Valley Jobs with Justice
Musicians Union, Local 99 (AFM)
Neighborhood Pride Team of Portland
Oregon Coalition on Housing and Homelessness
Oregon Food Bank
Oregonians for a Living Wage

Portland Jobs with Justice
Progressive Investment Management
Rogue Valley Community Dev. Corp.
SW Oregon Community Action
The Community Development Network
White Bird Clinic

Pennsylvania
1260 Housing Development Corporation
A Second Chance, Inc.
Adams Co. Interfaith Housing Corp.
AFGE Local 644
AFM Local 82-545
American Friends Service Committee
Asociacion Puertorriquenos en Marcha, Inc.
Beaver Co. Building and Construction Trades
Bethesda Project
Blueprint to End Homelessness
Carbondale Local 130 Musician Protective Association
Catherine McAuley Center
Citizens Budget Campaign of Western
COLT Coalition CDC
Community Action Commission
Community Action Committee of the Lehigh Valley
Community Human Services Corp.
Community Mosque, Inc.
Community Shelter Services, Inc.
Cooperative Parenting for Divided Families
Down to Earth
Fresh Start Community Development Corporation
Glenwood Community Dev. Corporation
Homeless Advocacy Project
Hunting Park Community Dev. Corporation
IBEW Local 1957
IBEW Local Union #56
Indiana Armstrong Clarion Central Labor Council
Indiana CLC AFL-CIO
Just Harvest
Labor Religion Coalition of PA
Liberty Street Café
Little Britain Monthly Meeting of Friends
Mental Health Association of SEPA
Milagro House
National Council for Urban Peace and Justice
NUHHCE District 1199C
Pennsylvania Low Income Housing Coalition
People's Emergency Center
Philadelphia Committee to End Homelessness
Philadelphia Area Jobs with Justice

Pocono Healthy Communities Alliance
Program for Health Care to Underserved Populations
Project HOME
SEIU Local 668, PSS4
SEIU-F&O Local 22
The National Council for Urban Peace & Justice
The New Men Association
The Philadelphia Veterans Multi-Service & Education Center
The Sisters of St. Joseph NW PA
The Thomas Merton Center
Unitarian Universal Lists United for Faith in Action
VISION, Inc.
Welfare Rights-Housing
Western Pennsylvania Living Wage Coalition
Westmoreland Human Opportunities, Inc.
Wood Street Common
YWCA of Gettysburg & Adams County
YWCA of Williamsport, PA
Bucks County Housing Group
Citizens Budget Campaign of Western PA
Little Britain Monthly Meeting of Friends
People's Emergency Center
United Electrical, Radio and Machine Workers of America, District Council 6
United Labor Council of Reading & Berks Co.
YMCA of McKeesport
YWCA of Greater Harrisburg

Puerto Rico
Hogar Padre Venard, Inc.
Hogarde Ayuda Refugio, Inc.
La Fondita de Jesus
Manos Al Servicio de la Comunidad, Inc.
Municipality O-P Mayaguez
San Juan Continuum of Care Coalition
Sheet Metal Workers Local 41

Rhode Island
Rhode Island Coalition for the Homeless
Brown Hillel Foundation
Childhood Lead Action Project
Green Party of Rhode Island
Hunger Center
Mirror Image
New Hope Emergency Shelter
Ocean State Action
Opportunities Unlimited, Inc.
Rhode Island Jobs with Justice
RI Carpenters Local Union 94

The Genesis Center
Travelers Aid

South Carolina
Sistercare, Inc.
Allen Temple Community Development Center
Anderson Sunshine House
Coastal Carolina Association of Professional Musicians, AFM 502
Concerned Citizens Assoc. of Saluda SC
Crisis Ministries
Elm Place Wedding Chapel
Family Shelter
Games Coalition for the Homeless
Little River Medical Center
Meg's House
Moresun Custom Woodworking, Inc.
Pee Dee Community Action Agency
St. Paul's Episcopal Church
The SC Institute on Poverty and Deprivation
Trinity Housing Corporation
Upstate Homeless Coalition of South Carolina

South Dakota
AFSC-South Dakota
American Indian Services
Mid-America Advocates for the Homeless
Road Home Inc.
Sioux Empire Homeless Coalition
Tulare United Church

Tennessee
Bethlehem-Wiley Church
Blount County Habitat for Humanity
Bradley-Cleveland Community Services
Bread Not Bombs
Cleveland Emergency Shelter
Greater Memphis Coalition for the Homeless
Knoxville Building and Construction Trades Council
Knoxville Jobs with Justice
Nashville Homeless Power Project
National Health Care for the Homeless Council
Progressive Student Alliance
Second Harvest Food Bank
Tennessee Network for Community Economic Development

Texas
Abiding Missionary Baptist Church
Abilene Big Country Central Labor Council

ACC American Federation of Teachers Local 6249
Advocacy Outreach
Agape Outreach Ministries Inc.
Alliance for a Feminist Option
Alliance for Multicultural Community Service
Amalgamated Transit Union #1091
Amalgamated Transit Union Local 1549
American Friends Service Committee (TX, AK, OK area office)
American Video Tape Service Center
Anderson Co. Area CLF, AFL-CIO
Antur LLC, dba Cartridge World Setex
Art From the Streets
Austin American Civil Liberties Union
Austin Area Homeless Task Force
Austin Area Interreligious Ministries
Austin Assoc of Profess Fire Fighters # AFL-CIO 975
Austin Center for Peace & Justice
Austin Federation of Musicians
Austin Labor Council of the AFL-CIO
Austin Latina/Latino Lesbian, Gay, Bisexual, & Transgender Organization ALLGO
Austin Living Wage Coalition
Austin Musicians
Austin Peace and Justice Coalition
Austin Recovery
Austin Tenants Council
Austin Travis County MHMR
Austin, Texas NAACP
Austin Families / Austin Area Employers Collaborative
Banner Sign and Graphics
Bark for Peace!, LLC
Bay Area Homeless Services
Bicycle Sport Shop
Bikes Not Bombs
Brazos Valley Central Labor Council
Brazos Valley Workforce Centers
Brick Oven Restaurant
Brownsville Housing Authority
C Van R Automotive
Capital Area Homeless Alliance
Cardiovascular On-Call Specialists, Inc.
Casa Marianella
Cecilia Wood Law Practice
Cen-Tex Silicone Implant Support, Inc.
CEO
Citizens for Social Democracy
City of Austin
City of Rollingwood - Texas
Clayworks Studio/Gallery
Clip Joint Natural Hair Salon and Spa

Cohen and Associate
Colonias Unidas
Colores del Pueblo
Communities In Schools-Central Texas
Corpus Christi American Federation of Teachers
Corpus Christi Universal Living Wage Warriors
Crime Prevention Institute
CWA Local 6132
Dallas Homeless Neighborhood Association
DC Mitchell Construction
Democratic Party of Collin County, Texas
Dorothy Day Catholic Worker of Corpus Christi
Dr. Namkee Choi's Social Policy Analysis Class - UT Austin
Dr. Singha's Natural Therapeutics, Inc.
Dynamics of Organization & Community Class UT, School of Social Work
Eco-Wise
Education Austin
El Franco Lee - County Commissioner - Harris County
El Paso Center on Family Violence
Environmental Science & Policy St. Edward's University
Family Connections
Family Forward
Flick Report
Forbidden Fruit
Fort Worth Bldg. & Const. Trades Council
GCIU Local 428M
Gray Panthers of Austin
Gray Panthers of Houston
Green Party of Brevard, TX
Guadalupe Economics
Harris County Green Party
Hatch Partnership Architect
Hays County Green Party
Healthcare for the Homeless - Houston
Holy Rosary Catholic Church
Homeless Task Force-Austin
House the Homeless, Inc.
Houston Area Women's Center
Houston Gulf Coast Building & Construction Trades Council
HSR Construction, Inc.
IBEW Local 301
IBEW Local 716
INNU SALON
Interfaith Hospitality Network, Humble Area
International Union of Operating Engineers Local 178
International Union of Operating Engineers Local 450
Jacinto City United Methodist Church
Jobs with Justice - Austin
Keep the Land

KOOP 91.7 FM Community Radio
Life Works
LULAC
Magnificent Houses, Inc.
Manos de Cristo
Mentoring for Homeless Self-Sufficiency / AmeriCorps Project
Mind Science Foundation
Mission San Francisco De La Espada
Mission Waco
Motor Blade Postering
National Consumer Advisory Board
National Organization for Human Services
Native American Center of Texas, Inc.
North Texas Jobs with Justice
Nueces County Department of Human Services
Pax Christi Austin
People Organized in Defense of the Earth's Resources PODER
PHOGG Phoundation / Planet K
Pickett Fence Learning - CTE
Plenty Austin
PODER People Organized in Defense of the Earth's Resources
Poetic Healings Productions
Prince of Peace Lutheran Church
Proyecto Azteca
Public Citizen (Texas Office)
Push Up Foundation
Rollingwood City Council
San Fernando Cathedral
SEED Coalition
Services for the Elderly, Inc
Serving San Antonio
Sisters & Brothers, Inc.
Southeast Texas Community Development Corp., Inc.
St. Edward's Universal Living Wage Warriors
St. Alphonsus Church
St. Martin De Porres Church
Steelbeam
Students Toward A New Democracy
Sweet Home for the Homeless
Tank Town LLC
Teamsters Local Union #657
Texans Standing Tall
Texas ACLU
Texas AFL-CIO
Texas Association of CDCs
Texas Civil Rights Project
Texas Coalition to Abolish the Death Penalty
Texas Conference of Churches
Texas Council on Family Violence

Texas Development Institute
Texas Fair Trade Coalition
Texas Federation of Teachers TFT
Texas Gray Panthers
Texas Homeless Network
Texas Legal Services Center
Texas Low Income Housing
Texas Moratorium Network
Texas NOW
Texas State Democratic Executive Committee
Texas State Employees Union/CWA Local 6168
Texas Tenants' Union
The Good Life
The Green Party of Texas
The Green Party USA
The Learning Center at Westlake High School
The Natural Gardener
The Rose Garden
The Social Welfare Action Alliance
The Stew Pot
Timon's Ministries
Transformations Remodeling
Transport Workers Union Local 555
Travis County
Travis County Democratic Party
Travis County Green Party
Travis County Veterans Service Office
Triangle Neighborhood Association
United East Austin Coalition
United Farm Workers of Texas
University of TX at Austin School of Social Work
UT School of Social Work
UT Students for a Universal Living Wage
Venus Rouhani DDS PC Dental Practice
Veterans for Peace, Austin Chapter 66
Volunteer Legal Services of Central Texas
Western Regional Organization for Human Services Professionals
Wheatsville Co-Op
White Mountain Foods.com
Whole Earth Body Works
Women's International League for Peace and Freedom
Workers Assistance Programs, Inc.
Workers Defense Project/Proyecto Defensa Laboral
YES Inc.
YWCA of Greater Austin
Push Up Foundation
Texas Homeless Network
United Food & Commercial Workers Local 540

Richard R. Troxell

Utah
Bricklayers Tile Setters & Allied Crafts Local #1
Coalition of Religious Communities
Crossroads Urban Center
IBEW Local 354
IBEW Local 354
Jedi Women
Jobs with Justice - Utah
Mormons for Equality & Social Justice MESJ
UMWA Local 8622
Union of Roofers Local 91

Virginia
American Medical Student Association
Arlington Street Peoples Assistance Network
Body Harmony
CARES, Inc.
Carpenter's Shelter
Community Lodgings
CWA Local 2201
CWA Local 2204
Disabled Action Committee (DAC)
Giles Co. Housing & Dev. Corp.
Giovanni Leather Works
GLU-CWA
Hampton Roads Building & Construction Trades Council
Homestretch, Inc.
Miriam's House, Inc.
Moonrise Jewelry, Inc.
Mountain Mystic Trading Co.
Norfolk Homeless Consortium
Northern Virginia Interfaith coalition for Justice
Our Lady Queen of Peace RC Church
Project Community, Inc.
RPJ Housing Development CORP
Salvation Army
Social Action Linking Together (SALT)
Social Justice and Outreach Minister
Staff Union of University of Virginia (SUUVA)/CWA
Tenants and Workers Committee
Tomorrow's World
VA AFL-CIO
Virginia Coalition for the Homeless
Virginia Interfaith Center for Public Policy
Virginia Organizing Project
YWCA of Roanoke Valley

Vermont
Ben & Jerry's Foundation
Brattleboro Area Community Land Trust
Brattleboro Housing and Human Resources Council
Central Vermont Community Action Council
COTS
Good Samaritan Haven
LineSync Architecture
Page Designs, Inc.
Randolph Area Community Development Corporation
Roofers Local 9
Rutland County Community Land Trust
Seventh Generation
Sisters of Mercy, Vermont Leadership Team
The Old Spokes Home
The Vermont Center for Independent Living
Vermont Affordable Housing Coalition
Vermont Coalition for the Homeless
Vermont Livable Wage Campaign
Vermont Workers' Center/ Jobs with Justice

Washington
Aloha Inn
American Friends Service Committee Pacific Northwest Regional Office
Catherine Booth House
Families in Shelters
First Place School
Helping Hand House
International District Housing Alliance
Jubilee Women's Center
Katherine Booth House
Metropolitan Development Council
Musicians' Association of Seattle
Northern Olympia Veterans for Peace
One Childhood
Our Brothers Keeper
Peace & Justice Action League / Spokane
Progressive Kid
Resident Peaceniks
SAMCO
St. Martin De Porres
Street News Service
Tacoma/Pierce County Coalition for Homeless
Unite Here Local #791
Washington Association of Churches
Washington Low Income Housing Alliance
Washington State Coalition for the Homeless
Yakima County Coalition for the Homeless
Seattle Musicians Assoc. AMF Local 76-493

Wisconsin
Brown County Coalition for the Homeless
Dane County Homeless Coalition
Hunger Task Force
Mfd. Home Owners Association, Inc.
Sheet Metal Workers' Local #18
Shelter of the Fox Valley
Southeastern Wisconsin Housing Corp
St. Benedict Community Meal
Teamster Local 200
The Harlington Poynette Area Clergy Association
Wisconsin Partnership for Housing Dev. Inc.

West Virginia
Community Action of South East West Virginia
CWA West Virginia
Genoa Christian Center
Global Village Enterprises
Huntington W. VA. Housing Authority
Iron Workers Local 787
REDEEM Realizing Economic Development Through Education, Enterprise and Morals
Roofers Local Union #242 AFL-CIO
SAFE
Southern Appalachian Labor School
Teamsters Local Union #505
The Religious Coalition for Community Renewal
West Virginia Economic Justice Project

Wyoming
Cheyenne Crossroads Clinic
Christ Chapel Apostolic Church
Health Care for the Homeless
Interfaith Good Samaritan
Wyoming Coalition for the Homeless
Wyoming Winds

Endnotes

1 "Todd Tries to Ban Camping in Public." *Austin American Statesman*, Mar. 9, 1995.

2 *Daily Texan*, July 12, 1995.

3 *Hunger and Homelessness Survey*. Rep. United States Conference of Mayors, Dec. 2007. Accessed on web: July 11, 2010. www.usmayors.org/hhsurvey2007/hhsurvey07.pdf.

4 "Camp Residents Decry Crackdown." *Austin American Statesman*, May, 1995.

5 "Camping Ban Not Designed as Attack on Homeless People." *Austin American Statesman*, May, 1995.

6 HUD 1995 Report — *Out of Reach*.

7 See www.NationalHomeless.org to read the *NCH Annual Hate Crimes Reports*.

8 Salinas, Miguel M. 1993 (re: Ricardo Davila), *Austin American Statesman*.

9 Milam, Sue. "Briefing to the Austin City Council," July 12, 1995, item #45, *Daily Texan*, July, 21, 1995.

10 Lindell, Chuck. "Homeless Hearing Draws Crowd," *Austin American Statesman*, June 21, 1995.

11 McLeese, Don. *"Camping Ban Punishes Those Without Power,"* Austin American Statesman, July 30, 1995.

12 "The City Council Moves Toward Public Encampment Ban." *Austin Chronicle*, Nov. 17, 1995.

13 "Nofziger Casts Deciding Vote In Stormy Council Meeting." *Austin American Statesman*, July, 1995.

14 "City's Heart Hard to Find in Camp Ban." Don Mcleese, *Austin American Statesman* Jan. 7, 1996.

15 "Foes of Camping Ban Denounce it as Cruel." *Austin American Statesman* January 1, 1996.

16 "Mayor Takes Active Role."*Austin American Statesman* Feb. 3, 1996.

17 "Repeal Camping Ban" *Austin American Statesman*, Feb. 15, 1996.

18 Duff, Audrey, "This Ain't No KOA." *Austin Chronicle*, Feb. 16, 1996.

19 "End Likely for Ban on Camping in Public, *Austin American Statesman*, July 13, 1997.

20   "Camping Ban Data to be Shared," *Austin American Statesman*, May 21, 1996.

21   "Judge Upholds City Camping Ban." *Austin American Statesman*, June 27, 1996.

22   Ibid.

23   "Camping Ordinances Costs." Report COA Health Dept., February 14, 1997.

24   "Council Back Camping Ban. Members also vote to find city land for a homeless campground where services could be provided." *Austin American Statesman*, July, 28, 1995.

25   Bruner, Henry, and Medard Gabel. *Globalinc: An Atlas of the Multinational Corporation*. The New Press, New York, 2003.

26   Van Scoy, Kayte."Class War." *Austin Chronicle*, August 8, 1997.

27   Ibid.

28   "Camping Ordinances City Camping Ban." *Austin American Statesman* June, 1996.

29   McLeese, Don. "As the Wind Blows, So Goes Garcia." *Austin American Statesman*, August 17, 1997.

30   Earle, Ronnie. "Dig Deeper for Solutions, Ideas to Safeguard Austin's Qualities" (Public Forum). *Austin American Statesman*, August, 1997.

31   McLeese, Don. "As the Wind Blows so Goes Garcia," *Austin American Statesman*, August 17, 1997.

32   Wear, Ben. "Council Approves Downtown Proposal," *Austin American Statesman*, December 4, 1998.

33   "Public Camping Law Revised," *Austin American Statesman*, Sept. 30, 2000.

34   Henly, Sally. "Prosecutions of Camping Ordinance Violations." Letter to Richard Troxell. Oct. 11, 2002. Manuscript. City of Austin Law Department, Austin, Texas.

35   Waltman, Jerold L. *The Case for the Living Wage*. Algora Publications, New York, 2004, pp. 117-118.

36   2000 U.S. Census

37   *How Many People Experience Homelessness?* Rep. National Coalition for the Homeless, July 2009. Accessed on web: July 7, 2010, www.

nationalhomeless.org/factsheets/How_Many.html.

38   Willis, Jesse. "How We Measure Poverty." *Oregon Center for Public Policy*. Feb. 2000. Accessed on web: July 16, 2010, www.ocpp.org/poverty/how.htm.

39   Pollin, Robert, and Stephanie Luce. *The Living Wage: Building a Fair Economy*. New York: The New Press, 2000. pp. 26-27.

40   Ibid.

41   Ibid., pp 26-28.

42   Ibid.

43   Ibid.

44   *Next Century Economy*. Rep. San Rafael, CA: ICF Kaiser Economic Strategy Group, 1988.

45   *The History of Tipping – From Sixteenth Century England to United States in the 1910s, Ofer H. Azars*, http://129.3.20.41/eps/eh/papers/0309/0309001.

46   Ibid.

47   Brenner, Mark L. *Tipping for Success!: Secrets for How to Get in and Get Great Service*. Brenmark House, Sherman Oaks, CA, 2001.

48   Pollin, Robert, and Stephanie Luce. *The Living Wage: Building a Fair Economy*. The New Press, New York, 2000.

49   Bernstein, Jared, and John Schmitt. Issue brief. Economic Policy Institute, June 1, 1997. Accessed on web. July 10, 2010. www.epi.org.

50   Bernstein, Jared. *America's Well Targeted Raise*. Issue brief no. 118. Economic Policy Institute, Sept. 2,1997. Accessed on web: July 11, 2010. www.epi.org/page/-/old/Issuebriefs/ib118.pdf.

51   Bernstein, Jared, and John Schmitt. *Http://www.epi.org*. Issue brief. Economic Policy Institute, June 1, 1997. Accessed on web: July 10, 2010. http://epi.3cdn.net/12b3330cc427b9fa7f_h9m6b5d4e.pdf.

52   "Concerned with Decisiveness." Web log post. *ArtsJournal.com*. Blog Riley, Feb. 17, 2006. Accessed on web: July 7, 2010. www.artsjournal.com/riley/2006/02/.

53   Pollin, Robert, and Stephanie Luce. *The Living Wage: Building a Fair Economy*. The New Press, New York, 2000.

54   Ibid.

55   Ibid.

56   Shulman, Beth. *The Betrayal of Work: How Low-wage Jobs Fail 30 Million Americans and their Families*. The New Press, New York, London, 2003.

57   "HUD Historical Background." *Locating New Page…*. U.S. Department of

Housing and Urban Development, May 18, 2007. Accessed on web: July 16, 2010. www.hud.gov/offices/adm/about/admguide/history.cfm#1970.

58   "Multifamily Housing - Renting - HUD." *Locating New Page....* U.S. Department of Housing and Urban Development, June 2007. Accessed on web: July 16, 2010. www.hud.gov/offices/hsg/mfh/gendocs/factsrap.pdf.

59   "Summary." *Fair Market Rents.* U.S. Department of Housing and Urban Development. Accessed on web: July 16, 2010. www.huduser.org/ periodicals/ushmc/winter98/summary-2.html.

60   "BAH Levels and Increases." *OSD Military Compensation (militarypay. defense.gov).* Accessed on web: July 16, 2010. http://militarypay.defense. gov/pay/bah/.

61   Koidin, Michelle, *San Antonio Express News,* Sept.29, 2002.

62   Pollin, Robert, and Stephanie Luce. *The Living Wage: Building a Fair Economy.* The New Press, New York, 2000.

63   2000 US Census.

64   Pollin, Robert, and Stephanie Luce. *The Living Wage: Building a Fair Economy.* The New Press, New York, 2000.

65   Ibid.

66   "Protesters Interrupt City Council Meeting." *Austin American Statesman,* June 6, 1997.

67   Shulman, Beth. *The Betrayal of Work: How Low Wage Jobs Fail 30 Million Americans and Their Families.* The New Press, New York: London, 2003.

68   Ibid.

69   Pollin, Robert, and Stephanie Luce. *The Living Wage: Building a Fair Economy.* The New Press, New York, 2000.

70   Schlosser, Eric. *Fast Food Nation/The Dark Side of the All-American Meal.* New York, Harper Collins, Perennial, New York, 2002.

71   Ibid.

72   Ibid.

73   Pollin, Robert, and Stephanie Luce. *The Living Wage: Building a Fair Economy.* The New Press, New York.

74   Ibid.

75   "The Sky Hasn't Fallen." Economic Policy Institute in Washington, DC.

76   Pollin, Robert, and Stephanie Luce. *The Living Wage: Building a Fair Economy.* The New Press, New York, 2000.

77   2000 US Census.

78   Pollin, Robert, and Stephanie Luce. *The Living Wage: Building a Fair Economy.* The New Press, New York, 2000.

79   *"The Realities of Poverty in Delaware 2001 - 2002." Welcome to DHC. N.p.,* *2002. Web. July 11, 2010.* www.housingforall.org/rop_0102.htm.

80   "Bring America Home Act." National Coalition for the Homeless. National Coalition for the Homeless, 2008. Accessed on web: July 8, 2010. www.nationalhomeless.org/advocacy/baha.html.

81   House The Homeless. Accessed on web. July 11, 2010. www. housethehomeless.org/.

82   Zeleny, Jeff. "Obama Takes Economic Detour from Health Care." Web log post. The Caucus Blogs. The New York Times, Mar. 2, 2010. Accessed on web: July 11, 2010. http://thecaucus.blogs.nytimes.com/2010/03/02/obama-takes-economic-detour-from-health-care/.

About the Author

Richard R. Troxell has been striving to end homelessness since he first witnessed it as a self made mortgage foreclosure preventionist in Philadelphia in the 1980s.

Troxell initiated Jobs Plus in Austin, Tex., a program that helps the homeless transition into housing. In addition, Troxell spearheaded a paradigm shift for homeless service delivery and was awarded a $100,000 grant from former Texas Gov. George Bush for the jobs component of Project Fresh Start. This Continuum of are model is now the premier case management blueprint for Austin's homeless citizens.

As a social engineer, Troxell has created scores of other programs to address a multitude of social problems. In Philadelphia, Troxell conceived of the "Blue Gray Task Force," in which retired police officers solve "cold cases." He also created the Mobile Mini Police Station, an emergency impact mobile police station designed to quickly establish a "beach-head" in areas with a high incidence of violence— a model which has been replicated in multiple cities. In addition, he developed "The Philadelphia Stabilization Plan" to first stabilize the city's abandoned housing stock and then provide a mechanism for banks to bring them back into the market.

Currently, Troxell sits on the Board and Executive Committee of the National Coalition for the Homeless. His work has culminated in the drive to "fix the Federal Minimum Wage" as the National Chairman of the Universal Living Wage Campaign. Using existing government guidelines, he designed a single national formula, based on the local cost of housing, that ensures that if a person works a 40-hour week, they will be able to afford basic food, clothing, and shelter (including utilities), regardless of where that work is performed throughout the United States. For the ninth year, he has again organized homeless advocates from all 50 states for two National Days of Action to promote the concept of the Universal Living Wage.

In addition, Troxell wrote the Homeless Protected Class Resolution for the National Coalition for the Homeless and recently pressed for State legislation to prevent hate crimes against people experiencing homelessness.

Troxell's work has been recognized by the Pennsylvania Senate, the Philadelphia Bar Association, the U.S. Department of Housing and Urban Development, La Salle University, the late Texas Governor Ann Richards, and the United Nations. He has received the National Jefferson Service Award and was honored by the Texas Civil Rights Commission. He has also received the Five Who Care Award, the JC Penny Golden Rule Award, and the Texas Homeless Network Outstanding Community Service Award, among many others.

Today, Troxell works with people with disabilities and homeless citizens of Austin, Texas, as the founder and director of Legal Aid for the Homeless. He is also president and founder of House the Homeless, Inc. (nonprofit 501c3) which he established in 1989. HtH is comprised of homeless and formerly homeless citizens struggling to protect their civil rights and find solutions that will end homelessness in their lifetime.

Richard Troxell earned a B.A. in sociology with honors from St. Edward's University.

LaVergne, TN USA
06 October 2010
199750LV00001B/17/P